DIGNITY, MENTAL H[...]
AND HUMAN RIGI[...]

This book is dedicated to Regina.

Dignity, Mental Health and Human Rights

Coercion and the Law

BRENDAN D. KELLY
University College Dublin, Ireland
and
Mater Misericordiae University Hospital, Ireland

Routledge
Taylor & Francis Group

LONDON AND NEW YORK

First published 2015 by Ashgate Publishing

Published 2016 by Routledge
2 Park Square, Milton Park, Abingdon, Oxon OX14 4RN
711 Third Avenue, New York, NY 10017, USA

First issued in paperback 2017

Routledge is an imprint of the Taylor & Francis Group, an informa business

British Library Cataloguing in Publication Data
A catalogue record for this book is available from the British Library.

The Library of Congress has cataloged the printed edition as follows:
Kelly, Brendan (Brendan D.), author.
 Dignity, mental health, and human rights : coercion and the law / by Brendan D. Kelly.
  pages cm
 Includes bibliographical references and index.
 ISBN 978-1-4724-5032-6 (hardback)
1. People with mental disabilities--Legal status, laws, etc.--England. 2. People with mental disabilities--Legal status, laws, etc.--Ireland. 3. Convention on the Rights of Persons with Disabilities and Optional Protocol (2007 March 30) 4. Mental health laws--England.
5. Mental health laws--Ireland. 6. Human rights--England. 7. Human rights--Ireland. I Title.
 KJC1020.K45 2015
 346.41701'38--dc23

2015004773

ISBN 13: 978-1-138-09445-1 (pbk)
ISBN 13: 978-1-4724-5032-6 (hbk)

Contents

List of Abbreviations

AMHP	Approved mental health professional
CRPD	Convention on the Rights of Persons with Disabilities
ECHR	European Convention on Human Rights (Convention for the Protection of Human Rights and Fundamental Freedoms)
ECT	Electroconvulsive therapy
EU	European Union
GDP	Gross domestic product
HRB	Health Research Board
IMCA	Independent Mental Capacity Advocate
NHS	National Health Service
OECD	Organisation for Economic Cooperation and Development
UK	United Kingdom
UN	United Nations
US	United States
WHO	World Health Organization

List of Legislation

European Union

European Union, 'Treaty on European Union', *Official Journal*, 1992, C191.

European Union, 'Treaty of Amsterdam amending the Treaty of the European Union, the Treaties establishing the European Communities and certain related acts', *Official Journal*, 1997, C340.

European Union, 'Charter of Fundamental Rights of the European Union', *Official Journal*, 2007, C303.

European Union, 'Consolidated versions of the Treaty on European Union and the Treaty on the Functioning of the European Union', *Official Journal*, 2008, C115.

England

Magna Carta 1215.

De Praerogativa Regis 1324.

Petition of Rights 1628.

Habeas Corpus Act 1679.

Bill of Rights 1689.

Vagrancy Act 1744.

Criminal Lunatics Act 1800.

Lunacy Act 1890.

Lunacy Act 1891.

Mental Deficiency Act 1913.

Mental Treatment Act 1930.

Mental Health Act 1959.

Mental Health (Amendment) Act 1982.

Mental Health Act 1983.

Mental Health Act 1983 (Remedial) Order 2001 (SI 2001/3712).

Data Protection Act 1998.

Human Rights Act 1998.

Freedom of Information Act 2000.

Criminal Justice Act 2003.

Civil Partnership Act 2004.

Domestic Violence, Crime and Victims Act 2004.

Mental Capacity Act 2005.

Mental Health Act 2007.

Health and Social Care Act 2008.
Equality Act 2010.

Republic of Ireland
Criminal Lunatics (Ireland) Act 1838.
Lunacy Regulations (Ireland) Act 1871.
Constitution of Ireland (*Bunreacht na hÉireann*) 1937.
Mental Treatment Act 1945.
Public Authorities Judicial Proceedings Act 1954.
Courts (Supplemental Provisions) Act 1961.
Domestic Violence Act 1996.
Powers of Attorney Act 1996.
Freedom of Information Act 1997.
Data Protection Act 1998.
Human Rights Commission Act 2000.
Mental Health Act 2001.
European Convention on Human Rights Act 2003.
Criminal Law (Insanity) Act 2006.
Mental Capacity and Guardianship Bill 2008.
Mental Health Act 2008.
Health (Miscellaneous Provisions) Act 2009.
Assisted Decision-Making (Capacity) Bill 2013.

Scotland
Mental Health (Scotland) Act 1984.
Adults with Incapacity (Scotland) Act 2000.
Mental Health (Care and Treatment) (Scotland) Act 2003.
Mental Health (Scotland) Bill 2014.

Northern Ireland
Mental Health (Northern Ireland) Order 1986.
Mental Capacity Bill (2014).

List of Cases

European Court of Human Rights

Aerts v Belgium (1998) 29 EHRR 50.

Ashingdane v UK (1985) 7 EHRR 528.

Benjamin v UK (2002) 36 EHRR 1.

Croke v Ireland (2000) ECHR 680.

DD v Lithuania (2012) ECHR 254.

De Wilde, Ooms and Versyp v Belgium (1972) 1 EHRR 438.

E v Norway (1990) 17 EHRR 30.

Fox, Campbell and Hartley v UK (1990) 13 EHRR 157.

Guzzardi v Italy (1980) 3 EHRR 333.

Herczegfalvy v Austria (1991) 15 EHRR 437.

HL v UK (Bournewood) (2004) 40 EHRR 761.

HM v Switzerland (2004) 38 EHRR 314.

Hutchison Reid v UK (2003) 37 EHRR 211.

Johnson v UK (1997) 27 EHRR 296.

Kolanis v UK (2006) 42 EHRR 12.

LR v France App no 33395/96 (ECHR, 27 June 2002).

Megyeri v Germany (1992) 15 EHRR 584.

Munjaz v UK App no 2913/06 (ECHR, 17 July 2012).

Nikolova v Bulgaria (2001) 31 EHRR 3.

Nowicka v Poland (2003) 1 FLR 417.

Osman v UK (2000) 29 EHRR 245.

Pereira v Portugal (2003) 36 EHRR 49.

Stanev v Bulgaria (2012) EHRR 46.

Van der Leer v Netherlands (1990) 12 EHRR 567.

Winterwerp v Netherlands (1979) 2 EHRR 387.

X v UK (1981) 4 EHRR 181.

X v UK (1981) 4 EHRR 188.

England

Aston Cantlow and Wilmcote with Billesley PCC Church Council v Wallbank [2003] UKHL 37 [2004] 1 AC 546.

Campbell v Mirror Group Newspapers Ltd. [2004] UKHL 22 [2004] 2 AC 457 (HL).

R v Deputy Governor of Parkhurst Prison, ex parte Hague and Weldon [1992] 1 AC 58.

Republic of Ireland

Acknowledgements

Parts of this book are reproduced and/or adapted from the following sources:

- *The International Journal of Law and Psychiatry*, Volume 34, Issue 6, Brendan D. Kelly, 'Mental health legislation and human rights in England, Wales and the Republic of Ireland', Pages 439–454, Copyright 2011, with permission from Elsevier.
- With kind permission from Springer Science+Business Media: *Irish Journal of Medical Science*, 'The Assisted Decision-Making (Capacity) Bill 2013: content, commentary, controversy', Volume: 184, Year of publication: 2015, Pages 31–46, Author: Brendan D. Kelly.
- Part of Table 1 (see Appendix) is reproduced, with permission of the publisher, from: World Health Organization, *WHO Resource Book on Mental Health, Human Rights and Legislation*, Geneva: World Health Organization, 2005 (ISBN 92 4 156282 X; http://www.who.int/mental_health/policy/resource_book_MHLeg.pdf, accessed 7 December 2014) (pages 121–154; i.e., most of Annex 1, 'WHO Checklist on Mental Health Legislation').
- This book contains public sector information licensed under the Open Government Licence v1.0 and the Open Government Licence v2.0.

I am very grateful to the *Guardian* for permission to quote from: Harding, E., 'Acts of contradiction', *Guardian (Society)*, 2010, 31 March.

I am very grateful to Professor José Miola and Professor Elizabeth Wicks at the School of Law, University of Leicester and Professor Jean V. McHale (now at Birmingham Law School, University of Birmingham). I wish to acknowledge the educational influences of my colleagues in clinical and academic psychiatry, the doctors, nurses, social workers, occupational therapists, psychologists, lecturers, administrators and students with whom I work. I also wish to express my appreciation to Professor Patricia Casey, Dr John Sheehan, Dr Eugene Breen, Dr John Bruzzi and Dr Larkin Feeney. In addition, I have benefitted enormously from my contact with mental health service-users and their families, carers, advocates and legal advisors.

I greatly appreciate the teaching and guidance of my teachers at Scoil Chaitríona, Renmore, Galway, Ireland; St Joseph's Patrician College, Nun's Island, Galway; and the School of Medicine at NUI Galway.

Most of all, I appreciate deeply the support of my wife (Regina), children (Eoin and Isabel), parents (Mary and Desmond), sisters (Sinéad and Niamh) and nieces (Aoife and Aisling).

Introduction

This is a book about human rights, law and mental disorder. More specifically, this book explores the human rights consequences of recent and ongoing revisions of mental health legislation in England and Ireland explicitly in the context of the World Health Organization (WHO) human rights standards,[1] recent case-law from the European Court of Human Rights and the United Nations (UN) Convention on the Rights of Persons with Disabilities (CRPD).[2]

This book's main themes are dignity, human rights and mental health law. The book's key objectives are to:

- determine to what extent, if any, human rights concerns have influenced recent and ongoing revisions of mental health legislation in England and Ireland; and
- determine to what extent, if any, recent developments in mental health law in both jurisdictions have assisted in protecting and promoting the human rights of the mentally ill.

Chapter 1 commences by introducing key concepts such as mental disorder, human rights, human dignity and paternalism, with particular emphasis on the economic, social, and personal consequences of mental disorder. There is strong emphasis on human rights as applied in the specific context of mental disorder, with reference to the Universal Declaration of Human Rights,[3] European Convention on Human Rights (Convention for the Protection of Human Rights and Fundamental Freedoms) (ECHR)[4] and the UN Principles for the Protection of Persons with Mental Illness and the Improvement of Mental Health Care.[5] Later chapters return to these concepts and explore them in greater depth, examining how issues of rights, dignity and paternalism relate

---

1 WHO, *WHO Resource Book on Mental Health, Human Rights and Legislation*, Geneva: WHO, 2005.

2 UN, *Convention on the Rights of Persons with Disabilities*, Geneva: UN, 2006.

3 UN, *Universal Declaration of Human Rights*, Geneva: UN, 1948.

4 Council of Europe, *European Convention on Human Rights (Convention for the Protection of Human Rights and Fundamental Freedoms)*, Strasbourg: Council of Europe, 1950.

5 UN, *Principles for the Protection of Persons with Mental Illness and the Improvement of Mental Health Care*, New York: UN, Secretariat Centre For Human Rights, 1991.

to mental health legislation in England and Ireland (Chapters 2 and 5) and standards outlined by the WHO (Chapter 3) and UN (Chapter 4), as well as the broader relevance of these concepts in terms of the European dimension to mental health law and policy (Chapter 6).

Chapter 2 examines mental health legislation in England and Ireland in some detail, with particular focus on human rights. This examination (and this book in general) focuses on civil rather than criminal detention, and provisions relating to adults rather than children. Against this background, Chapter 2 explores the background to relevant mental health legislation in both jurisdictions, as well as key issues driving recent reforms. Specific legislative provisions are outlined and explored (e.g., criteria for detention, mental health tribunals, etc.) and an overall assessment of both jurisdictions is provided.

Chapter 3 moves the analysis forward by providing a critical discussion of the WHO's 'Checklist on Mental Health Legislation' outlined in its Resource Book on Mental Health, Human Rights and Legislation[6] and goes on to explore the extent to which mental health legislation in England and Ireland meets or fails to meet specific WHO standards. This analysis is presented both in the text and in Table 1 (see Appendix). A summary assessment is also provided, concluding that mental health legislation in England meets 92 (55.4%) of the 166 relevant WHO standards and Ireland meets 81 (48.8%).

Areas of high compliance include definitions of mental disorder and other key terms, involuntary admission procedures and clarity regarding offences. Areas of medium compliance relate to capacity and consent (with a particular deficit regarding capacity legislation in Ireland), review procedures (which exclude long-term voluntary patients and lack robust complaint procedures) and rules governing special treatments. Areas of low compliance relate to economic and social rights, voluntary patients (especially non-protesting, incapacitated patients), vulnerable groups and emergency treatment.

Chapter 4 examines the CRPD[7], which is the most significant development in the field of mental disability, mental disorder and human rights in recent years. More specifically, this chapter explores the implications of the CRPD for mental health legislation in England and Ireland and concludes that the CRPD strongly discourages, if not precludes, *any* deprivation of liberty based on mental disorder. This is a dramatic change in the human rights landscape for people with mental disorder in England and Ireland and will have far-reaching implications for current and future revisions of mental health and capacity legislation in both jurisdictions.

Chapter 5 goes on to explore the revision of mental capacity legislation currently underway in Ireland, focusing on the Assisted Decision-Making

---

6 WHO, 2005.

7 UN, 2006.

(Capacity) Bill 2013, which proposes an entirely new legislative framework to govern decision-making by persons with impaired mental capacity. This process of legislative reform is interesting not only in relation to Ireland, but also for the potential lessons it holds for other jurisdictions contemplating similar reform, especially in the context of evolving interpretations of the CRPD.

Based on the analyses presented in the preceding chapters and the broader literature, Chapter 6 explores three key themes relating to the evolving relationship between human rights and mental health law; namely, (a) growing international influences on mental health policy and law, with particular emphasis on human rights; (b) key values underpinning human rights in mental health, with particular emphases on human dignity and human capabilities theory; and (c) the relevance of the 'third wave'[8] of human rights in mental health law and policy.

To conclude, Chapter 7 summarises key arguments presented throughout the book, chapter by chapter, placing particular emphasis on the centrality of human dignity and the necessity to integrate mental health policy with legislation in order to provide meaningful protection and promotion of rights in practice. This chapter presents overall conclusions stemming from the book, and outlines useful themes for future research including placing increased emphasis on studying the *outcome* of mental health legislation, the precise relevance of the 'third wave' of human rights in the context of mental health, and the increasing relevance of trans-national influences on national mental health law (e.g., WHO, UN, European Union [EU]).

Ultimately, this book seeks to articulate better, clearer and more connected ways to protect and promote the rights of the mentally ill though both law and policy.

---

8 Klug, F., *Values for a Godless Age: The History of the Human Rights Act and Its Political and Legal Consequences*, London: Penguin, 2000; Klug, F., 'The Human Rights Act – a "third way" or "third wave" Bill of Rights', *European Human Rights Law Review*, 2001, 4, 361–372.

Chapter 1
Mental Disorder and Human Rights

Background

In 1817, the House of Commons of Great Britain and Ireland established a committee to investigate the plight of the mentally ill in Ireland. The committee reported a disturbing situation:

> When a strong man or woman gets the complaint [mental disorder], the only way they have to manage is by making a hole in the floor of the cabin, not high enough for the person to stand up in, with a crib over it to prevent his getting up. This hole is about five feet deep, and they give this wretched being his food there, and there he generally dies.[1]

The situation in nineteenth-century Ireland was not unique, as the majority of individuals with mental disorder in Ireland, England and many other countries lived lives of vagrancy, destitution, physical and mental illness and early death.[2]

Two centuries later, in 2010, the *Guardian* newspaper reported on the death of a man with schizophrenia in central London:

> Mayan Coomeraswamy was found dead on 9 January last year, having died from heart disease. Ulcers in his stomach were a strong sign of hypothermia. The 59-year-old, who had schizophrenia, lived in a dirty, damp and freezing flat, with mould growing on the floor and exposed electrical wires hanging off the walls. His boiler had broken, the bathroom ceiling had collapsed, and neighbours began to complain about the smell. His brother, Anthony Coombe, describing the scene as 'squalor', said: 'Even an animal couldn't have lived in that'.

---

1 Quoted in Shorter, E., *A History of Psychiatry*, New York: John Wiley and Sons, 1997; pp. 1–2.

2 Porter, R., *Madness*, Oxford: Oxford University Press, 2002; Robins, J., *Fools and Mad*, Dublin: Institute of Public Administration, 1986; Torrey, E.F., Miller, J., *The Invisible Plague*, New Brunswick, NJ: Rutgers University Press, 2001; Kelly, B.D., 'Dignity, human rights and the limits of mental health legislation', *Irish Journal of Psychological Medicine*, 2014, 31, 75–81.

The disturbing circumstances of Coomeraswamy's death have exposed serious flaws in the way mental health law is implemented in the case of vulnerable people. … Everyone knew the conditions Coomeraswamy was living in, but he refused to move for cleaning and refurbishment work to be done. Despite four years of pleading from his family, NHS [National Health Service] care staff would not intervene – wrongly thinking they would be violating his human rights.[3]

Against the background of these reports, separated by almost two centuries but disturbingly similar in other respects, this book examines two key questions. First, to what extent, if any, have human rights concerns influenced recent revisions of mental health legislation in England and Ireland?[4] Second, to what extent, if any, have recent developments in mental health law in both jurisdictions truly assisted in protecting and promoting the rights of the mentally ill?

The remainder of this introductory chapter outlines the background to this book's exploration of these two questions. The chapter commences by presenting an overview of the nature and burden of mental disorder in society and goes on to examine key concepts in human rights as applied to mental disorder, with particular reference to the Universal Declaration of Human Rights,[5] European Convention on Human Rights (Convention for the Protection of Human Rights and Fundamental Freedoms) (ECHR)[6] and the UN Principles for the Protection of Persons with Mental Illness and the Improvement of Mental Health Care.[7] The chapter concludes by providing an exploration of key theoretical constructs underpinning much of the rest of the book, including human dignity, especially as it relates to human capabilities, and paternalism.

The Nature and Burden of Mental Disorder

A medical *disorder* is disease or ailment.[8] A *mental* disorder, according to the WHO, is a clinically recognisable group of symptoms or behaviours associated

---

3 Harding, E., 'Acts of contradiction', *Guardian (Society)*, 2010, 31 March; p. 3.

4 For the remainder of this book, 'Ireland' refers to the Republic of Ireland except where specified otherwise.

5 UN, 1948.

6 Council of Europe, 1950.

7 UN, 1991.

8 Pearsall, J., Trumble, B. (eds), *The Oxford Reference English Dictionary (Second Edition)*, Oxford and New York: Oxford University Press, 1996; p. 408.

in the majority of cases with interference with personal functions and distress.[9] In the absence of personal dysfunction, social deviance or conflict on their own are not sufficient to constitute mental disorder, according to the WHO.

Notwithstanding the emergence of this WHO definition of mental disorder towards the end of the twentieth century, the evolution of the concept of 'mental disorder' has been, and remains, a highly contested process,[10] as mental disorders are variously conceptualised as spiritual or religious manifestations, legal conundrums, medical diseases, social issues, or all of the above, with the balance between competing conceptualisations varying over time.[11] In recent decades, re-definition and expansion of diagnostic categories have proven especially controversial.[12]

Since this book is primarily concerned with mental health *law*, it maintains a strong focus not on *clinical* definitions of mental disorder, such as that developed by the WHO, but on *legal* definitions provided in mental health legislation in England and Ireland. These definitional issues are extremely important, not least because involuntary detention of the mentally ill has been a long-standing feature of their experience in all societies in which such matters are recorded.[13] As a result, various jurisdictions have developed dedicated mental health legislation to govern this practice.[14]

Today, involuntary admission to psychiatric facilities under civil mental health legislation remains relatively common: in the year from 1 April 2010 to 31 March 2011 there were 49,365 episodes of involuntary psychiatric admission in England,[15] and by 2012/13 this had increased to 50,408 detentions in NHS

9 WHO, *International Classification of Mental and Behavioural Disorders*, Geneva: WHO, 1992; p. 5.

10 Shorter, 1997; Stone, M.H. *Healing the Mind*, London: Pimlico, 1998.

11 Millon, T., *Masters of the Mind*, Hoboken, NJ: John Wiley & Sons, 2004; p. 2; Shorter, 1997; Stone, 1998; Millon, 2004; Porter, R. *Madmen: A Social History of Madhouses, Mad-Doctors and Lunatics*, Gloucestershire, UK: Tempus, 2004; Scull, A., *The Most Solitary of Afflictions*, New Haven: Yale University Press, 2005.

12 Horowitz, A.V., *Creating Mental Illness*, Chicago and London: University of Chicago Press, 2002; Watters, E., *Crazy Like Us*, New York: Free Press, 2010.

13 Shorter, 1997; Stone, 1998; Millon, 2004; Porter, 2004; Scull, 2005; Gostin, L., McHale, J., Fennell, P., Mackay, R.D., Bartlett, P., 'Preface', in Gostin, L., McHale, J., Fennell, P., Mackay, R.D. and Bartlett, P. (eds), *Principles of Mental Health Law and Policy* (pp. v–viii), Oxford: Oxford University Press, 2010.

14 Torrey & Miller, 2001; Kelly, B.D., 'Mental health law in Ireland, 1821–1902: building the asylums', *Medico-Legal Journal*, 2008, 76, 19–25.

15 NHS Information Centre for Health and Social Care, *In-patients Formally Detained in Hospitals under the Mental Health Act 1983*, London: NHS/National Statistics, 2011; p. 9.

and independent hospitals.[16] In Ireland, there were 1,602 involuntary admissions in 2010[17] and by 2013 this had increased to 2,039; in addition, the *rate* of involuntary admission in Ireland increased from 41.9 per 100,000 population in 2012 to 44.4 in 2013.[18]

In this context of a long-standing history of involuntary admission and treatment, it is clear that legal definitions of mental illness are of considerable significance. Such definitions are examined in some depth later in this book (Chapters 2 and 3). It is important to note at the outset, however, that mental disorder, as defined by the WHO, is relatively common and imposes considerable costs and burdens on individuals, families and societies.

Worldwide, approximately 450 million people suffer from mental disorder at any given time.[19] The 12-month prevalence of mental disorder varies from 6% in Nigeria to 27% in the United States (US).[20] The Organisation for Economic Cooperation and Development (OECD) estimates that 5% of the working-age population have a severe mental health condition, and a further 15% are affected by a more common condition.[21]

Mental disorder exerts considerable economic costs. The OECD estimates that direct and indirect costs of mental disorder can exceed 4% of gross domestic product (GDP).[22] In England, the annual economic cost of mental disorder is approximately £77 billion, of which 16% is attributable to care provision, 30% to lost productivity, and the remainder to reduced quality and quantity of life.[23] According to the OECD, mental disorder accounts for 40% of the 370,000 new claims for disability benefit each year.[24] In Ireland, the annual

---

16   Health and Social Care Information Centre, *In-patients Formally Detained in Hospitals under the Mental Health Act 1983 and Patients Subject to Supervised Community Treatment*, London: Health and Social Care Information Centre, 2013.

17   Daly, A., Walsh, D., *HRB [Health Research Board] Statistics Series 15: Activities of Irish Psychiatric Units and Hospitals 2010*, Dublin: Health Research Board, 2011; p. 47.

18   Daly, A, Walsh D., *HRB Statistics Series 25: Activities of Irish Psychiatric Units and Hospitals 2013*. Dublin: Health Research Board, 2014; p. 57.

19   O'Donovan, D., *The Atlas of Health*, London: Earthscan, 2008.

20   Twelve-month prevalence means that the individual has suffered from a mental disorder within the past twelve months (Kessler, R.C., Üstün, T.B., *WHO World Mental Health Surveys*, Cambridge: Cambridge University Press, 2008).

21   OECD, 'Making mental health count', *Focus on Health*, 2014, July.

22   OECD, 'Making mental health count', *Focus on Health*, 2014, July.

23   Sainsbury Centre for Mental Health, *Mental Health At Work*, London: Sainsbury Centre for Mental Health, 2007; Knapp, M., 'Mental ill-health: cost implications', in Cooper, C.L., Field, J., Goswami, U., Jenkins, R. and Sahakian, B.J. (eds), *Mental Capital and Wellbeing* (pp. 515–527), Chichester, West Sussex: Wiley-Blackwell, 2010.

24   Elliott, L., 'Mental health issues "cost UK £70bn a year", claims thinktank', *Guardian*, 2014, 11 February.

cost of mental health problems exceeds €3 billion (£2.4 billion), or 2% of gross national product.[25] This figure includes over €1 billion (£0.8 billion) for health and social care, and over €2 billion (£1.6 billion) from lost economic output.

The true cost of mental disorder, of course, stems chiefly from the untold suffering experienced by patients and their families, in addition to the measurable economic and societal costs. This cost in terms of human suffering is difficult, if not impossible, to estimate with any degree of accuracy, but is undoubtedly substantial and underlines the need to provide treatments that are acceptable, effective and evidence-based to all persons with mental disorder, and appropriate support to their families and carers.

Human Rights and Mental Health

While ideas underpinning current conceptualisations of human rights have lengthy histories in many political and religious traditions,[26] there was renewed focus on human rights during the eighteenth-century Enlightenment, in the writings of Thomas Hobbes (1588–1679), among others, and England's Habeas Corpus Act 1679,[27] which built on the Magna Carta (1215) and Petition of Right (1628) in articulating key ideas about the rights of the individual.[28] In 1776, the concept of individual rights was further endorsed by the US Declaration of Independence[29] and in 1789 the French Declaration of the Rights of Man and of the Citizen strengthened and transformed the language of human rights substantially.[30]

In essence, a *right* is an entitlement, a thing one may morally or legally claim.[31] The term 'human rights' refers specifically to particular rights which a human being possesses simply because he or she *is* a human being.[32] Human rights do not need to be granted or earned; they are the birth-right of *all* human beings

25   O'Shea, E., Kennelly, B., *The Economics of Mental Health Care in Ireland*, Dublin: Mental Health Commission/Irish Centre for Social Gerontology/Department of Economics, NUI Galway, 2008; p. ix.

26   Ishay, M.R., *The History of Human Rights*, Berkeley and Los Angeles: University of California Press, 2004.

27   Adams, G.B., *The Origin of the English Constitution*, New Haven: Yale University Press, 1912.

28   Hunt, L., *Inventing Human Rights*, New York and London: W.W. Norton and Company, 2007; p. 114.

29   Hunt, 2007.

30   Hunt, 2007; p. 133.

31   Pearsall & Trumble, 1996; p. 1240.

32   Edmundson, W., *An Introduction to Rights*, Cambridge: Cambridge University Press, 2004; Ishay, 2004; Hunt, 2007.

simply because they *are* human beings.[33] Human rights recognise *extraordinarily* special interests, and this is what sets them apart from other claims or rights.[34] Today, the term 'human rights' is most commonly understood by reference to statements of human rights dating from the twentieth century, including, most notably, the Universal Declaration of Human Rights adapted by the UN General Assembly in 1948[35] (see below).

Throughout the 1800s, however, notwithstanding the emergence of new ideas about human rights in Europe, America and elsewhere, the majority of people with mental disorder continued to live lives of poverty, destitution and indignity, generally untouched by changing trends in political thought.[36] In Ireland, a predominantly Roman Catholic country, the Roman Catholic Church, interestingly, played little role in providing for the mentally ill during this period, although there is evidence that the Church in Ireland did *not* support witch-hunts against the mentally ill, as occurred in many other European countries.[37] In England, by contrast, there is greater evidence of pro-active involvement of religious groups in caring for the mentally ill: in 1792, for example, William Tuke, a Quaker, founded the York Retreat for individuals with mental illness, following the death of a Quaker woman in York Asylum.[38]

More broadly, public authorities moved with remarkable uniformity across Europe and the US to provide institutional solutions to the 'hurried weight of human calamity' that the mentally ill appeared to present to communities and societies during the eighteenth and nineteenth centuries.[39] These initiatives, however, stemmed chiefly from welfare-based impulses and philanthropic concerns rather than ideas about empowerment of the mentally ill, recognition of rights or enhancement of dignity.[40] This theme of paternalism as opposed to empowerment is one which emerges repeatedly throughout the histories of psychiatry in England and Ireland, from the 1700s to the present day, and it is a key theme of this book.

This nineteenth-century approach to the problems presented by the mentally ill, centred on institutional provision, produced a dramatic growth in asylum populations in England and Ireland: in 1859, there were 1.6 asylum

---

33 Edmundson, 2004; p. 3.

34 Edmundson, 2004; p. 191.

35 UN, 1948.

36 Shorter, 1997: p. 2; Psychiatrist, 'Insanity in Ireland', *The Bell*, 1944, 7, 303–310; p. 304.

37 Robins, 1986; pp. 18–22.

38 Torrey & Miller, 2001; p. 28.

39 Hallaran, W.S. *An Enquiry into the Causes producing the Extraordinary Addition to the Number of Insane*, Cork: Edwards and Savage, 1810; p. 10.

40 Torrey & Miller, 2001; pp. 124–129.

inmates per 1,000 population in England and by 1909 this had risen to 3.7.[41] In Ireland, there were 3,234 individuals in asylums in 1851, and by 1914 this had risen to 16,941.[42] The relative absence of mental disorder from emerging discussion about human rights during this era (when such discussion was very much needed) is likely related to a number of different factors, including the absence of clear definitions of 'lunacy' or mental disorder, the paucity of effective treatments, stigma, and the customary exclusion of persons with mental disorder from many strands of political and societal activity.[43]

From today's perspective, these historical trends emphasise strongly the role of welfare-based concerns and paternalism towards the mentally ill, rather than empowerment or enhancement of dignity, as key motivators in service development, both in the past and, arguably, today. This leads to one of the key questions explored in this book: to what extent do today's mental health laws in England and Ireland perpetuate the approaches of the 1800s, and to what extent do they, by contrast, protect and promote the rights of the mentally ill? Have these two approaches – one based on welfare-based provision of care to the afflicted, the other based on empowerment though human rights – been reconciled? These themes emerge repeatedly throughout this book in the specific contexts of the mental health laws of England and Ireland and how they are interpreted by the courts.

Of course, the emerging interest in human rights throughout the eighteenth and nineteenth centuries should have automatically included and promoted the rights of people with mental disorder. The historical experiences of the mentally ill, however, repeatedly highlight the need for *pro-active* consideration of protections for their human rights and dignity.[44] The need to provide dedicated safeguards for the rights of the mentally ill was not to be formally recognised, however, until well into the twentieth century, with the publication of the UN Principles for the Protection of Persons with Mental Illness and the Improvement of Mental Health Care in 1991.[45] The pathway to this important development is considered next, commencing with the UN's iconic Universal Declaration of Human Rights.[46]

---

41 Shorter, 1997; p. 47.

42 Walsh, D., Daly, A., *Mental Illness in Ireland 1750–2002*, Dublin: Health Research Board, 2004; p. 21.

43 Shorter, 1997; Kelly, B.D., 'Structural violence and schizophrenia', *Social Science and Medicine*, 2005, 61, 721–730; Scull, 2005.

44 Shorter, 1997; Porter, 2004; Scull, 2005.

45 UN, 1991.

46 UN, 1948.

The Universal Declaration of Human Rights

The early decades of the twentieth century saw substantially increased attention being devoted to the concept of human rights.[47] In light of the unprecedented carnage and atrocities of the Second World War, the UN was established in October 1945 in order to promote international peace and security. One of the key aims of the new organisation was to develop a political, legal and intellectual framework that would support the observance of human rights among member states and promote a culture of human rights throughout the world.

In order to promote these goals, the Universal Declaration of Human Rights was adopted by the UN General Assembly at Palais de Chaillot in Paris on 10 December 1948.[48] The Declaration was presented as a non-binding statement of rights, the first stage in a process which continued with the drafting of the International Covenant on Civil and Political Rights and International Covenant on Economic, Social and Cultural Rights, adapted by the UN General Assembly in 1966.

The 1948 Declaration comprises 30 articles, with a preamble which recognises that 'the inherent dignity and ... the equal and inalienable rights of all members of the human family is the foundation of freedom, justice and peace in the world' and 'it is essential, if man is not to be compelled to have recourse, as a last resort, to rebellion against tyranny and oppression, that human rights should be protected by the rule of law'.[49]

The Declaration states that 'all human beings are born free and equal in dignity and rights. They are endowed with reason and conscience and should act towards one another in a spirit of brotherhood'.[50] The latter statement seems especially relevant to the mentally ill: does the link which the UN draws between 'human beings' and being 'endowed with reason' mean that the mentally ill, whose mental disorder may occasionally impair their reason, do not necessarily possess the rights outlined? Such a conclusion would appear contrary to the spirit of the Declaration, especially Article 2, which emphasises the universal nature of rights:

Everyone is entitled to all the rights and freedoms set forth in this Declaration, without distinction of any kind, such as race, colour, sex, language, religion, political or other opinion, national or social origin, property, birth or other status.[51]

---

47 Ishay, 2004.

48 UN, 1948; Morsink, J., *The Universal Declaration of Human Rights*, Philadelphia: University of Pennsylvania Press, 1999; Ishay, 2004; p. 221.

49 Universal Declaration of Human Rights, preamble.

50 Universal Declaration of Human Rights, article 1.

51 Universal Declaration of Human Rights, article 2.

Mental disorder was not mentioned explicitly in this list of factors, which were *not* to form the basis of discrimination, but presumably is included under the term 'other status'. In 1991, the UN made this more explicit in its Principles for the Protection of Persons with Mental Illness and the Improvement of Mental Health Care:

> Every person with a mental illness shall have the right to exercise all civil, political, economic, social and cultural rights as recognized in the *Universal Declaration of Human Rights*, the *International Covenant on Economic, Social and Cultural Rights*, the *International Covenant on Civil and Political Rights* and in other relevant instruments, such as the *Declaration on the Rights of Disabled Persons* and the *Body of Principles for the Protection of All Persons under Any Form of Detention or Imprisonment.*[52]

Articles 3 to 19 of the Universal Declaration of Human Rights go on to articulate rights related to the principle of liberty, including 'the right to life, liberty, and security of person'.[53] Deprivation of liberty in the context of involuntary psychiatric treatment is considered in greater depth later in this book (Chapters 2, 3 and 4).

Before moving on from the Universal Declaration of Human Rights, however, it is useful to consider some general controversies relating to the Declaration. In the first instance, eight countries abstained from ratifying the Declaration in 1948, owing chiefly to concerns about specific rights (e.g., freedom of movement) and the possibility that the non-binding Declaration might challenge their domestic jurisdictions.[54] This concern was compounded by perceived Western bias,[55] and some Islamic commentators were especially concerned that the Declaration allegedly failed adequately to reflect Islamic culture, religion and tradition, resulting in the Cairo Declaration on Human Rights in Islam.[56]

The Universal Declaration of Human Rights also generated controversy owing to the exclusion of certain rights such as, for example, an explicit right to conscientious objection and 'the right to refuse to kill'.[57] Various other rights

---

52   UN, 1991; principle 1, article 5.

53   Universal Declaration of Human Rights, article 3.

54   Byelorussia, Czechoslovakia, Poland, Saudi Arabia, South Africa, Ukraine, the Soviet Union and Yugoslavia abstained. See also: Ishay, 2004; p. 223.

55   Cassese, A., 'The General Assembly', in Alston, P. (ed.), *The United Nations and Human Rights* (pp. 25–54), Oxford: Clarendon Press, 1992.

56   Organisation of the Islamic Conference, *Cairo Declaration on Human Rights in Islam*, Cairo: Organisation of the Islamic Conference, 1990.

57   MacBride, S., 'The Imperatives of Survival' in Abrams, I. and Frängsmyr, T. (eds), *Nobel Lectures: Peace, 1971–1980* (pp. 86–101), Singapore: World Scientific Publishing Company, 1997; p. 99.

also generated concern as the twentieth century progressed; for example, the right to a clean environment[58] and rights of specific groups such as gay, lesbian and transgender individuals.[59] Many of these issues came to prominence in the later decades of the twentieth century, and reflect the ongoing evolution of both socio-political concerns and concepts of rights.[60]

Other controversies surrounding the Universal Declaration of Human Rights focussed on the inclusion of certain rights, such as economic and social rights, given their inevitable relationship with a state's political and economic situations.[61] Neier argued that placing economic and social rights at the same level as civil and political rights brought areas in which compromise is essential into the arena of rights adjudication.[62] This issue had been the subject of debate during initial drafting,[63] and in 1966 two separate covenants were adapted by the UN General Assembly: the International Covenant on Civil and Political Rights and the International Covenant on Economic, Social and Cultural Rights. According to this paradigm, civil and political rights were to be implemented immediately, while social and cultural rights were to be realised progressively, consistent with other programmes in various countries.[64] In the meantime, however, the ECHR had been adopted by the Council of Europe in 1950, and this is considered next.

The European Convention on Human Rights

In 1950, the Council of Europe adopted the Convention for the Protection of Human Rights and Fundamental Freedoms, more commonly known as the ECHR. In essence, the ECHR aims to protect human rights and the fundamental freedoms 'which are the foundation of justice and peace in the world and are best maintained on the one hand by an effective political democracy and on the other by a common understanding and observance of the human rights upon which they depend'.[65]

---

58   Tomuschat, C., *Human Rights (Second Edition)*, Oxford: Oxford University Press, 2008; pp. 56–57.

59   Smith, R.K.M., *Textbook on International Human Rights (Third Edition)*, Oxford: Oxford University Press, 2007; p. 191.

60   Freeman, M., *Human Rights*, Cambridge: Polity Press, 2002; pp. 51–54.

61   Freeman, 2002; pp. 164–166.

62   Neier, A., 'Social and economic rights', *Human Rights Brief*, 2006, 13, 1–3: p. 2.

63   Morsink, 1999; p. 2; Puta-Chekwe, C., Flood, N., 'From division to integration' in Merali, I. and Oosterveld, V. (eds), *Giving Meaning to Economic Social and Cultural Rights* (pp. 39–51), Philadelphia: University of Pennsylvania Press, 2001.

64   Ishay, 2004; p. 224.

65   ECHR, preamble.

The EHCR outlines a range of individual rights including rights to life,[66] liberty, security and a fair trial[67]; respect for private and family life;[68] freedom of thought, conscience, religion,[69] expression,[70] assembly and association;[71] the right to marry;[72] and the right to 'an effective remedy before a national authority notwithstanding that the violation has been committed by persons acting in an official capacity'.[73] There are prohibitions on torture,[74] slavery, forced labour,[75] discrimination[76] and abuse of rights.[77]

Under the ECHR, the European Court of Human Rights[78] was established in 1959, and by 2007 held jurisdiction over 47 states. The number of applications to the court has increased steadily since the 1970s, and in 2007 there were 49,750 applications.[79] By the end of 2007, there were some 80,000 cases pending;[80] this backlog developed despite a doubling of court resources since 2002. By 2008, the court employed 629 people and had a budget of £46 million, almost a quarter of the budget of the Council of Europe. In addition to these logistical issues, there are also significant difficulties enforcing certain court judgments, especially when violations are attributable to poor standards of legal or political order in participating states.[81]

Despite these concerns, the European Court of Human Rights has still become a significant world leader in human rights protections,[82] and there is substantial evidence that it provides enhanced protections for basic human

---

66 ECHR, article 2.
67 ECHR, article 5.
68 ECHR, article 8.
69 ECHR, article 9.
70 ECHR, article 10.
71 ECHR, article 11.
72 ECHR, article 12.
73 ECHR, article 13.
74 ECHR, article 3.
75 ECHR, article 4.
76 ECHR, article 14.
77 ECHR, article 17.
78 ECHR, article 19.
79 Tomuschat, 2008.
80 Barber, L., 'Spread of freedom leaves human rights court fighting fires', *Financial Times*, 2008, 19/20 April; p. 9.
81 Tomuschat, 2008; p. 256.
82 Tomuschat, 2008; p 239.

rights in ratifying states,[83] albeit that its performance varies between issues,[84] and there can be inefficiencies and delays.[85]

Notwithstanding these challenges, there is now a significant body of ECHR jurisprudence in relation to mental illness.[86] The European Court of Human Rights delivered its first significant decision in this area in 1979, and between 2000 and 2004 delivered 4y judgments in this area, with a particular focus on the right to liberty.[87]

The key provisions of the ECHR in this respect are presented in Articles 5(1) and 5(4). Article 5(1) states:

> Everyone has the right to liberty and security of person. No one shall be deprived of his liberty save in the following cases and in accordance with a procedure prescribed by law ... [including] (e) the lawful detention of persons for the prevention of the spreading of infectious diseases, of persons of unsound mind, alcoholics or drug addicts or vagrants.

Article 5(4) states that 'everyone who is deprived of his liberty by arrest or detention' shall be entitled to 'take proceedings by which the lawfulness of his detention shall be decided speedily by a court'. The relevance of these and other key provisions of the ECHR in relation to mental disorder are explored further in Chapter 2 of this book, with reference to relevant judgments of the European Court of Human Rights. First, however, it is useful to explore another statement of human rights which constitutes a important element of the human rights background to mental health cases from recent decades: the UN Principles for the Protection of Persons with Mental Illness and the Improvement of Mental Health Care.[88]

---

83 Smith, 2007.

84 Letsas, G., *A Theory of Interpretation of the European Convention on Human Rights*, Oxford: Oxford University Press, 2007.

85 Helfer, L.R., 'Redesigning the European Court of Human Rights', *European Journal of International Law*, 2008, 19, 125–159; p. 125.

86 In relation to international human rights instruments and mental disability, see: Perlin, M.L., Kanter, A.S., Treuthart, M.P., Szeli, E., Gledhill, K., *International Human Rights and Comparative Mental Disability Law*, Durham, NC: Carolina Academic Press, 2006; Perlin, M.L., Kanter, A.S., Treuthart, M.P., Szeli, E., Gledhill, K., *International Human Rights and Comparative Mental Disability Law: Documents Supplement*, Durham, NC: Carolina Academic Press, 2006. In relation to the ECHR and mental disability, see: Bartlett, P., Lewis, O., Thorold, O., *Mental Disability and the European Convention on Human Rights (International Studies in Human Rights, Volume 90)*, Leiden/Boston: Martinus Nijhoff Publishers, 2007.

87 Bartlett et al., 2007; p. 1.

88 UN, 1991.

United Nations Principles for the Protection of Persons with Mental Illness and the Improvement of Mental Health Care

In 1991, the UN introduced its Principles for the Protection of Persons with Mental Illness and the Improvement of Mental Health Care, the first substantial declaration of rights to focus specifically on people with mental disorder.[89] The UN principles emphasise that all people are entitled to receive the best mental health care available, and to be treated with humanity and respect. In addition, there shall be no discrimination on the grounds of mental disorder: all persons with mental disorder have the same rights to medical and social care as other people, and rights to live, work and receive treatment in the community, as far as possible.

The principles state that mental health care shall be based on internationally-accepted ethical standards, and not on political, religious or cultural factors, and that the treatment plan for each patient shall be reviewed regularly with the patient. Mental health skills and knowledge shall not be misused, and medication shall meet the health needs of the patient (i.e., medication shall not be administered for the convenience of others or as a punishment).

For voluntary patients, no treatment shall be administered without their informed consent, subject to some exceptions (e.g., patients with personal representatives empowered by law to provide consent). For involuntary patients, every effort shall be made to inform the patient about treatment. Physical restraint or involuntary seclusion shall be used only in accordance with official guidelines. The principles also require that records are kept of all treatments and mental health facilities are appropriately structured and resourced. Finally, an impartial review body shall, in consultation with mental health practitioners, review the cases of involuntary patients; this is consistent with the requirements of the ECHR.[90]

The WHO re-stated many of these key principles in 1996 in its Ten Basic Principles of Mental Health Care Law,[91] which emphasise that every person should benefit from the best possible measures possible to prevent mental disorders and promote mental well-being, and have access to basic mental health care. All mental health assessments should be made in accordance with accepted medical principles and procedures, and all persons with mental disorder should receive health care which is the least restrictive possible.

The WHO's Ten Basic Principles also state that consent to treatment is required, and if a person has difficulty appreciating the consequences of

---

89 UN, 1991.

90 ECHR, article 5(4).

91 Division of Mental Health and Prevention of Substance Abuse (WHO), *Mental Health Care Law: Ten Basic Principles*, Geneva: WHO, 1996.

a decision, he or she shall benefit from the assistance of an informed third party. There must be a review mechanism in place for any decision made by a representative (e.g., family member), official (e.g., judge) or health-care provider. If such a decision affects liberty (e.g., hospitalisation) or integrity (e.g., treatment) and has a lasting impact, there must be an automatic periodical review mechanism, and decisions must be in accordance with law (and not on an arbitrary basis).

Against the background of these publications and positions, the WHO went on, in 2005, to publish the most detailed systematic set of human rights standards for national mental health legislation assembled to date, in its WHO Resource Book on Mental Health, Human Rights and Legislation.[92] This WHO checklist for mental health legislation forms the framework for the detailed examination of mental health legislation in England and Ireland presented in Chapter 3 of this book, which also presents a critique of the WHO standards.

Before proceeding further, however, it is necessary to examine some of the key *concepts* which underpin statements of human rights, the application of such rights in the specific context of mental disorder, and the arguments presented throughout the remainder of this book. These concepts include, most importantly, human dignity and paternalism, both of which are considered next.

Human Rights, Human Dignity and Paternalism

The concepts underlying human rights have a lengthy history in society in general, but a substantial and specific focus on the rights of the mentally ill was not apparent until the UN produced its Principles for the Protection of Persons with Mental Illness and the Improvement of Mental Health Care in 1991.[93] More recently, many of the values underpinning the UN principles were again re-emphasised in the UN Convention on the Rights of Persons with Disabilities (CRPD), adopted by the UN General Assembly in 2006.[94] The CRPD commits signatory countries 'to promote, protect and ensure the full and equal enjoyment of all human rights and fundamental freedoms by all persons with disabilities, and to promote respect for their inherent dignity'.[95]

The contents and implications of the CRPD as they relate to mental disorder are explored in detail in Chapter 4 of this book. At this point, however, it is worth noting that while the United Kingdom (UK) signed the CRPD in 2007 and ratified it in 2009, Ireland signed the CRPD in 2007 but has yet to ratify it.

---

92   WHO, 2005.
93   UN, 1991.
94   UN, 2006; Bartlett et al., 2007.
95   CRPD, article 1.

Even following ratification, however, detailed observance of *specific measures* within the CRPD is highly likely to vary between signatory countries[96] and, ultimately, the key importance of the CRPD may well lie in its articulation of a broader set of values, including respect for the dignity, equality and worth of all human beings, rather than precise observance of specific provisions.[97]

The realisation of these values (dignity, equality and worth) clearly requires a dynamic balance between support and autonomy, and this is a balance that may vary over time, especially (but not exclusively) among persons with mental disorder: everyone, including persons with and without mental disorder, seeks to achieve a delicate balance between relying on the support of others and enjoying personal freedom and autonomy in various areas of life.[98] The importance of dignity in this matrix is underscored by Klug[99] and, especially, Osiatyński, who argues that the protection of dignity is one of the most important functions of *all* rights,[100] consistent with the emphasis that the Universal Declaration of Human Rights places on the 'inherent dignity' of all persons.[101] Underpinning this point further, Maritain maintains that dignity is an inherent quality which *all* human beings possess by virtue of the fact of being human.[102]

While concepts such as dignity are occasionally difficult to define, Beyleveld and Brownsword outline two useful conceptualisations of 'dignity

---

96   Lewis, O., 'The expressive, educational and proactive roles of human rights', in McSherry, B., and Weller, P. (eds), *Rethinking Rights-Based Mental Health Laws* (pp. 97–128), Oxford and Portland, Oregon: Hart Publishing, 2010; pp. 127–128.

97   Kämpf, A., 'Involuntary treatment decisions: using negotiated silence to facilitate change?', in McSherry, B., and Weller, P. (eds), *Rethinking Rights-Based Mental Health Laws* (pp. 129–150), Oxford and Portland, Oregon: Hart Publishing, 2010; p. 150; Carozza, P., 'Human dignity and judicial interpretation of human rights: a reply', *European Journal of International Law*, 2008, 19, 931–944.

98   Minkowitz, T., 'Abolishing mental health laws to comply with the Convention on the Rights of Persons with Disabilities', in McSherry, B., and Weller, P. (eds), *Rethinking Rights-Based Mental Health Laws* (pp. 151–177), Oxford and Portland, Oregon: Hart Publishing, 2010; p. 176.

99   Klug, F., *Values for a Godless Age: The History of the Human Rights Act and Its Political and Legal Consequences*, London: Penguin, 2000; pp. 100–101.

100   Osiatyński, W., *Human Rights and Their Limits*, Cambridge: Cambridge University Press, 2009; p. 189. See also: Edmundson, 2004; Ishay, 2004; Hunt, 2007; Boutros Boutros Ghali, quoted in: Tacket, A., *Health Equity, Social Justice and Human Rights*, London and New York, Routledge, 2012; p. 7.

101   Universal Declaration of Human Rights, preamble.

102   Maritain, J. *The Rights of Man and Natural Law*, New York: Charles Scribner's Sons, 1951; p. 65.

as empowerment' and 'dignity as constraint'.[103] The idea of 'dignity as empowerment' centres on individual dignity as the key foundation for human rights, consistent with the Universal Declaration of Human Rights. According to this conceptualisation, dignity reinforces claims to self-determination rather than limiting free choice.

Beyleveld and Brownsword also argue that a somewhat contrasting conception of 'dignity as constraint' is implicated in certain thinking about the limits to be placed on contemporary biomedicine, reflecting the belief that biomedical practice should be shaped, at least in part, by a shared conceptualisation of dignity that extends *beyond individuals*.[104] They cite various examples of this trend relating to body parts,[105] genes[106] and clinical ethics committees,[107] all converging on the idea that dignity is an objective value or good that reaches beyond the individual in such a fashion that if this value is violated, dignity is compromised *regardless of whether or not the person in questions freely performed the act in question*.[108]

While the optimal balance between 'dignity as empowerment' and 'dignity as constraint' may be difficult to attain, the concepts are nonetheless useful ones[109] and applicable in the context of mental disorder, when dignity may be undermined by either mental disorder itself or, on occasion, its treatment (e.g., involuntary detention), and interventions may have significant implications for both of Beyleveld and Brownsword's conceptualisations of dignity. In particular, many individuals with mental disorder may be socially marginalised and vulnerable,[110] suggesting that a dynamic balance between Beyleveld and Brownsword's two conceptualisations of dignity may be both relevant and helpful in understanding and resolving situations which are often highly complex, changeable and contested.

---

103 Beyleveld, D., Brownsword, R., *Human Dignity in Bioethics and Biolaw*, Oxford: Oxford University Press, 2001; p. vii.

104 Beyleveld & Brownsword, 2001; p. 29. See also: Beyleveld, D., Brownsword, R., Wallace, S., 'Clinical ethics committees: clinician support or crisis management?', *HEC Forum*, 2002, 14, 13–25; p. 13.

105 Beyleveld & Brownsword, 2001; p. 30. See also: Beyleveld, D., Brownsword, R., 'My body, my body parts, my property?', *Health Care Analysis*, 2000, 8, 87–99.

106 Beyleveld & Brownsword, 2001; pp. 38–41. See also: Beyleveld, D., Brownsword, R., 'Human dignity, human rights, and human genetics', *Modern Law Review*, 1998, 61, 661–680.

107 Beyleveld et al., 2002.

108 Beyleveld & Brownsword, 2001; p. 34.

109 Ashcroft, R.E., 'Making sense of dignity', *Journal of Medical Ethics*, 2005, 31, 679–682; p. 681.

110 Ashcroft, 2005; p. 681. See also: Kelly, B.D., 'The power gap: freedom, power and mental illness', *Social Science and Medicine*, 2006, 63, 2118–2128.

In the context of clinical care, Seedhouse and Gallagher propose a conceptualisation of dignity largely consistent with Beyleveld and Brownsword's idea of 'dignity as empowerment',[111] based on careful consideration of the capabilities and circumstances of the person.[112] Seedhouse and Gallagher argue that a person has dignity if is he or she is in a situation where he or she can apply his or her capabilities effectively. Since the ability to apply capabilities is dependent on circumstances, a health-worker can increase dignity by enhancing the person's capabilities, circumstances or both.

Consistent with this, Shotton and Seedhouse link loss of dignity with the extent to which specific circumstances prevent exercise of capabilities.[113] They articulate various levels of loss of dignity including trivial loss (when dignity is easily restored), serious loss (when substantial effort is required to restore dignity) and devastating loss (when it is impossible to regain dignity without help). Creating appropriate circumstances to support dignity in clinical settings involves developing an awareness of the importance of respect, weighing the balance between independence and dependence, and promoting the individual's own priorities and interests in the context of staff practices, clinical environments, health-care resources and various other aspects of care.[114]

Dworkin takes a slightly different approach and argues that a person's right to be treated with dignity is equivalent to the right to expect others to acknowledge his or her genuine critical interests.[115] Shotton and Seedhouse, however, argue that acknowledging such interests is not sufficient and that there is an obligation pro-actively to *protect* such interests, in order properly to maintain and promote dignity.[116] Consistent with this, Gallagher argues that dignity refers to the worth and value felt by *and* bestowed upon individuals.[117] She argues convincingly that we are *all* vulnerable to loss of dignity throughout our lives and that an Aristotlean 'ethic of aspiration' is required in order to acknowledge such vulnerability, aspire to be and do better, and develop awareness of the subtle effects of everyday activities on dignity.

In order to promote dignity in clinical practice, Gallagher points to the importance of people (e.g., clinicians), professional practice (what clinicians do),

111 Beyleveld & Brownsword, 2001; p. vii.

112 Seedhouse, D., Gallagher, A., 'Clinical ethics: undignifying institutions', *Journal of Medical Ethics*, 2002, 28, 368–372; p. 371.

113 Shotton, L., Seedhouse, D., 'Practical dignity in caring', *Nursing Ethics*, 1998, 5, 246–255.

114 Gallagher, A., Seedhouse, D., 'Dignity in care: the views of patients and relatives', *Nursing Times*, 2002, 98, 38–40.

115 Dworkin, R., *Life's Dominion*, London: Harper Collins, 1995; p. 236.

116 Shotton & Seedhouse, 1998; p. 253.

117 Gallagher, A., 'Dignity and respect for dignity – two key health professional values: implications for nursing practice', *Nursing Ethics*, 2004, 11, 587–599; p. 587.

place (clinical environments) and processes (for patients, families and staff). This is consistent with the approach of Cass and colleagues, who argue that dignity in care means providing the kind of care that supports and promotes a person's self-respect regardless of any perceived difference.[118] Against the background of these various approaches, Häyry suggests that the existence of a plurality of competing conceptualisation of dignity can be regarded as an opportunity, provided that relevant parties can muster some conceptual leniency towards each other.[119]

Mental health care, for example, can be characterised by both provision of care and deprivation of liberty, and is clearly likely to require a dynamic balance between Beyleveld and Brownsword's conceptualisations of 'dignity as empowerment' and 'dignity as constraint'.[120] At the point of delivery of care, however, the conceptualisation of dignity provided by Seedhouse and Gallagher appears especially useful, based on the idea that a person will have dignity when he or she can apply his or her capabilities effectively, and health workers can respect dignity by enhancing capabilities, circumstances or both.[121] This, broadly, is the approach to dignity applied throughout the remainder of this book.

This approach to dignity is also consistent with Nussbaum's theory of human capabilities, which proposes that human history demonstrates that certain human capabilities are essential to the very definition of a 'human being'.[122] This human capabilities approach involves an open-ended list of necessary human functions, capabilities and limitations. Developing such a list involves recognising a range of facts about being human, including that humans are born, have bodies, and die. We require food and shelter. We have the capabilities to drink, eat, move, work, play, reason, laugh and so forth. All of these qualities and capabilities define our common humanity.

Human capabilities theory, then, is based on a common conception of humanity, combined with an awareness of cultural difference and a need for

---

118   Cass, E., Robbins, D., Richardson, A. *Dignity in Care*, London: Social Care Institute for Excellence, 2006; p. 6. For an examination of philosophical underpinnings of various definitions of dignity, see: Rosen, M., *Dignity: Its History and Meaning*, Cambridge, MA: Harvard University Press, 2012.

119   Häyry, M., 'Another look at dignity', *Cambridge Quarterly of Healthcare Ethics*, 2004, 13, 7–14; p. 11.

120   Beyleveld & Brownsword, 2001; p. vii.

121   Seedhouse, D., Gallagher, A., 'Clinical ethics: undignifying institutions', *Journal of Medical Ethics*, 2002, 28, 368–372; p. 371.

122   Nussbaum, M.C., 'Human functioning and social justice: in defence of Aristotelian essentialism', *Political Theory*, 1992, 20, 202–246; Nussbaum, M.C., *Women and Human Development: The Capabilities Approach*, Cambridge: Cambridge University Press, 2000.

participatory dialogue among those who interpret its conception of humanity in different ways. In addition, according to Nussbuam, the human capabilities approach provides a basis for moral action because human capabilities, as presented in the theory, provide a basis for respect, and the idea of shared vulnerabilities provides a similar basis for compassion.[123]

The human capabilities theory also suggests that certain *values* are of particular importance; that is, by including the ability to reason as a fundamental human capability, this theory consequently respects the value of autonomy.[124] Nussbaum is, however, wary of linking capabilities directly with rights, believing that the idea of capabilities is clearer and more applicable across cultures. Nonetheless, Nussbaum acknowledges that her theory may provide a basis for certain rights claims; for example, the ability to reason suggests a right to freedom of conscience.[125]

As a general basis for governing human conduct, however, the human capabilities theory presents some potential difficulties, including its minimal guidance for making difficult moral distinctions between what is 'good' and 'bad', and the absence of a comprehensive method for reaching resolution when the needs of one person are incompatible with those of another.[126] Even in these circumstances, however, the human capabilities approach can provide at least some guidance. For example, by establishing minimal conditions for human flourishing, the theory would suggest that art is more conducive to human flourishing than torture (which is undeniably true).[127] In situations of conflict between the rights of individuals, the theory can again assist by prioritising basic capabilities over more developed ones. Ultimately, according to this approach, justice requires the realisation of fundamental human capabilities, and many dilemmas can be ameliorated by applying its principles in a flexible, considered and culturally sensitive fashion.[128]

Most importany for the present book, Nussbaum's human capabilities theory is notably consistent with the conceptualisation of dignity outlined by Seedhouse and Gallagher, centered on optimising both human capabilities and circumstances in order to enhance dignity.[129] This conceptualisation of dignity as being inextricably linked with capabilities is one of the key ideas throughout this book, hand-in-hand with the concept of human rights. There is, in addition,

---

123 Nussbaum, 1992.

124 Freeman, 2002; p. 67.

125 Nussbaum, 2000; pp. 96–101.

126 Gray, J., *Liberalism*, Milton Keynes: Open University Press, 1986; pp. 47–49.

127 Freeman, 2002; p. 67.

128 Nussbaum, M.C., *Creating Capabilities: The Human Development Approach*, Cambridge, MA: Harvard University Press, 2011.

129 Seedhouse & Gallagher, 2002; p. 371.

a third key concept (in addition to rights and dignity) which is central to this book's arguments, and this is the concept of paternalism, especially in relation to the human rights implications of apparently paternalistic interpretations of mental health legislation. This chapter concludes with a brief introduction to this third key concept, paternalism, before Chapters 2 and 3 present detailed examinations of mental health legislation in England and Ireland and elaborate further on this and other key themes.

Paternalism involves a claim by government or others to take responsibility for defining someone else's welfare, so that paternalism centres not on what a person wants for himself or herself, but on what others believe to be good for him or her.[130] In psychiatry, mental health legislation can appear paternalistic by interfering with the right to autonomy, ostensibly owing to concerns for the patient's mental health, the protection of others, and the patient's right to treatment.[131] Paternalistic attitudes towards the mentally ill may also be evident in other settings; for example, when employers insist that individuals may only return to work if they are monitored while taking medication.[132]

Ireland provides a good example of how paternalism can be enshrined in law, owing, in large part, to article 40 of the Constitution of Ireland (Bunreacht na hÉireann).[133] This article explicitly establishes equality before the law, but also articulates a need for 'due regard' for certain differences between persons:

> All citizens shall, as human persons, be held equal before the law. This shall not be held to mean that the State shall not in its enactments have due regard to differences of capacity, physical and moral, and of social function.[134]

The Constitution is even more explicit about the need to 'protect' certain individuals:

---

130 Feldman, D., *Civil Liberties and Human Rights in England and Wales (Second Edition)*, Oxford: Oxford University Press, 2002; p. 26. See also: McHale, J., Fox, M., Gunn, M., Wilkinson, S., *Health Care Law: Text and Materials (Second Edition)*, London: Sweet and Maxwell, 2006; p. 124.

131 Rosen, A., Rosen, T., McGorry, P., 'The human rights of people with severe and persistent mental illness', in Dudley, M., Silove, D. and Gale, F. (eds), *Mental Health and Human Rights* (pp. 297–320), Oxford: Oxford University Press, 2012; p. 299.

132 Sayce, L., *From Psychiatric Patient to Citizen*, Basingstoke: Palgrave, 2000; pp. 170–171.

133 Hogan, G., Whyte, G., *J.M. Kelly: The Irish Constitution (Fourth Revised Edition)*, Dublin: Tottel Publishing, 2003.

134 Constitution of Ireland, article 40(1).

The State shall, in particular, by its laws protect as best it may from unjust attack and, in the case of injustice done, vindicate the life, person, good name, and property rights of every citizen.[135]

The Irish Supreme Court made this paternalistic approach explicit in *Re A Ward of Court*, a case involving medical treatment for a person who lacked capacity, in which the Court determined that 'the Court should approach the matter from the standpoint of a prudent, good and loving parent'.[136] Against this background, many argue that Irish courts have interpreted Ireland's mental health legislation in an excessively paternalistic fashion, resulting in significant criticism (see Chapter 2).[137]

It is also argued, however, that this criticism stems from a misunderstanding of the legal Latin term *parens patriae*, which is the common law principle that the State (*patriae*) has parental (*parens*) obligations to care for the vulnerable, as enshrined in the Constitution.[138] Kennedy, a professor of forensic psychiatry in Ireland, presents a compelling argument that paternalistic interpretation of legislation is a method whereby the judiciary can hold the executive to account in relation to these welfare obligations towards vulnerable citizens, including those with mental disorder.

This issue, apparent paternalism in the content and interpretation of mental health legislation, especially in Ireland, forms the third key theme of this book, along with human rights and dignity (especially as linked with human capabilities). To commence this discussion, Chapter 2, examines mental health legislation in England and Ireland in some detail, with particular focus on human rights. It explores the background to current mental health legislation in both jurisdictions as well as key issues driving current and recent reform. Specific legislative provisions in key areas are outlined (e.g., criteria for detention, mental health tribunals), and an overall assessment of both jurisdictions is provided.

This is followed, in Chapter 3, by a detailed, point-by-point examination of the extent to which mental health legislation in England and Ireland meets (or fails to meet) the human rights standards for national mental health legislation presenten by the WHO in its Resource Book on Mental Health, Human Rights and Legislation.[139]

---

135 Constitution of Ireland, article 40(3).

136 *Re A Ward of Court (Withholding Medical Treatment) (No. 2)* [1996] 2 IR, [1995] 2 ILRM 40; p. 99.

137 Whelan, D., *Mental Health: Law and Practice*, Dublin: Round Hall, 2009; pp. 26–31.

138 Kennedy, H., '"Libertarian" groupthink not helping mentally ill', *Irish Times*, 2012, 12 September.

139 WHO, 2005.

Chapter 2
Mental Health Legislation in England and Ireland: Background to Current Mental Health Legislation

Regulatory control of people with mental disorder in England dates from at least the fourteenth century.[1] The Vagrancy Act 1744 made the first specific legislative provision for this group,[2] and this was later built upon to establish an era of asylum care in the 1800s, with the Lunacy Acts of 1890 and 1891 substantially revising admission criteria.[3] A shift to community care was signalled as early as 1926 by the Royal Commission on Lunacy and Mental Disorder,[4] and the Mental Treatment Act 1930 introduced voluntary admission status, as was also introduced in France, Germany, and elsewhere around this time.[5]

The establishment of the NHS in 1948 added further impetus to the move to a community-based model of care,[6] as did the 1957 Royal Commission on the Law Relating to Mental Illness and Mental Deficiency.[7] The Commission's conclusions were supported by the Mental Health Act 1959, which placed particular emphasis on voluntary admission[8] and increased clinical inputs into decisions.[9] Despite criticism of the perceived inadequacy of certain elements of

---

1   Bowen, P., *Blackstone's Guide to The Mental Health Act 2007*, Oxford: Oxford University Press, 2007; p. 10.

2   Bowen, 2007; p. 11.

3   Shorter, 1997; p. 231.

4   Royal Commission, Report of the Royal Commission on Lunacy and Mental Disorders (Cmd. 2700), London: Stationery Office, 1926.

5   Shorter, 1997; p. 230.

6   Mulholland, C., *A Socialist History of the NHS*, Saarbrücken: VDM Verlag, 2009.

7   Department of Health and Social Security, 1957.

8   Bowen, 2007; p. 13.

9   Unsworth, C., *The Politics of Mental Health Legislation*, Oxford: Clarendon Press, 1987; Moncrieff, J., 'The politics of a New Mental Health Act', *British Journal of Psychiatry*, 2003, 183, 8–9; Fennell, P., *Mental Health: The New Law*, Bristol: Jordan Publishing Limited, 2007; pp. 2–3.

community provision,[10] community care remained at the heart of government mental health policy throughout the 1970s and 1980s.[11] At the same time, there was growing awareness of the importance of human rights in health in general and mental health in particular,[12] stemming from a range of legal and medical sources.[13]

Against this background, the Mental Health Act 1983 introduced important reforms to mental health legislation in England, many of which had significant implications in terms of human rights. For example, the 1983 Act provided new definitions of 'mental disorder', 'severe mental impairment', 'mental impairment', and 'psychopathic disorder'.[14] Nobody was to be deemed to suffer from a mental disorder 'by reason only of promiscuity or other immoral conduct, sexual deviancy or dependence on alcohol or drugs'.[15]

The 1983 Act permitted involuntary 'admission for assessment' for people with mental disorder for up to 28 days, provided admission was supported by medical opinion.[16] 'Admission for treatment' was for up to six months[17] and required two medical opinions, as well as assurance that, 'in the case of psychopathic disorder or mental impairment, such treatment is likely to alleviate or prevent a deterioration of his condition';[18] and admission 'is necessary for the health or safety of the patient or for the protection of other persons that he

---

10   Fadden et al., 1987; Dyer, 1996.

11   Department of Health and Social Security, *Better Services for the Mentally Ill. Cmnd 6233*, London: Her Majesty's Stationery Office, 1975; Department of Health and Social Security, *Care in the Community. A Consultative Document on Moving Resources for Care in England*, London: Her Majesty's Stationery Office, 1981.

12   Gostin, L.O., *A Human Condition: The Mental Health Act from 1959 to 1975, Volume 1*, Leeds: National Association for Mental Health (MIND), 1975.

13   *X v UK* (1981) 4 EHRR 181; Bowen, 2007; p. 14; Bluglass, R., 'The origins of The Mental Health Act 1983', *Bulletin of the Royal College of Psychiatrists*, 1984, 8, 127–134; p. 128; Gostin, L.O., *A Human Condition: The Law Relating to Mentally Abnormal Offenders. Observations, Analysis and Proposals for Reform, Volume 2*, Leeds: National Association for Mental Health (MIND), 1975; Gunn, J., 'Reform of mental health legislation', *British Medical Journal*, 1981, 283, 1487–1488; Department of Health and Social Security, *Review of the Mental Health Act 1959*, London: Her Majesty's Stationery Office, 1975; Department of Health and Social Security, *Reform of Mental Health Legislation*, London: Her Majesty's Stationery Office, 1981.

14   Mental Health Act 1983, section 1(2).

15   Mental Health Act 1983, section 1(3). See also: *Winterwerp v Netherlands* (1979) 2 EHRR 387; *X v UK* (1981) 4 EHRR 188.

16   Mental Health Act 1983, section 2(3); *Winterwerp v Netherlands* (1979) 2 EHRR 387; *X v UK* (1981) 4 EHRR 188.

17   Mental Health Act 1983, section 3(2)(a).

18   Mental Health Act 1983, section 3(2)(b).

should receive such treatment'.[19] The legislation also contained provisions for 'guardianship',[20] which were significantly more limited in scope than those for involuntary admission.[21]

Detained patients could apply to the Mental Health Review Tribunal for a review of detention following admission for assessment (within 14 days), admission for treatment (within six months) or being received into guardianship (within six months).[22] The Tribunal could direct the discharge of a patient detained for assessment if not satisfied that the patient had a 'mental disorder of a nature or degree which warrants his detention in a hospital for assessment' and 'his detention as aforesaid is justified in the interests of his own health or safety or with a view to the protection of other persons'.[23]

The Tribunal could direct discharge of a patient otherwise detained if the tribunal was not satisfied '(i) that he is then suffering from mental illness, psychopathic disorder, severe mental impairment or mental impairment or from any of those forms of disorder of a nature or degree which makes it appropriate for him to be liable to be detained in a hospital for medical treatment; or (ii) that it is necessary for the health and safety of the patient or for the protection of other persons that he should receive such treatment; or (iii) in the case of [certain applications] that the patient, if released, would be likely to act in a manner dangerous to other persons or to himself'.[24]

The 1983 Act also outlined a mechanism for 'after-care under supervision' outside of hospital, once specific conditions were met and it was deemed medically advisable.[25] The benefits of compulsory treatment in the community are, however, far from established[26] and, while such an arrangement has the undoubted merit of permitting treatment in less restrictive settings, the practice supports the idea that individuals who are not detained within an institution can be subject to restrictions and requirements which impinge significantly on their freedoms.[27]

---

19 Mental Health Act 1983, section 3(2)(c).

20 Mental Health Act 1983, section 7(2)(a).

21 Gunn,1981; p. 1487.

22 Mental Health Act 1983, section 66).

23 Mental Health Act 1983, section 72(1)(a).

24 Mental Health Act 1983, section 72(1)(b).

25 Mental Health Act 1983, section 25B(5)–(6).

26 Kisely, S., Campbell, L.A., Preston, N., 'Compulsory community and involuntary outpatient treatment for people with severe mental disorders', *Cochrane Database of Systematic Reviews*, 2005, 3, CD004408; Lawton-Smith, S., Dawson, J., Burns, T., 'Community treatment orders are not a good thing', *British Journal of Psychiatry*, 2008, 193, 96–100.

27 Kelly, B.D., 'Community treatment orders under the Mental Health Act 2007 in England and Wales: what are the lessons for Irish mental health legislation?', *Medico-*

Ireland, by contrast, does not have, and has never had, explicit provision for compulsory treatment of mental disorder outside hospital settings. The history of mental health services in Ireland is, however, otherwise quite similar to that in England, at least to the extent that there was relatively scant provision of systematic care throughout the seventeenth and eighteenth centuries,[28] followed by the establishment of a large network of public asylums during the nineteenth.[29] In Ireland, the trend toward continually increasing admission rates persisted well into the mid-twentieth century: by 1961, one in every 70 Irish people above the age of 24 was in a psychiatric hospital,[30] a notably high proportion by international standards.[31]

Ireland's Mental Treatment Act 1945 aimed to address this situation and was to remain the cornerstone of Irish mental health legislation until the Mental Health Act 2001 was fully implemented in November 2006. Most notably, the 1945 Act increased medical involvement in the detention process and introduced a voluntary admission status,[32] a change which had already taken place in Great Britain (1930) and Northern Ireland (1932).[33] The 1945 Act also introduced new procedures for involuntary admission, one for 'temporary chargeable patients' and the other for 'persons of unsound mind'. Both involuntary admission processes required that a family member, relative or other person apply for admission of the individual concerned and that a doctor then examine the individual, who was then brought to the psychiatric hospital (by police, if necessary) where the involuntary admission order could be completed by a doctor, following another examination.

The 'temporary chargeable patient' procedure resulted in detention and involuntary treatment for up to six months (although this could be extended if clinically indicated), while the 'person of unsound mind' procedure resulted

---

Legal Journal of Ireland, 2009, 15, 43–48.

28   Psychiatrist, 1944; Robins, 1986; Kelly, B.D., 'Mental illness in nineteenth century Ireland: a qualitative study of workhouse records', *Irish Journal of Medical Science*, 2004, 173, 53–55.

29   Hallaran, 1810; Inspectors of Lunatics, *The Forty-Second Report (With Appendices) of the Inspector of Lunatics (Ireland)*, Dublin: Thom & Co. for Her Majesty's Stationery Office, 1893; Finnane, P., *Insanity and the Insane in Post-Famine Ireland*, London: Croon Helm, 1981.

30   Lyons, 1985.

31   Shorter, 1997; US Bureau of the Census, *Historical Statistics of the United States, Colonial Times to 1970, Bicentennial Edition, Part 2*, Washington, DC: GPO, 1975. Kelly, B.D., 'Mental health law in Ireland, 1945 to 2001: Reformation and renewal?' *Medico-Legal Journal*, 2008; 76, 65–72.

32   Mental Treatment Act 1945, part 15.

33   O'Neill, 2005; Kelly, B.D., 'The Mental Treatment Act 1945 in Ireland: an historical enquiry', *History of Psychiatry*, 2008, 19, 47–67.

in detention and involuntary treatment for an indefinite period. While either detention order could be revoked at any time by the psychiatrist, neither procedure was followed by automatic review by a tribunal or other independent body.

In order to challenge his or her detention, the patient had to either write to the 'Inspector of Mental Hospitals' or various other named parties,[34] or else instigate legal action in the Irish courts under the Constitution of Ireland.[35] Moreover, even when a detained patient accessed legal representation in order to challenge the detention in the High Court, the 1945 Act (as amended by section 2(3) of the Public Authorities Judicial Proceedings Act 1954) placed significant limitations on such civil proceedings, which could only be taken 'by leave of the High Court', and such leave could only be granted if the High Court was 'satisfied that there are substantial grounds for contending that the person against whom the proceedings are to be brought acted in bad faith or without reasonable care'.[36]

Issues Driving Reform of Mental Health Legislation

In the late 1900s, it was apparent that there was a need for reform of mental health legislation in both England and Ireland. In England, the Mental Health Act 1983 had raised a series of issues relating to both public safety and human rights, and there was a growing case for significant updating and reform of the Act.[37] With regard to public safety in particular, there had been a long-standing perception that people with mental disorder presented a substantial risk to public safety,[38] despite the fact that, at population level, the proportion of violent crime attributable to mental disorder is extremely low,[39] and much

---

34 The Minister for Health, President of the High Court, Registrar of Wards of Court, Health Board (i.e., local health authority), a Visiting Committee of a district mental hospital or the Inspector of Mental Hospitals (Mental Treatment Act 1945, section 266; Cooney, T., O'Neill, O., *Kritik 1: Psychiatric Detention: Civil Commitment in Ireland*, Delgany, Wicklow: Baikonur, 1996); p. 300.

35 Constitution of Ireland, article 40.

36 Mental Treatment Act 1945, section 260(1); Spellman, J., 'Section 260 of the Mental Treatment Act, 1945 Reviewed', *Medico-Legal Journal of Ireland*, 1998, 4, 20–24.

37 Richardson, 2005.

38 Shorter, 1997; Torrey, E.F., *Surviving Schizophrenia (Fourth Edition)*, New York: Quill/HarperCollins, 2001; Foley, S., Kelly, B.D., Clarke, M., McTigue, O., Gervin, M., Kamali, M., Larkin, C., O'Callaghan, E., Browne, S., 'Incidence and clinical correlates of aggression and violence in patients with first episode psychosis', *Schizophrenia Research*, 2005, 72, 161–168.

39 Walsh, E., Buchannan, A., Fahy, T., 'Violence and schizophrenia', *British Journal of Psychiatry*, 2001, 180, 490–495.

of that risk is attributable to co-occurring drug misuse rather than mental disorder itself.[40] Moreover, owing to the rarity of violence in mental disorder, prediction is impossible.[41]

Despite these facts, the issue of public safety featured prominently in considerations and reconsiderations of mental health law following the Mental Health Act 1983.[42] The issue of public safety was further emphasised following the case of Christopher Clunis, a man with a history of mental disorder who killed a musician in London in 1992.[43] Public safety was subsequently a strong feature in the deliberations of the 'Expert Committee', chaired by Professor Genevra Richardson, which advised the government on revising the 1983 Act.[44] This concern was duly reflected in England's Mental Health Act 2007 (see below).[45]

Concern about public safety was, however, accompanied by specific human rights concerns raised by the 1983 Act, and subsequent national and international cas-law. Key human rights concerns that emerged over this period included:

- The fact that the burden of proof in the Mental Health Review Tribunal lay with the patient,[46] a situation which the Court of Appeal deemed incompatible with article 5(1) of the ECHR;[47] the Mental Health Act 1983 (Remedial) Order 2001 (SI 2001/3712) remedied the matter.

---

40 Steadman, H.J., Mulvey, E.P., Monahan, J., Clark Robbins, P., Applebaum, P.S., Grisso, T., Roth, L.H., Silver, E., 'Violence by people discharged from acute psychiatric inpatient facilities and by others in the same neighbourhoods', *Archives of General Psychiatry*, 1998, 55, 393–401.

41 Szmukler, G., 'Homicide enquiries', *Psychiatric Bulletin*, 2000, 24, 6–10; Foley et al., 2005.

42 Bowen, 2007; pp. 10–23; Fennell, 2007; pp. 6–7. See also: Bartlett, P., Sandland, R., *Mental Health Law: Policy and Practice (Third Edition)*, Oxford: Oxford University Press, 2007; p. 151.

43 Court, C., 'Clunis inquiry cites "catalogue of failure"', *British Medical Journal*, 1994, 308, 613; Ritchie, J.H., Dick, D., Lingham, R., *The Report of the Inquiry into the Care and Treatment of Christopher Clunis*, London: Her Majesty's Stationery Office, 1994; Coid, J.W., 'The Christopher Clunis enquiry', *Psychiatric Bulletin*, 1994, 18, 449–452.

44 Expert Committee, 1999; p. 19.

45 Mental Health Act 2007, section 1(2).

46 Mental Health Act 1983, sections 72 and 73; R *(H) v Mental Health Review Tribunal* [2002] EWHC 1522 (Admin), [2002] QB 1; Dyer, C., 'Ruling could free dozens of mentally ill offenders', *Guardian*, 2001, 29 March.

47 Specifically, the 'reverse burden of proof' violated the ECHR right to liberty (article 5(1)).

- The ECHR right to respect for 'private and family life',[48] which led to a series of cases in which judgments emphasised the patient's right to select his or her 'nearest relative';[49] that recording of telephone calls in a high secure setting might not breach this right;[50] and that considerable (although not absolute) importance is to be accorded to codes of practice in relation to matters such as seclusion and mechanical restraint.[51]
- Section 6(1) of the Human Rights Act 1998, which makes it 'unlawful for a public authority to act in a way which is incompatible with a Convention right';[52] in one case concerning the suicide of a detained psychiatric inpatient, the House of Lords concluded that the NHS Trust had a duty to reasonably protect patients from taking their own lives[53] and, in a second, the Supreme Court declared that this obligation can extend to voluntary patients, even when on home leave.[54]
- Other cases relating to the 1983 Act focused on the powers of tribunals to release patients,[55] adequate resourcing[56] and flexible timing

---

48 ECHR, article 8.

49 *R (M) v Secretary of State for Health* [2003] EWHC 1094 (Admin), [2003] 1 MHLR 88; Mental Health Act 1983, section 26.

50 *R (N) v Ashworth Special Hospital Authority* [2001] EWHC 339 (Admin), [2001] HRLR 46.

51 *R (Munjaz) v Mersey Care NHS Trust* [2003] EWCA Civ 1036 [2004] QB 395; *R (Munjaz) v Mersey Care NHS Trust* [2005] UKHL 58 [2006] 2 AC 148; *Munjaz v UK* App no 2913/06 (ECHR, 17 July 2012). Department of Health, 2008; p. 2. See also: *R v Deputy Governor of Parkhurst Prison, ex parte Hague and Weldon* [1992] 1 AC 58. For comparison with Ireland, see: Mental Health Commission, *Rules Governing the Use of Seclusion and Mechanical Means of Bodily Restraint*, Dublin: Mental Health Commission, 2009.

52 Human Rights Act 1998, section 6(1).

53 *Savage v South Essex Partnership NHS Foundation Trust* [2008] UKHL 74; *Savage v South Essex Partnership NHS Foundation Trust* [2010] EWHC 865 (QB).

54 *Rabone and Anor v Pennine Care NHS Trust* [2012] UKSC 2. See also: Bowcott, O., 'Hospital breached duty of care to psychiatric patient, supreme court rules', *Guardian*, 2012, 8 February; Madden, E., 'Important UK Supreme Court decision on human rights', *Irish Medical Times*, 2012, 18, 26.

55 *R (D) v Secretary of State for the Home Department* [2002] EWHC 2805 (Admin) [2003] 1 WLR 1315; see also: *Benjamin v UK* (2002) 36 EHRR 1, and Criminal Justice Act 2003; section 295.

56 *R (KB) v Mental Health Review Tribunal* [2003] EWHC 193 (Admin) [2004] QB 936; Richardson, G., 'The European convention and mental health law in England and Wales', *International Journal of Law and Psychiatry*, 2005, 28, 127–139.

of tribunals,[57] various issues regarding treatment[58] and a range of other matters.[59]

The development of the Mental Health Act 2007 was fuelled by worries about public safety and these kinds of human rights concerns,[60] many of which were further emphasised by concerning service-related data indicating, for example, high rates of psychiatric detention among Black compared to White patients,[61] different rates of appeal after detention in different ethnic groups,[62] and low levels of understanding among consultant psychiatrists regarding their roles at tribunals[63] and among general hospital doctors regarding assessing capacity

---

57 *R (C) v London South and West Region Mental Health Review Tribunal* [2001] EWCA Civ 1110 [2002] 1 WLR 176.

58 *R (PS) v Responsible Medical Officer* [2003] EWHC 2335 (Admin); *Hutchison Reid v UK* (2003) 37 EHRR 211. For a discussion of 'dangerous and severe personality disorder', see: Buchanan, A., Grounds, A., 'Forensic psychiatry and public protection', *British Journal of Psychiatry*, 2011, 198, 420–423; Duggan, C., 'Dangerous and severe personality disorder', *British Journal of Psychiatry*, 2011, 198, 431–433.

59 Mental Health Act 1983, section 2. *R (M) v Secretary of State for Health* [2003] EWHC 1094 (Admin) [2003] 1 MHLR 88.

60 Bindman, J., Maingay, S., Szmukler, G., 'The Human Rights Act and mental health legislation', *British Journal of Psychiatry*, 2003, 182, 91–94; Curtice, M.J.R., 'Medical treatment under Part IV of the Mental Health Act 1983 and the Human Rights Act 1998', *Psychiatric Bulletin*, 2009, 33, 111–115; Kingdon, D., Jones, R., Lönnqvist, J., 'Protecting the human rights of people with mental disorder', *British Journal of Psychiatry*, 2004, 185, 277–279; Council of Europe, *Recommendation (818) on the Situation of the Mentally Ill*, Strasbourg: Council of Europe, 1977; Council of Europe, *Recommendation R(83)2 of the Committee of Ministers to Member States Concerning the Legal Protection of Persons Suffering from Mental Disorder Placed as Involuntary Patients*, Strasbourg: Council of Europe, 1983; Council of Europe, *Recommendation 1235 on Psychiatry and Human Rights*, Strasbourg: Council of Europe, 1994; Council of Europe, *White Paper Regarding a Draft Recommendation on Legal Protection of Persons Suffering from Mental Disorder*, Strasbourg: Council of Europe, 2000; Council of Europe, *White Paper on the Protection of the Human Rights and Dignity of People Suffering from Mental Disorder*, Strasbourg: Council of Europe, 2000.

61 Singh, S.P., Greenwood, N., White, S., Churchill, R., 'Ethnicity and the Mental Health Act 1983', *British Journal of Psychiatry*, 2007, 191, 99–105.

62 Nilforooshan, R., Amin, R., Warner, J., 'Ethnicity and outcome of appeal after detention under the Mental Health Act 1983', *Psychiatric Bulletin*, 2009, 33, 288–290.

63 Nimmagadda, S., Jones, C.N., 'Consultant psychiatrists' knowledge of their role as representatives of the responsible authority at mental health review tribunals', *Psychiatric Bulletin*, 2008, 32, 366–369.

under the 1983 Act,[64] despite increased committal rates.[65] Interestingly, the issue of patient dignity did not feature prominently in discussion leading up to the 2007 Act which focused chiefly on a perceived need to balance patients' rights to autonomy and non-discrimination with public protection and paternalism,[66] with, arguably, a greater emphasis on public safety than on protecting rights.

These key drivers of change in England contrast somewhat with the drivers of change in Ireland, where human rights concerns took centre-stage and public safety was essentially absent from public discussion. In 2008, for example, the Irish Supreme Court found Ireland's Mental Treatment Act 1945 had been inconsistent with the Irish Constitution all along, as it restricted grounds for challenging detention to two specific grounds (acting in 'bad faith' or proceeding 'without reasonable care'), and thus represented a disproportionate restriction on the patient's right to access the courts where a fundamental right, liberty,[67] had been restricted.[68]

In 1999, the Irish Law Society highlighted this and several other problems with the 1945 Act[69] and, based on a review of case law and international human rights standards, proposed that criteria for involuntary commitment be more clearly defined; a 'least restrictive alternative' principle be introduced, along with a right to a minimum level of psychiatric service; formal safeguards be extended to voluntary patients; and measures be introduced to enable reviews of detention orders. These ideas were strongly consistent with the government's 1995 White Paper, which proposed introducing new legislation and admitted that the 1945 Act did not accord with Ireland's obligations under international law.[70] The changes required included 'a redefinition of the criteria for detention of mentally disordered persons'; 'the introduction of procedures to review the

---

64 Richards, F., Dale, J., 'The Mental Health Act 1983 and incapacity', *Psychiatric Bulletin*, 2009, 33, 176–178.

65 Information Centre, *In-patients Formally Detained in Hospitals Under the Mental Health Act 1983 and Other Legislation: 1995–96 to 2005–06*, London: Information Centre/ Government Statistical Service, 2007: p. 4; NHS Information Centre for Health and Social Care, 2011; p. 9; Singh, D.K., Moncrieff, J., 'Trends in mental health review tribunal and hospital managers' hearings in north-east London 1997–2007', *Psychiatric Bulletin*, 2009, 33, 15–17.

66 Mental Health Alliance, *Mental Health Act 2007: Report Stage Briefing, House of Commons*, London: Mental Health Alliance, 2006; p. 1.

67 Constitution of Ireland, article 6.

68 *Blehein v The Minister for Health and Children and others* [2008] IESC 40; Madden, E., 'Section of Mental Health Act was unconstitutional', *Irish Medical Times*, 2009, 30, 15.

69 Law Reform Committee, *Mental Health: The Case for Reform*, Dublin: The Law Society, 1999.

70 Department of Health, 1995; p. 13.

decision to detain a person'; 'an automatic review of long-term detention'; and 'greater safeguards for the protection of detained persons'.[71]

In marked contrast with England, then, the Irish reforms were explicitly driven by human rights; concerns about public safety did not shape the reform process to any significant extent at any stage. International influences were, however, clearly to the fore, as the Irish government explicitly sought to achieve 'full compliance with our obligations under the European Convention',[72] and the Law Society explicitly relied on the ECHR and UN Principles for the Protection of Persons with Mental Illness and the Improvement of Mental Health Care[73] in its recommendations.[74]

The centrality of human rights in this process was emphasised yet again in 2000, when the lack of automatic review of detention under the Mental Treatment Act 1945 formed the focus of an important case in the European Court of Human Rights.[75] In the course of these proceedings, the Irish Supreme Court declared that the lack of an automatic, independent review of psychiatric detention did not violate the Irish Constitution, and so the applicant took his case to the European Court of Human Rights arguing that his ECHR rights were being violated. In a 'friendly settlement' in 2000, the Irish state noted its obligations under the ECHR and paid an agreed compensatory sum to the applicant. The state also noted that the applicant's claim had been initiated prior to the publication of the Mental Health Bill 1999, which was progressed with notably greater urgency after this case was instigated in the Irish courts in 1994 and later in the European Court of Human Rights.[76] This process eventually resulted in the Mental Health Act 2001, which currently forms the centre-piece of Ireland's civil mental health legislation.

Interestingly, human rights standards, especially as reflected in the ECHR, continued to dominate this reform process not only during the drafting of the Mental Health Act 2001, but also after the new legislation had passed through the Oireachtas (Irish parliament) on 8 July 2001 and full implementation was awaited.[77] The 2001 Act was finally, fully implemented on 1 November 2006,

---

71   Department of Health, 1995; p. 15.

72   Department of Health, 1995; p. 15.

73   UN, 1991.

74   Law Reform Committee, 1999.

75   *Croke v Smith* [1994] 3 IR 529; *Croke v Smith (No. 2)* [1998] 1 IR 101; *Croke v Ireland* (2000) ECHR 680.

76   *Croke v Smith* [1994] 3 IR 529; Rutherdale, A., 'Detention in mental hospital after 6 month period without new order invalid', *Irish Times*, 1994, 26 September; Department of Health, 1995; *Croke v Smith (No. 2)* [1998] 1 IR 101; Law Reform Committee, 1999.

77   Coulter, C., 'Legal rights of mental health sufferers ignored', *Irish Times*, 2005, 1 November; Kelly, B.D., 'Irish mental health law', *Irish Psychiatrist*, 2006, 7, 29–30; Owens, J., 'Mental health services crying out for reform', *Irish Times*, 2005, 21 November.

and key provisions of the new legislation are discussed and compared with the corresponding provisions in English mental health legislation next.

Specific Legislative Provisions in England and Ireland

Definition of Mental Disorder

In England, the Mental Health Act 2007, which amended but did not replace the Mental Health Act 1983, removed the four categories of mental illness outlined in the 1983 Act[78] and redefined 'mental disorder' as 'any disorder or disability of the mind'.[79] Individuals with a learning disability 'shall not be considered by reason of that disability' to be suffering from mental disorder 'unless that disability is associated with abnormally aggressive or seriously irresponsible conduct on his part'.[80] These changes were broadly in line with recommendations of the Richardson Committee[81] and Mental Health Act Commission.[82]

The 2007 Act also amended the exclusion criteria: whereas the Mental Health Act 1983 stated that somewhat was to be deemed to have a mental disorder 'by reason only of promiscuity or other immoral conduct, sexual deviancy or dependence on alcohol or drugs',[83] the 2007 Act replaced these exclusion criteria with the following: 'Dependence on alcohol or drugs is not considered to be a disorder or disability of the mind'.[84] This reform may reflect the current unlikeliness of anyone being diagnosed as mentally ill owing to 'promiscuity or other immoral conduct' or 'sexual deviancy',[85] but it also means that it is no longer explicitly unlawful under mental health legislation to do so.[86] There also remains, of course, considerable clinical discretion about whether or not any provisions of legislation are applied in a particular case;[87] that is, not everyone who fulfils criteria for mental disorder is so diagnosed, and not everyone who fulfils criteria for detention is detained.

---

78   Mental Health Act 1983, section 1(2).

79   Mental Health Act 2007, section 1(2).

80   Mental Health Act 2007, section 2(2).

81   Expert Committee, 1999.

82   Mental Health Act Commission, *Placed amongst Strangers*, London: The Stationery Office, 2003; para. 7.31, pp. 85–86.

83   Mental Health Act 1983, section 1(3).

84   Mental Health Act 2007, section 1(3).

85   Mental Health Act 2007, section 1(3).

86   Mental Health Act 2007, section 1(3).

07   Hall, I., Ali, A., 'Changes to the Mental Health and Mental Capacity Acts', *Psychiatric Bulletin*, 2009, 33, 226–230.

In Ireland, the Mental Health Act 2001 defined 'mental disorder' to include 'mental illness, severe dementia or significant intellectual disability' where 'there is a serious likelihood of the person concerned causing immediate and serious harm to himself or herself or to other persons' or 'the judgment of the person concerned is so impaired that failure to admit the person to an approved centre [inpatient psychiatric facility] would be likely to lead to a serious deterioration in his or her condition or would prevent the administration of appropriate treatment that could be given only by such admission'.[88] In addition, detention and treatment must 'be likely to benefit or alleviate the condition of that person to a material extent'.[89]

'Mental illness' is further defined a' 'state of mind of a person which affects the person's thinking, perceiving, emotion or judgment and which seriously impairs the mental function of the person to the extent that he or she requires care or medical treatment in his or her own interest or in the interest of other persons'.[90]

'Severe dementia' is 'a deterioration of the brain of a person which significantly impairs the intellectual function of the person thereby affecting thought, comprehension and memory and which includes severe psychiatric or behavioural symptoms such as physical aggression'.[91] 'Significant intellectual disability' is 'a state of arrested or incomplete development of mind of a person which includes significant impairment of intelligence and social functioning and abnormally aggressive or seriously irresponsible conduct on the part of the person'.[92]

Overall, these Irish definitions are substantially consistent with day-to-day clinical definitions, such as, for example, the WHO definition of intellectual

---

88 Mental Health Act 2001, section 3(1). The phrase 'serious likelihood' of harm has been interpreted by the High Court to represent a standard of proof of a high level of probability which is beyond the normal standard of proof in civil actions (i.e., more likely, or probable, to be true) but below the standard in criminal prosecution (i.e., beyond reasonable doubt); i.e., 'proof to a standard of a high level of likelihood as distinct from simply being more likely to be true' (*MR v Cathy Byrne, administrator, and Dr Fidelma Flynn, clinical director, Sligo Mental Health Services, Ballytivnan, Co. Sligo* [2007] IEHC 73; p. 16). In the same case, the meaning of the word 'serious' in the phrase 'immediate and serious harm' was interpreted as differing depending on whether the harm is directed at one's self or others: 'Clearly, the infliction of any physical injury on another could only be regarded as "serious" harm, while the infliction of a minor physical injury on the person themselves could be regarded as not "serious"' (p. 17).

89 Mental Health Act 2001, section 3(1).

90 Mental Health Act 2001, section 3(2).

91 Mental Health Act 2001, section 3(2).

92 Mental Health Act 2001, section 3(2).

disability.[93] The Mental Health Act 2001 adds a requirement for 'abnormally aggressive or seriously irresponsible conduct',[94] chiefly because once an individual fulfils the definition of 'significant intellectual disability', which is a form of 'mental disorder', that individual can be detained and involuntarily treated.

The Mental Health Act 2007 introduced a similar requirement in England, where individuals with learning disability 'shall not be considered by reason of that disability' to be suffering from mental disorder 'unless that disability is associated with abnormally aggressive or seriously irresponsible conduct on his part'.[95]

Interestingly, the definitions in Ireland's Mental Health Act 2001 are significantly more similar to those in England's original Mental Health Act 1983 than the Mental Health Act 2007. The original 1983 Act defined 'mental disorder' as 'mental illness, arrested or incomplete development of mind, psychopathic disorder and any other disorder or disability of mind',[96] which is notably similar to the definition in Ireland's 2001 Act. England's Mental Health Act 2007, however, removed these four categories and redefined 'mental disorder' as 'any disorder or disability of the mind',[97] in marked contrast with Ireland.

In addition, a person cannot be detained under Ireland's Mental Health Act 2001 solely because he or she 'is suffering from a personality disorder;[98] and, while England's 2007 Act removed the need for 'abnormally aggressive or seriously irresponsible conduct' for a diagnosis of psychopathic disorder',[99] detention can still occur if 'it is necessary for the health or safety of the patient or for the protection of other persons that he should receive such treatment'.[100]

Criteria for Detention

In England, the Mental Health Act 2007 introduced significant amendments to involuntary detention processes. The original Mental Health Act 1983 had permitted the civil committal of persons with 'psychopathic disorder or mental impairment' under section 3 only if 'treatment is likely to alleviate or prevent a deterioration of his condition';[101] this criterion also applied to renewal orders for

---

93 WHO, *ICD-10 Guide for Mental Retardation*, Geneva: WHO, 1996; p. 1.

94 Mental Health Act 2001, section 3(2).

95 Mental Health Act 2007, section 2(2).

96 Mental Health Act 1983, section 1(2).

97 Mental Health Act 2007, section 1(2).

98 Mental Health Act 2001, section 8(2).

99 Mental Health Act 1983, section 1(2).

100 Mental Health Act 1983, section 3(2)(c).

101 Mental Health Act 1983, section 3(2)(b).

all forms of mental disorder.[102] If this condition was not met, a renewal order could still be made for a patient with 'mental illness or severe mental impairment' if 'the patient, if discharged, is unlikely to be able to care for himself, to obtain the care which he needs or to guard himself against serious exploitation'.[103]

The Mental Health Act 2007 replaced these 'treatability and care tests' with a more autonomy-focused 'appropriate treatment test' which applies to all forms of mental disorder; that is, orders[104] can be made or renewed only if 'appropriate medical treatment is available'.[105] The 2007 Act also expanded the areas of application of the new 'appropriate treatment test' to include accused individuals on remand to hospital for treatment,[106] transfer directions for remand prisoners and other detainees,[107] and 'hospital orders'.[108] Renewal orders, too, must now meet this condition[109] and, if it is not met, a tribunal can discharge the patient.[110] This test does not, however, apply to those detained under sections 2 ('admission for assessment'), 35 ('remand to hospital for report on accused's mental condition'), 135 ('warrant to search for and remove patients') or 136 ('mentally disordered persons found in public places'). The provision to make a renewal order under section 20(4) of the 1983 Act (i.e., 'the patient, if discharged, is unlikely to be able to care for himself, to obtain the care which he needs or to guard himself against serious exploitation') was repealed by the 2007 Act.[111]

The 2007 Act also amended the definition of the term 'medical treatment' so as to include, in addition to 'nursing',[112] 'psychological intervention and specialist mental health habilitation, rehabilitation and care'.[113] 'Medical treatment' refers to 'medical treatment the purpose of which is to alleviate,

---

102   Mental Health Act 1983, section 20(4)(b).

103   Mental Health Act 1983, section 20(4).

104   Under sections 3, 37, 45A and 47.

105   Mental Health Act 2007, section 4; amending Mental Health Act 1983, sections 3(2)(b); 3(4)(b); 37(2)(a)(i); 45A(2)(c); 47(1).

106   Mental Health Act 2007, section 5(2); amending Mental Health Act 1983, section 36(1).

107   Mental Health Act 2007, section 5(3); amending Mental Health Act 1983, section 48(1).

108   Mental Health Act 2007, section 5(4); amending Mental Health Act 1983, section 51(6)(a).

109   Mental Health Act 2007, section 4(4); amending Mental Health Act 1983, section 20(4).

110   Mental Health Act 2007, section 5(8); amending Mental Health Act 1983, section 72(1)(b)(ii).

111   Mental Health Act 2007, section 4(4)(c).

112   Mental Health Act 1983, section 145(1).

113   Mental Health Act 2007, section 7(2).

or prevent a worsening of, the disorder or one or more of its symptoms or manifestations'[114] and, for each patient, such treatment must be 'appropriate in his case, taking into account the nature and degree of the mental disorder and all other circumstances of his case'.[115]

The 2007 Act's amendment of the 'treatability test' proved controversial during the Act's passage through parliament.[116] Under the final, compromise provisions, it is no longer necessary to demonstrate that treatment is 'likely' to help, but rather that it has the 'purpose' of helping, regardless of likely efficacy. Even so, the introduction and expansion of the 'appropriate treatment test' appears to go beyond the requirements of the ECHR, which does not outline *any* treatability test for persons of 'unsound mind' who are detained, once the detention is 'in accordance with a procedure prescribed by law'.[117]

Overall, it appears unlikely that these changes in England will usher in a period of preventive detention, not least because if treatment is not benefitting a patient, doctors are ethically bound to discharge the patient.[118] It is possible, however, that widening the role of 'responsible clinician'[119] to include other professionals (e.g., clinical psychologists) may ultimately result in greater decision-making by individuals trained in settings with different priorities, such as prisons, where issues of public safety may hold greater sway, and this could potentially increase the custodial element within services.[120]

Overall, however, it appears equally arguable that the new 'appropriate treatment test' has, in fact, set the threshold for detention in England *higher* than previously, as it is now necessary that the proposed treatment is truly available to the patient at the time of admission; this is generally protective of both the right to liberty and a patient's reasonable expectation of treatment when detained (i.e., a principle of reciprocity).

In Ireland, the Mental Health Act 2001 specifies that a person can be involuntarily admitted to an 'approved centre' (i.e., registered psychiatric inpatient facility) on the grounds that he or she is suffering from a 'mental disorder';[121] a person *cannot* be so detained solely on the grounds that he or she '(a) is suffering from a personality disorder, (b) is socially deviant, or (c) is addicted to drugs or intoxicants'.[122]

---

114 Mental Health Act 2007, section 7(3).
115 Mental Health Act 2007, section 4(3).
116 Bowen, 2007; p. 47.
117 ECHR, section 5(1)(e).
118 Bowen, 2007; p. 55.
119 Mental Health Act 2007, sections 9–17.
120 Bowen, 2007; p. 55.
121 Mental Health Act 2001, section 8(1).
122 Mental Health Act 2001, section 8(2).

An application for detention can be made by a spouse, relative, 'authorised officer',[123] member of the Garda Síochána (Irish police force) or, in circumstances where no one in these categories is available, anyone else, subject to specific conditions.[124] In all cases, the applicant must have observed the person within 48 hours of signing the application.[125]

The next step involves examination by a registered doctor (e.g., general practitioner) with a view to a 'recommendation' for involuntary admission.[126] If this 'recommendation' is provided, the person can be conveyed to the psychiatric unit or hospital,[127] with the assistance of 'staff of the approved centre', if required.[128] If 'there is a serious likelihood of the person concerned causing immediate and serious harm to himself or herself or to other persons', members of the police force can enter the person's home by force and ensure the removal of the person to the approved centre.[129]

Once the person arrives at the inpatient facility, a consultant psychiatrist 'shall, as soon as may be, carry out an examination of the person' and shall either (a) complete an 'admission order' if 'he or she is satisfied that the person is suffering from a mental disorder' or (b) decline to complete an 'admission order'.[130] The person can be detained for up to 24 hours for such an examination to occur. If an admission order is made, it authorises 'the reception, detention and treatment of the patient concerned and shall remain in force for a period of 21 days';[131] this may be extended by a 'renewal order' for up to three months;[132] this may then be extended for up to 6 months; and each further extension can be for up to 12 months.[133]

---

123 Mental Health Act 2001, section 9(8).

124 Mental Health Act 2001, section 9(2).

125 Mental Health Act 2001, section 9(4).

126 Mental Health Act 2001, sections 10(2) and 10(5).

127 Mental Health Act 2001, section 13(1).

128 Mental Health Act 2001, section 13(2). See also: *EF v The Clinical Director of St Ita's Hospital* [2007] JR 816; and the Health (Miscellaneous Provisions) Act 2009; section 63.

129 Mental Health Act 2001, section 13(3).

130 Mental Health Act 2001, section 14(1).

131 Mental Health Act 2001, section 15(1).

132 Mental Health Act 2001, section 15(2). See also: *MD v Clinical Director of St Brendan's Hospital & Anor* [2007] IEHC 183; and Madden, E., 'Involuntary detention found admissible in the High Court', *Irish Medical Times*, 2007, 28, 20.

133 Mental Health Act 2001, section 15(3); renewal orders should be completed by the consultant psychiatrist responsible for the care and treatment of the patient; more than one consultant psychiatrist may meet that description (e.g., if a detained patient is under the care of a consultant forensic psychiatrist in Dublin's Central Mental Hospital, an inpatient forensic psychiatry facility, but their catchment area (non-

Following the completion of an involuntary admission order, the consultant psychiatrist is under an obligation to inform the Mental Health Commission, which can then (a) refer the matter to a mental health tribunal; (b) assign a legal representative to the patient, 'unless he or she proposes to engage one'; and (c) arrange that an independent psychiatrist examine the patient, interview the consultant psychiatrist and review the records.[134] Within 21 days, a mental health tribunal reviews the detention of the patient.

Ireland's 2001 Act also permits the clinical director to arrange for the transfer of a patient 'detained in that centre for treatment to a hospital or other place and for his or her detention there for that purpose' and the 'detention of a patient in a hospital or other place under this section shall be deemed for the purposes of this Act to be detention in the centre from which he or she was transferred'.[135]

Finally, Ireland's 2001 Act states that when a voluntary patient 'indicates at any time that he or she wishes to leave the approved centre', a staff member may, if 'of opinion that the person is suffering from a mental disorder', detain him or her for up to 24 hours.[136] During this period, the consultant psychiatrist responsible for the care of the patient 'shall either discharge the person or arrange for him or her to be examined by another consultant psychiatrist'[137] and, if the second psychiatrist 'is satisfied that the person is suffering from

---

forensic) psychiatrist is also involved in their treatment) (*JB v The Director of the Central Mental Hospital and Dr Ronan Hearne and the Mental Health Commission and the Mental Health Tribunal* [2007] IEHC 201). See also: *MM v Clinical Director Central Mental Hospital* [2008] IESC 31; Madden, E., 'Supreme Court rules on Mental Health Act', *Irish Medical Times*, 2008, 22, 26.

134 Mental Health Act 2001, section 17(1).

135 Mental Health Act 2001, section 22(1); the legislation states that such transfers must be arranged by the clinical director, but the High Court found that, in cases of medical emergency, it would be 'manifestly absurd and contrary to the whole spirit and intention of the Act' (p. 7) to potentially jeopardise the health of a detained patient owing to the non-availability of the clinical director to personally 'arrange' such transfer to a medical facility; other staff may do so under such circumstances (*Patrick McCreevy v The Medical Director of the Mater Misericordia Hospital in the City of Dublin, and the Clinical Director of St Aloysius Ward Psychiatric Unit of the Mater Misericordia Hospital in the City of Dublin and the Health Service Executive and, by order, the Mental Health Tribunal* [2007] SS 1413).

136 Mental Health Act 2001, section 23(1); the individual must express a desire to leave for this procedure to be invoked; other expressions of disagreement with treatment plans (e.g., declining medication) do not constitute grounds for detention under this section (*Q v St Patrick's Hospital* [2006] O'Higgins J., *ex tempore*, 21 December 2006).

137 Mental Health Act 2001, section 24(1).

a mental disorder, he or she shall issue a certificate in writing';[138] then, the consultant psychiatrist responsible for the care of the patient shall make a 21-day admission order[139] which will be subject to review by a mental health tribunal within 21 days.[140]

Overall, the criteria and provisions for involuntary detention in both England and Ireland appear, on the face of it, to meet the *Winterwerp* requirement that a diagnosis of 'mental disorder' must be based upon 'objective medical expertise'.[141] The extent to which these procedures accord with the more detailed human rights standards outlined in the WHO's 'Checklist on Mental Health Legislation', in its Resource Book on Mental Health, Human Rights and Legislation,[142] is examined in Chapter 3.

Professional Roles

In England, the Mental Health Act 2007 introduced significant changes to the professional roles of a range of individuals in relation to involuntary admission and treatment. Under the 1983 Act, each detained patient was under the care of a 'responsible medical officer'[143] who had to be a 'registered medical practitioner'.[144] In the Mental Health Act 2007, references to 'responsible medical officer' were replaced by 'responsible clinician',[145] who is now 'the approved clinician with overall responsibility for the case',[146] and, in relation to guardianship, is 'the approved clinician authorised by the responsible local social services authority to act (either generally or in any particular case or for any particular purpose) as the responsible clinician'.[147]

The Mental Health Act 2007 Explanatory Notes clarify that 'approval need not be restricted to medical practitioners, and may be extended to practitioners

---

138 Mental Health Act 2001, section 24(2)(a).

139 Mental Health Act 2001, section 24(3).

140 Mental Health Act 2001, section 24(4).

141 *Winterwerp v Netherlands* (1979) 2 EHRR 387; see also *X v UK* (1981) 4 EHRR 188; the court stated that 'national authorities are better placed to evaluate the evidence adduced before them'; this is consistent with the court's general reliance on national courts for the determination of facts and on medical doctors for medical opinions.

142 WHO, 2005.

143 Mental Health Act 1983, section 34(1).

144 Mental Health Act 1983, section 55(1).

145 Mental Health Act 2007, section 9(9); amending Mental Health Act 1983, section 34(1).

146 Mental Health Act 2007, section 12(7)(a); amending Mental Health Act 1983, section 64(1).

147 Mental Health Act 2007, section 10; amending Mental Health Act 1983, section 34(1).

from other professions, such as nursing, psychology, occupational therapy and social work'.[148] Under the 2007 Act, the 'responsible clinician' will take over the roles previously performed by the 'responsible medical officer', as well as additional roles in relation to supervised community treatment.

The 2007 Act does not change the requirement that *medical* recommendations' (italics added) are needed to support *admission* for 'assessment'[149], 'treatment'[150] or guardianship[151] and must be provided by 'registered medical practitioners'.[152] This is consistent with the requirement, enunciated by the European Court of Human Rights, that there must be objective medical evidence that an individual is of 'unsound mind' if he or she is to be deprived of liberty on that basis.[153]

The 2007 Act does, however, change the legal situation regarding *renewal* orders. Under the original 1983 Act, the making of a renewal order, like an admission order, required an examination and report by a 'responsible medical officer',[154] but, following the 2007 Act, the 'responsible clinician' (who may or may not be a medical doctor) can now make out a renewal order, although they must consult with another 'professional' connected with the case before doing so.[155]

The 2007 Act also introduced significant changes to the roles of the 'approved social worker' who, under the Mental Health Act 1983, had a range of involvements, most notably in making applications for detention for 'assessment',[156] 'treatment'[157] or guardianship.[158] The 2007 Act replaced the term 'approved social worker' with 'approved mental health professional',[159] who must have 'appropriate competence in dealing with persons who are suffering from mental disorder';[160] this individual need not necessarily be a social worker, but must *not* be 'a registered medical practitioner'.[161]

---

148 Department of Health and Social Security, *Mental Health Act 2007 Explanatory Notes*, London: Her Majesty's Stationery Office, 2007; paragraph 48.

149 Mental Health Act 1983, section 2.

150 Mental Health Act 1983, section 3.

151 Mental Health Act 1983, section 7.

152 Mental Health Act 1983, section 12(2).

153 ECHR, article 5(1). *Winterwerp v Netherlands* (1979) 2 EHRR 387.

154 Mental Health Act 1983, sections 20(3) and (4).

155 Mental Health Act 2007, section 9(4)(b); amending Mental Health Act 1983, section 20(5A).

156 Mental Health Act 1983, sections 2 and 11.

157 Mental Health Act 1983, sections 3 and 11.

158 Mental Health Act 1983, sections 7 and 11.

159 Mental Health Act 2007, section 18.

160 Mental Health Act 2007, section 18; amending Mental Health Act 1983, section 114(3).

161 Mental Health Act 2007, section 18; amending Mental Health Act 1983, section 114(2).

This expansion of professional roles met with concern from the British Medical Association[162] and, if implemented, would represent a radical departure from the traditional dominance of psychiatrists in directing care. The most potentially dramatic change is that the 2007 Act indicated that a renewal order could be made out by a 'responsible clinician' (who is not necessarily a medical doctor), after consultation with another professional (who may not be a medical doctor either), possibly resulting in a renewal *without any evidence from a medical doctor at any point*.[163] It is decidedly unclear whether or not this will meet the requirement for objective medical evidence if liberty is to be denied on the grounds of 'unsound mind'.[164]

This matter may not be definitively resolved for some time, not least because of the extremely low numbers of mental health professionals taking up these new roles. In July 2012, the Department of Health reported that it did not know how many approved clinicians there were who are not doctors, and went on to note that 'inspections of the 22 AMHP [approved mental health professional] training courses in England found that of the 936 candidates who had completed their training since November 2008, 84% were social workers and 15% nurses'.[165] The pace of change is, then, slow; the first non-doctor 'responsible clinician' in London, a consultant clinical psychologist, was only approved in May 2013.[166] These issues do not arise at all in Ireland, interestingly: Ireland's Mental Health Act 2001 did not introduce any expansion or redefinitions of professional roles analogous to those in England's 2007 Act.

The Role of Families

In England, the Mental Health Act 1983 accorded significant roles to a patient's 'nearest relative', permitting him or her to make an application for detention for 'assessment',[167] 'treatment',[168] or guardianship;[169] prevent the

---

162 Bamrah, J.S., Datta, S., Rahim, A., Harris, M., McKenzie, K., 'UK's Mental Health Bill', *Lancet*, 2007, 370, 1029; Hall and Ali, 2009; p. 228.

163 Mental Health Act 2007, section 9(4)(b); amending Mental Health Act 1983, section 20(5A).

164 *Winterwerp v Netherlands* (1979) 2 EHRR 387; Bowen, 2007; p. 134; ECHR, article 5(1).

165 Department of Health, Post-Legislative Assessment of the Mental Health Act 2007 (Cm 8408). London: The Stationery Office, 2012; p. 7.

166 http://www.oxleas.nhs.uk/news/2013/5/londons-first-non-medical-appr/.

167 Mental Health Act 1983, sections 2 and 11.

168 Mental Health Act 1983, sections 3 and 11.

169 Mental Health Act 1983, sections 7 and 11.

making of an application detention for 'treatment'[170] or guardianship[171] by an 'approved social worker'; apply to a tribunal on the patient's behalf, under certain circumstances;[172] and make 'an order for discharge' from detention for assessment,[173] treatment[174] or guardianship.[175] The 1983 Act also provided definitions of 'relative' and 'nearest relative',[176] and consequently patients did not have a choice in determining who was their 'nearest relative'; moreover, civil partners under the Civil Partnership Act 2004 were excluded from the role.[177]

The Mental Health Act 2007 introduced several changes in this area, all of which advance patient autonomy and help address the incompatibility between the 1983 Act and the ECHR right to respect for 'private and family life'.[178] The critical changes include a right for the patient to apply to displace his or her nearest relative[179] and, if the person nominated by the patient 'is, in the opinion of the court, a suitable person to act as such and is willing to do so, the court shall specify that person'; 'otherwise, the court shall specify such person as is, in its opinion, a suitable person to act as the patient's nearest relative and is willing to do so'.[180]

Other amendments include a right for the patient to apply to discharge or vary an order appointing an acting 'nearest relative'[181] and inclusion of civil partners within the definition.[182] These changes represent a significant advance on the 1983 Act in terms of patient autonomy and the right to respect for 'private and family life',[183] although it is arguably excessively paternalistic that

---

170   Mental Health Act 1983, sections 3 and 11(4).

171   Mental Health Act 1983, sections 7 and 11(4).

172   Mental Health Act 1983, section 66(1)(ii).

173   Mental Health Act 1983, section 23(2)(a).

174   Mental Health Act 1983, section 23(2)(a).

175   Mental Health Act 1983, section 23(2)(b).

176   Mental Health Act 1983, sections 26–30.

177   Bowen, 2007; p. 62.

178   ECHR, article 8; R (M) v Secretary of State for Health [2003] EWHC 1094 (Admin) [2003] 1 MHLR 88.

179   Mental Health Act 2007, section 23(2); amending Mental Health Act 1983, section 29(1); Mental Health Act 2007, section 23(4); amending Mental Health Act 1983, section 29(2).

180   Mental Health Act 2007, section 23(3); amending Mental Health Act 1983, section 29(1A).

181   Mental Health Act 2007, section 24(2); amending Mental Health Act 1983, section 30(1).

182   Mental Health Act 2007, section 26, amending Mental Health Act 1983, section 26.

183   ECHR, article 8.

the patient's nominee for 'nearest relative' must be, 'in the opinion of the court, a suitable person to act as such'.[184]

Nonetheless, these changes are still positive ones in terms of human rights, and they contrast with the position in Ireland, where mental health legislation has no equivalent to 'nearest relative'. Indeed, the absence of any clear or articulated rights for families in Ireland is highlighted in the analysis of Ireland's level of accordance with the WHO human rights standards[185] presented in Chapter 3 of this book.

Supervised Community Treatment

In England, the Mental Health Act 1983, as originally enacted, contained detailed provisions for compulsory treatment in the community including granting 'leave to be absent' for detained patients,[186] subject to certain conditions,[187] and the responsible medical officer could recall the patient if needed.[188] Alternatively, section 25 of the 1983 Act (amended in 1996) outlined a process for 'after-care under supervision', which was subject to myriad conditions[189] and the process involved was outstandingly complex.[190]

The Mental Health Act 2007 repealed sections 25A-J of the 1983 Act and introduced a new 'supervised community treatment order', which can only be used when detained patients are leaving hospital; that is, it cannot be instigated de novo in the community.[191] Under the 2007 Act, 'the responsible clinician may by order in writing discharge a detained patient from hospital subject to his being liable to recall' under certain circumstances.[192] This requires the agreement of 'an approved mental health professional'[193] and various specific criteria must be met before such an order is made.[194]

---

184 Mental Health Act 2007, section 23(3); amending Mental Health Act 1983, section 29(1A).

185 WHO, 2005.

186 Mental Health Act 1983, section 17(1).

187 Mental Health Act 1983, section 17(3).

188 Mental Health Act 1983, section 17(4).

189 Mental Health Act 1983, section 25A(4).

190 Mental Health Act 1983, section 25A–J.

191 Mental Health Act 2007, sections 32–36.

192 Mental Health Act 2007, section 32(2); amending Mental Health Act 1983, section 17A(1).

193 Mental Health Act 2007, section 32(2); amending Mental Health Act 1983, section 17A(4).

194 The five criteria are: '(a) the patient is suffering from mental disorder of a nature or degree which makes it appropriate for him to receive medical treatment; (b) it is necessary for his health or safety or for the protection of other persons that he

If made, such an order 'shall specify conditions to which the patient is to be subject while the order remains in force' provided the responsible clinician and approved mental health professional agree that such conditions are 'necessary or appropriate' for specific purposes, including 'ensuring that the patient receives medical treatment'; 'preventing risk of harm to the patient's health or safety' and 'protecting other persons'.[195] Patients subject to such orders can be recalled to hospital if they require inpatient treatment, present a risk to themselves or others which can be addressed by recall, or fail to comply with the order's conditions.[196] Once the patient is recalled, the community treatment order can be revoked by the responsible clinician, with the agreement of an approved mental health professional,[197] and the patient again detained in hospital.[198] If the community treatment order is not revoked, the patient can be treated as a detained patient for up to 72 hours and then released from the hospital, but 'remains subject to the community treatment order'.[199]

If the community treatment order is not renewed, it expires (a) six months after it was made; (b) when the patient is discharged 'by the responsible clinician, by the managers of the responsible hospital, or by the nearest relative of the patient'[200] or by a tribunal;[201] (c) when the initial application for admission for treatment ceases to have effect;[202] or (d) when the order is revoked following recall to hospital.[203]

---

should receive such treatment; (c) subject to his being liable to be recalled as mentioned in paragraph (d) below, such treatment can be provided without his continuing to be detained in a hospital; (d) it is necessary that the responsible clinician should be able to exercise the power under section 17E(1) below to recall the patient to hospital; and (e) appropriate medical treatment is available for him' (Mental Health Act 2007, section 32(2); amending Mental Health Act 1983, section 17A(5)).

195 Mental Health Act 2007, section 32(2); amending Mental Health Act 1983, section 17B(2).

196 Mental Health Act 2007, section 32(2); amending Mental Health Act 1983, section 17E.

197 Mental Health Act 2007, section 32(2); amending Mental Health Act 1983, section 17F(4).

198 Mental Health Act 2007, section 32(2); amending Mental Health Act 1983, section 17G(3).

199 Mental Health Act 2007, section 32(2); amending Mental Health Act 1983, section 17F(7).

200 Mental Health Act 2007, schedule 3, section 10(4); amending Mental Health Act 1983, section 23(2)(c).

201 Mental Health Act 2007, schedule 3, section 20; amending Mental Health Act 1983; section 72.

202 Mental Health Act 2007, section 32(3); amending Mental Health Act 1983; section 20B.

203 Mental Health Act 2007, section 32(2); amending Mental Health Act 1983, section 17F(4).

Regarding the pre-existing provision for 'leave of absence' under the 1983 Act,[204] the Mental Health Act 2007 states that 'longer-term leave may not be granted to a patient unless the responsible clinician first considers whether the patient should be dealt with under section 17A instead' (i.e., community treatment order);[205] for this purpose 'longer-term leave of absence' is defined as 'a specified period of more than seven days'.[206]

These 'supervised community treatment' procedures in the 2007 Act[207] generated significant concern among patient groups at the time, some of whom felt the measures were excessively paternalistic and could lead to human rights abuses if used inappropriately or too widely.[208] On the day these changes were introduced, however, the Royal College of Psychiatrists and Department of Health moved swiftly to reassure the public that clinicians will use these provisions fairly and for the benefit of patients and families.[209]

From a human rights perspective, the European Court of Human Rights has already accepted the principle that conditions may be placed on discharge from psychiatric facilities in certain cases.[210] There are, however, other human rights concerns in relation to supervised community treatment, including the fact that such orders can be revoked by a 'responsible clinician'[211] or, in the case of a recalled patient, by the 'responsible clinician' once they have the agreement of an 'approved mental health professional',[212] and none of these individuals need be a medical doctor.[213]

Furthermore, mental health tribunals do not have the power to vary the conditions of a community treatment order, even though it is conceivable

---

204 Mental Health Act 1983, section 17(1).

205 Mental Health Act 2007, section 33(2); amending Mental Health Act 1983, section 17(2A).

206 Mental Health Act 2007, section 33(2); amending Mental Health Act 1983, section 17(2B).

207 Mental Health Act 2007, sections 32–36.

208 Butcher, J., 'Controversial Mental Health Bill reaches the finishing line', *Lancet*, 2007, 370, 117–118.

209 Bhugra, D., Appleby, L., 'Mental illness, the law and rudeness', *Guardian*, 2008, 3 November.

210 *Johnson v UK* (1997) 27 EHRR 296; Bowen, 2007; pp. 91–92.

211 Mental Health Act 2007, schedule 3, section 10(4); amending Mental Health Act 1983, section 23(2)(c); Bowen, 2007; p. 91.

212 Mental Health Act 2007, section 32(2); amending Mental Health Act 1983, section 17F(4).

213 It is a requirement that a diagnosis of 'mental disorder' must, for the purpose of initial detention at least, be based upon 'objective medical expertise' (*Winterwerp v Netherlands* (1979) 2 EHRR 387; see also *X v UK* (1981) 4 EHRR 188).

that such conditions could contravene ECHR rights.[214] As 'public authorities', tribunals have a duty to comply with ECHR rights under the Human Rights Act 1998,[215] but have a defence if the tribunal is giving effect to an Act of Parliament, although the tribunal must, firstly, ensure that the legislation 'cannot be read or given effect in a way which is compatible with the Convention rights'.[216] While this certainly affords the tribunal a considerable degree of responsibility in reading or giving effect to legislation, the tribunal may still be unable to prevent a contravention of ECHR rights, and the relevant legislation would then be subject to challenge.[217]

Some of these issues may not, however, prove to be actual violations of the ECHR because, notwithstanding the fact that the Tribunal cannot provide detailed guidance on which detained patients should be treated on community treatment orders and what the conditions of such orders should be, the Tribunal still has the key power to revoke the patient's detention if it appropriate. In addition, the *Winterwerp* criteria indicate that objective medical expertise is one of the criteria for compulsory *confinement*,[218] and proposed amendments in the 2007 Act which would have required the opinion of a medical doctor prior to *revoking* a community treatment order were explicitly rejected by the House of Commons as the legislation evolved.

All of this differs significantly from the position in Ireland which does not have, and has never had, explicit provision for compulsory treatment in the community. A patient detained under Ireland's 2001 Act may, however, be given leave 'subject to such conditions as [the consultant psychiatrist] considers appropriate'.[219] While this provision was not intended as a community treatment provision, it has been used as such[220] and has the merit that patients retain full

---

214 ECHR, article 5(4); Bowen, 2007; p. 92.

215 Human Rights Act 1998, section 6(1): 'It is unlawful for a public authority to act in a way which is incompatible with a Convention right'.

216 Human Rights Act 1998, section 6(2): 'Subsection (1) does not apply to an act if – (a) as the result of one or more provisions of primary legislation, the authority could not have acted differently; or (b) in the case of one or more provisions of, or made under, primary legislation which cannot be read or given effect in a way which is compatible with the Convention rights, the authority was acting so as to give effect to or enforce those provisions'.

217 Human Rights Act 1998, sections 3 and 4.

218 Winterwerp v Netherlands (1979) 2 EHRR 387.

219 Mental Health Act 2001, section 26.

220 Bainbridge, E., Byrne, F., Hallahan, B., McDonald, C., 'Clinical stability in the community associated with long term approved leave under the Mental Health Act 2001', *Irish Journal of Psychological Medicine*, 2014, 31, 143–148.

access to mental health tribunals,[221] as they do in England, and the period of 'leave' must end before the detention order expires, unless the detention order is renewed.

In both England and Ireland, then, there are provisions for supervised community treatment, albeit that these provisions are detailed and explicit in England, and brief to the point of laconic in the Irish legislation. The provisions in both jurisdictions are, however, really forms of supervised discharge (as patients need to be detained within hospitals firstly) and both are subject to the oversight of mental health tribunals. It remains the case, however, that the clinical usefulness of community treatment orders has yet to be firmly established,[222] and their use in the absence of such evidence raises a question that has more to do with the ethics of using treatment modalities that are not systematically proven rather than human rights issues stemming from legislation per se.

Safeguards Regarding Electroconvulsive Therapy

In England, the Mental Health Act 1983 as originally enacted, specified that a detained patient could receive electroconvulsive therapy (ECT) if the patient consented 'and either the responsible medical officer or a registered medical practitioner appointed for the purposes of this Part of this Act by the Secretary of State has certified in writing that the patient is capable of understanding its nature, purpose and likely effects and has consented to it'; or a registered medical practitioner (other than the responsible medical officer) 'has certified in writing that the patient is not capable of understanding the nature, purpose and likely effects of that treatment or has not consented to it but that, having regard to the likelihood of its alleviating or preventing a deterioration of his condition, the treatment should be given'.[223] Before making a certificate as outlined in section 58(b), the registered medical practitioner had to 'consult two other persons who have been professionally concerned with the patient's medical treatment, and of those persons one shall be a nurse and the other shall be neither a nurse nor a registered medical practitioner'.[224]

The Mental Health Act 2007 introduced a number of further safeguards in relation to ECT for specific groups, including that detained patients who lack

---

221 Kelly, B.D., 'Community treatment orders under the Mental Health Act 2007 in England and Wales', *Medico-Legal Journal of Ireland*, 2009, 15, 43–48.

222 Kisely et al., 2005; Lawton-Smith et al., 2008.

223 Mental Health Act 1983, section 58(3); Department of Health and Social Security, *Mental Health (Hospital, Guardianship and Consent to Treatment) Regulations*, London: Her Majesty's Stationery Office, 1983; regulation 16.

224 Mental Health Act 1983, section 58(4).

capacity can only receive ECT when a 'second opinion appointed doctor'[225] certifies that the patient lacks capacity; ECT is an appropriate treatment; and (for an adult) the treatment does not conflict with a valid advance directive or 'decision made by a donee or deputy or by the Court of Protection' (except in emergency situations).[226] Detained patients over the age of 18 years with capacity, can be administered ECT only when they consent and a 'second opinion appointed doctor'[227] certifies that they possess capacity (except in emergency situations).[228] The 2007 Act also restricts the grounds upon which emergency ECT is permitted to circumstances in which '(a) it is immediately necessary to save the patient's life; or (b) it is immediately necessary to prevent a serious deterioration of the patient's condition and is not irreversible'.[229]

These changes were generally consistent with the Richardson Committee's recommendations[230] and, overall, the 2007 Act managed to balance the retention of emergency ECT with new restrictions on the circumstances in which it can be so administered,[231] reflecting a complex, important balance between the autonomy and dignity of the patient, the paternalism inherent in involuntary treatment, and the right to medical care.[232]

The situation is somewhat similar in Ireland, where the Mental Health Act 2001 specifies that 'the consent of a [detained] patient shall be required for treatment' (in general) except when the patient is incapable for providing consent and the treating psychiatrist believes treatment 'is necessary to safeguard the life of the patient, to restore his or her health, to alleviate his or her condition, or to relieve his or her suffering'.[233] Psychosurgery can only be carried out if the detained patient consents in writing and surgery is authorised by a mental health tribunal.[234]

For a detained patient, ECT can be administered only if either (a) the patient consents in writing,[235] or (b) if the patient is 'unable or unwilling' to provide consent, the ECT is approved by the treating consultant psychiatrist

---

225   Mental Health Act 1983, part 4.

226   Mental Health Act 2007, section 27; amending Mental Health Act 1983, section 58A(5).

227   Mental Health Act 1983, part 4.

228   Mental Health Act 2007, section 27; amending Mental Health Act 1983, section 58A(2 and 3).

229   Mental Health Act 2007, section 35(1); amending Mental Health Act 1983, section 64C(5) and (6).

230   Expert Committee, 1999; pp. 5, 85.

231   Hall and Ali, 2009; p. 229.

232   Universal Declaration of Human Rights, article 25(1).

233   Mental Health Act 2001, section 57(1).

234   Mental Health Act 2001, section 58(1).

235   Mental Health Act 2001, section 59(1)(a).

and one other psychiatrist.[236] Similarly, if 'medicine has been administered to a [detained] patient for the purposes of ameliorating his or her mental disorder for a continuous period of 3 months, the administration of that medication shall not be continued' unless either the patient consents in writing, or, if the patient is 'unable or unwilling' to consent, the treatment is approved by the treating consultant psychiatrist and one other psychiatrist.[237]

In both jurisdictions, then, treatment with ECT is available for detained patients, albeit with specific protections. This is important: the National Institute for Clinical Excellence recommends ECT for 'rapid and short-term improvement of severe symptoms after an adequate trial of other treatment options has proven ineffective and/or when the condition is considered to be potentially life-threatening, in individuals with, severe depressive illness, catatonia, or a prolonged or severe manic episode'.[238] So while additional safeguards surrounding ECT in both jurisdictions are certainly important in terms of the right to bodily integrity, the availability of the treatment to detained patients is also important in terms of the right to medical care.[239]

Mental Health Tribunals and Other Reviews

In England, under the Mental Health Act 1983 as originally enacted, detained patients could apply to the Mental Health Review Tribunal following admission for assessment (within 14 days), admission for treatment (within six months) or being received into guardianship (within six months), among other circumstances.[240] Interestingly, the first declaration of incompatibility made under the Human Rights Act 1998 related to the 1983 Act and, specifically, the fact that the burden of proof in the Mental Health Review Tribunal lay with the patient,[241] a situation which the Court of Appeal deemed incompatible with article 5(1) of the ECHR;[242] the Mental Health Act 1983 (Remedial) Order 2001 (SI 2001/3712) remedied this matter.

---

236 Mental Health Act 2001, section 59(1)(b).

237 Mental Health Act 2001, section 60.

238 National Institute for Clinical Excellence, *Guidance on the Use of Electroconvulsive Therapy (Update: May 2010)*, London: National Institute for Clinical Excellence, 2010; p. 5.

239 Universal Declaration of Human Rights, article 25(1).

240 Mental Health Act 1983, section 66.

241 Mental Health Act 1983, sections 72 and 73; R *(H) v Mental Health Review Tribunal* [2002] EWHC 1522 (Admin) [2002] QB 1; Dyer, C., 'Ruling could free dozens of mentally ill offenders', *Guardian*, 2001, 29 March.

242 Specifically, the 'reverse burden of proof' violated the ECHR right to liberty (article 5(1)).

The Mental Health Act 2007 made further changes to these provisions to take account of various other revisions of the legislation, including the revised 'supervised community treatment' measures.[243] In addition, the 2007 Act introduced a requirement that hospital managers refer cases to the Tribunal within six months of admission, for patients admitted for assessment or treatment; community patients; patients whose community treatment orders were revoked (under section 17F); and patients 'transferred from guardianship to a hospital' (in pursuance of regulations made under section 19).[244] Hospital managers must now also refer all such cases to the 'Tribunal if a period of more than three years (or, if the patient has not attained the age of 18 years, one year) has elapsed since his case was last considered by such a tribunal, whether on his own application or otherwise'.[245]

This means that the 2007 Act introduced automatic referral to the Tribunal for patients admitted for assessment, albeit after six months of detention;[246] such patients are generally detained for only 28 days, but this period may be extended if there is an application to displace a nearest relative[247] and during such an extended period there was no right of appeal to the Tribunal.[248] The introduction of an automatic referral to the Tribunal after six months helps address concerns highlighted in *R (M) v Secretary of State for Health*,[249] although greater efficiency in processing requests to displace the 'nearest relative' would also help protect the ECHR right to respect for 'private and family life'.[250]

Overall, these changes appear likely to result in greater involvement in Tribunal hearings for clinicians in England, which may increase workloads but also increase emphasis on the 'best' rather than 'medical' interests; that is, possibly result in greater emphasis on autonomy and dignity, as opposed to a clinically-constructed 'right' to treatment.[251]

---

243 Mental Health Act 2007, sections 32–36.

244 Mental Health Act 2007, section 37(3); amending Mental Health Act 1983, section 68(1).

245 Mental Health Act 2007, section 37(3); amending Mental Health Act 1983, section 68(6).

246 Mental Health Act 2007, section 37, amending Mental Health Act 1983, section 2.

247 Mental Health Act 1983, section 29(4).

248 Bowen, 2007; p. 64. The House of Lords has found that this does not violate ECHR rights (R *(H) v Secretary of State for Health* [2005] UKHL 60 [2006] 1 AC 441).

249 R *(M) v Secretary of State for Health* [2003] EWHC 1094 (Admin) [2003] 1 MHLR 88.

250 ECHR, article 8.

251 Sarkar, S.P., Adshead, G., 'Black robes and white coats', *British Journal of Psychiatry*, 2005, 186, 96–98. ECHR principles have been evoked in relation to treatment, but while rulings indicate that treatment, when provided, must be based on medical

In Ireland, the Mental Health Act 2001 introduced mental health tribunals for the first time. Each tribunal comprises three members: one consultant psychiatrist, one barrister or solicitor (of not less than 7 years' experience), and one other person.[252] They make decisions by majority voting.[253] Prior to the tribunal hearing, the Mental Health Commission arranges that an independent psychiatrist examines the detained patient, interviews the consultant psychiatrist and reviews the records. Within 21 days of the involuntary admission, a tribunal reviews the detention and, 'if satisfied that the patient is suffering from a mental disorder' on the day of the tribunal, and that appropriate procedures have been followed, shall affirm the order; if the tribunal is not so satisfied, the tribunal shall 'revoke the order and direct that the patient be discharged from the approved centre concerned'.[254] Similar procedures apply for renewal orders.[255]

Overall, these changes in Ireland are strongly protective of the patient's right to liberty. Grounds for appeal are, however, limited: the patient 'may appeal to the Circuit Court against a decision of a tribunal to affirm an order made in respect of him or her on the grounds that he or she is not suffering from a mental disorder';[256] that is, the only grounds upon which an appeal to the Circuit Court can be made is that of not having 'mental disorder'; procedural aberrations, no matter how apparently serious, do not constitute grounds for appeal to the Circuit Court. In addition, however, the patient may appeal to the High Court, but only 'on a point of law';[257] that is, the patient cannot appeal to the High Court not on the grounds that he or she does not have a 'mental disorder'.

The introduction of tribunals to review all detention orders brings Irish legislation into greater accordance with the ECHR requirement that 'everyone who is deprived of his liberty by arrest or detention shall be entitled to take proceedings by which the lawfulness of his detention shall be decided speedily

---

necessity and in the patient's best interests (*R (PS) v Responsible Medical Officer* [2003] EWHC 2335 (Admin)), there is no automatic right to treatment (e.g., for an individual with untreatable personality disorder, detained on the basis of public protection) (*Hutchison Reid v UK* (2003) 37 EHRR 211).

252 Mental Health Act 2001, section 48(3).

253 Mental Health Act 2001, section 48(4).

254 Mental Health Act 2001, section 18(1).

255 The 21-day period within which the tribunal must be held commences on the date of the *making* of the renewal order, even if the renewal order does not come into effect on that day (i.e., if it has been made some days in advance of the expiry of the existing detention order) (*AMC v St Lukes Hospital, Clonmel* [2007] IEHC 65).

256 Mental Health Act 2001, section 19(1); see also: Mills, S., 'The Mental Health Act 2001', *Irish Psychiatrist*, 2004, 5, 49–55.

257 Mental Health Act 2001, section 19(16).

by a court and his release ordered if the detention is not lawful'.[258] To date, the European Court of Human Rights has found that delays of 55 days[259] and 24 days[260] are not sufficiently speedy, suggesting that a maximum delay of two or three weeks may be acceptable, in the absence of specific requests by the patient for deferral (e.g., to seek independent medical opinion).[261]

In Ireland, however, it came to light in 2007, that tribunals tended to be scheduled for as late as possible in the 21-day period in order to minimise costs.[262] This practice was criticised by the Department of Health and Children[263] and, in 2008, the Mental Health Commission affirmed that it is fully committed to arranging mental health tribunal hearings as early as possible.[264]

Tribunals in Ireland have the power to overlook certain procedural irregularities under certain circumstances, once 'the failure does not affect the substance of the order and does not constitute an injustice'.[265] It is not clear to what extent such discretionary powers are used by tribunals as there is no systematic record of tribunal reasoning made public. There is more evidence available from the courts, which hear appeals, and which do appear to overlook certain apparent irregularities which, in the opinion of the courts, do not constitute injustices.[266] This area requires greater transparency and study, especially in relation to tribunals.

With regard to the Circuit Court, concern has also been expressed that the burden of proof lies with the patient to show 'to the satisfaction of the Court that he or she is not suffering from a mental disorder'.[267] The European Court of Human Rights has previously ruled that section 64 of the Mental Health (Scotland) Act 1984, which placed the burden of proof on the patient in an

---

258 ECHR, article 5(4).

259 *E v Norway* (1990) 17 EHRR 30; in this case, E was transferred to a secure psychiatric setting on 21 July 1988; applied for a court hearing on 3 August 1988; and judgment was delivered on 27 September 1988.

260 *LR v France* App no 33395/96 (ECHR, 27 June 2002).

261 Bartlett et al., 2007; pp. 66–67.

262 McGuinness, I., 'Penny-pinching delays', *Irish Medical Times*, 2007, 25, 1; Department of Health and Children, *Review of the Operation of the Mental Health Act 2001*, Dublin: Department of Health and Children, 2007; p. 24.

263 Department of Health and Children, 2007; p. 24.

264 Mental Health Commission, *Report on the Operation of Part 2 of the Mental Health Act 2001*, Dublin: Mental Health Commission, 2008; p. 88.

265 Mental Health Act 2001, section 18(1)(a)(ii).

266 *Z v Khattak and Anor* [2008] IEHC 262; p. 8. See also: Mental Health Subcommittee, 'Advising a mentally disordered client', *Law Society Gazette*, 2009, 103, 44–45; p. 44.

267 Mental Health Act 2001, section 19(4).

appeal against detention, violated the ECHR.[268] In 2007, a detained patient in Ireland instigated judicial proceedings in the High Court arguing that the fact that the burden of proof lies with the patient in Circuit Court appeals was incompatible with the ECHR.[269] The High Court took account of relevant European case-law, as required under the European Convention on Human Rights Act 2003,[270] most notably *Hutchison Reid v UK*,[271] and concluded that that the burden of proof must not lie with the patient in a *first instance* review of detention (i.e., mental health tribunal) but that this did not apply to courts of further appeal (i.e., Circuit Court).[272] Despite this judgment, the Interim Report of the Steering Group on the Review of the Mental Health Act 2001 recommended in 2012 that the 2001 Act should be revised so that the burden of proof does not fall on the patient in the Circuit Court.[273]

In the Irish High Court, a detained patient can only lodge an appeal on a point of law, and 'no civil proceedings shall be instituted in respect of an act purporting to have been done in pursuance of this Act save by leave of the High Court and such leave shall not be refused unless the High Court is satisfied: (a) that the proceedings are frivolous or vexatious, or (b) that there are no reasonable grounds for contending that the person against whom the proceedings are brought acted in bad faith or without reasonable care'.[274]

As a result, the *detaining authority* must demonstrate that 'there are no reasonable grounds for contending that' the detaining authority 'acted in bad faith or without reasonable care',[275] thus effectively reversing the situation that pertained with the Mental Treatment Act 1945, under which the *patient* had to demonstrate to the High Court that there were 'substantial grounds for contending' that the detaining authority 'acted in bad faith or without reasonable care'.[276]

---

268 ECHR, article 5(4); see: *Hutchison Reid v UK* (2003) 37 EHRR 211.

269 *TS v Mental Health Tribunal, Ireland, The Attorney General, The Minister for Health and Children, The Mental Health Commission, Bola Oluwole and Ciaran Power* [2007] JR 1562.

270 European Convention on Human Rights Act 2003, section 4.

271 *Hutchison Reid v UK* (2003) 37 EHRR 211.

272 *TS v Mental Health Tribunal, Ireland, The Attorney General, The Minister for Health and Children, The Mental Health Commission, Bola Oluwole and Ciaran Power* [2007] JR 1562; p. 11. This is also the position held by the Department of Health and Children (2007; p. 16).

273 Steering Group on the Review of the Mental Health Act 2001, *Interim Report of the Steering Group on the Review of the Mental Health Act 2001*, Dublin: Department of Health, 2012; p. 29.

274 Mental Health Act 2001, section 73(1).

275 Mental Health Act 2001, section 73(1).

276 Mental Treatment Act 1945, section 290(1).

Overall, the Mental Health Act 2001 had the progressive effect of introducing mental health tribunals to Ireland, and, broadly, clarifying avenues of legal redress for individuals who object to their detention in psychiatric facilities.[277] There are significant similarities between the various appeal mechanisms in Ireland and England, but there are also certain differences, and one of the most potentially significant differences is the extent to which 'paternalism' influences the operation of these appeals mechanisms, especially in Ireland. This is considered next.

Paternalism

Paternalism involves a claim by government or others to take responsibility for defining someone else's welfare, so that paternalism centres not necessarily on what a person wants for himself or herself, but on what others believe to be good for him or her.[278] Mental health legislation can demonstrate paternalism by interfering with the right to autonomy, ostensibly owing to concerns for the patient's mental health or protection of others. While public safety has been a dominant theme in public discourse about mental health law in England (see above), paternalism has been an especially dominant theme in Ireland.

While Ireland's Mental Health Act 2001 undoubtedly opened up the possibility of greater observance of human rights and personal dignity, its interpretation by Irish Courts has repeatedly demonstrated evidence of a paternalistic approach to the mentally ill.[279] The High Court has specified that, in its 'opinion having regard to the nature and purpose of the Act of 2001 as expressed in its preamble and indeed throughout its provisions, it is appropriate that it is regarded in the same way as the Mental Treatment Act of 1945, as of a paternal character, clearly intended for the care and custody of persons suffering from mental disorder'.[280]

---

277   Ryan, 2010; pp. 96–98. This is not without complexity; see: Eldergill, A., 'The best is the enemy of the good', *Journal of Mental Health Law*, 2008, 5, 21–37; *T O'D. v Harry Kennedy and Others* [2007] IEHC 129. *D Han v The President of the Circuit Court and Doctor Malcolm Garland and Doctor Richard Blennerhassett and Doctor Conor Farren and Professor Patrick McKeon and the Mental Health Commission and the Mental Health Tribunal* [2008] IEHC 160.

278   Feldman, D., *Civil Liberties and Human Rights in England and Wales (Second Edition)*, Oxford: Oxford University Press, 2002; p. 26. See also: McHale, J., Fox, M., Gunn, M., Wilkinson, S., *Health Care Law: Text and Materials (Second Edition)*, London: Sweet and Maxwell, 2006; p. 124.

279   Craven, C., 'Signs of paternalist approach to the mentally ill persist', *Irish Times*, 2009, 27 July.

280   *MR v Cathy Byrne, administrator, and Dr Fidelma Flynn, clinical director, Sligo Mental Health Services, Ballytivnan, Co. Sligo* [2007] IEHC 73; p. 14.

The Supreme Court also holds that interpretation of the 2001 Act 'must be informed by the overall scheme and paternalistic intent of the legislation',[281] consistent with the Act's requirement that the 'best interests of the person shall be the principal consideration with due regard being given to the interests of other persons'.[282] Notwithstanding this explicit paternalism, however, it appears that there are limits on the extent to which the legislation, even when interpreted paternalistically, permits courts or tribunals to overlook non-compliance with the precise requirements of the Act; in 2007, for example, the High Court stated that, in its 'opinion, the best interests of a person suffering from a mental disorder are secured by a faithful observance of and compliance with the statutory safeguards put into the 2001 Act, by the Oireachtas … only those failures of compliance which are of an insubstantial nature and do not cause injustice can be excused by a Mental Health Tribunal'.[283]

At present, it is not possible to establish the extent to which tribunals overlook such aberrations 'of an insubstantial nature' or, indeed, act in a paternalistic fashion, owing to the fact that detailed data on reasons underlying decisions by tribunals are not collected, collated or published in Ireland.[284] Despite the paucity of such data, however, it is apparent that at least some tribunals are adversarial in nature and have significantly negative effects on the doctor-patient relationship.[285] This is, broadly, inconsistent with the intention of the legislators that the 'best interests of the person shall be the principal consideration' in all decisions made under the Act [286] and with the generally paternalistic interpretations of the High and Supreme Courts.[287]

Further evidence of paternalism was, arguably, in evidence in the Mental Health Act 2008, a piece of emergency legislation speedily enacted when it was discovered that one of the statutory forms provided by the Mental Health Commission for making renewal orders did not accord precisely with the 2001

---

281 *EH v St Vincent's Hospital and Ors* [2009] IESC 46; p. 12.

282 Mental Health Act 2001, section 4(1). See also: *T O'D. v Harry Kennedy and Others* [2007] IEHC 129; p. 21; *FW v Dept. of Psychiatry James Connolly Memorial Hospital* [2008] IEHC 283; Madden, E., 'Judge commends action of hospital staff in detention', *Irish Medical Times*, 2008, 37, 28; *PL v Clinical Director of St Patrick's University Hospital and Dr Séamus Ó Ceallaigh* [2012] IEHC 15; *EH v St Vincent's Hospital and Ors* [2009] IESC 46; *MR v Cathy Byrne, administrator, and Dr Fidelma Flynn, clinical director, Sligo Mental Health Services, Ballytivnan, Co. Sligo* [2007] IEHC 73.

283 *WQ v Mental Health Commission* [2007] IEHC 154; see also: *Q v St Patrick's Hospital* [2006] O'Higgins J, *ex tempore*, 21 December 2006.

284 For an interesting discussion about tribunals, see: Lee, G., 'Far from the madding crowd', *Law Society Gazette*, 2008, 6, 40–43.

285 Jabbar et al., 2010; Department of Health and Children, 2007; p. 24.

286 Mental Health Act 2001, section 4(1).

287 Craven, 2009.

Act.[288] The 2008 Act stated that any renewal orders that might be deemed to be without a basis in law for that reason would now be deemed lawful and *would be deemed (retrospectively) to have been lawful all along*.[289] Even in the case of the patient who took the proceedings which resulted in the 2008 Act, the judge did not order immediate release, owing to the fact that she was clearly mentally ill.[290]

In the end, the 2008 Act resulted in the continued detention of 209 patients for up to five working days on flawed forms; the completion of 209 replacement renewal detention orders during those five working days; and the subsequent examination of these 209 replacement renewal orders by 209 mental health tribunals, within 21 days. The resultant cost was estimated at €993,377 (£779,354), excluding the costs of the judicial review process itself and the indirect costs of tribunals, which amount to double the direct costs.[291] While the 2008 Act clearly avoided the possible abrupt release of 209 detained patients owing to a poorly-worded form, it is also possible to interpret the entire episode as reflecting the persistence of an excessively paternalistic approach to the mentally ill.

The issue of paternalism is, however, a complex one in Irish law[292] and Kennedy argues, convincingly, that criticism of alleged paternalism stems arises from a mistaken translation of the term *parens patriae*; that is, the common law principle that the State bears parental responsibilities to care for vulnerable citizens.[293] Notwithstanding these arguments, the Interim Report of the Steering Group on the Review of the Mental Health Act 2001 in 2012 stated that

---

288   Cummings, E., O'Conor, O., 'The SM Judgment and The Mental Health Act 2008', *Irish Medical Journal*, 2009, 7, 234; *SM v The Mental Health Commissioner, The Mental Health Tribunal, The Clinical Director of St Patrick's Hospital, Dublin, Attorney General and the Human Rights Commission* [2008] JR 749. See also: Carolan, M., 'Psychiatric patient takes case against involuntary detention in hospital', *Irish Times*, 2008, 16 October; Coulter, C., 'Government and judge combine to clear up loophole', *Irish Times*, 2008, 1 November; Carolan, M., 'Woman's hospital detention ruled unlawful by court', *Irish Times*, 2008, 1 November; Collins, S., 'Emergency mental health law rushed through Dáil', *Irish Times*, 2008, 31 October.

289   Mental Health Act 2008, section 3(1).

290   Carolan, M., 'Woman's hospital detention ruled unlawful by court', *Irish Times*, 2008, 1 November. This was not without precedent; see: *JH v Vincent Russell, Clinical Director of Cavan General Hospital* [2007] unreported High Court judgment; Nolan, N., 'Case law on the Mental Health Act 2001: part 1', *Irish Psychiatrist*, 2008, 3, 176–182; p. 177.

291   Cummings & O'Conor, 2009; Blumenthal, S., Wessely, S., 'The cost of Mental Health Review Tribunals', *Psychiatric Bulletin*, 1994, 18, 274–276.

292   Whelan, 2009; p. 28.

293   Kennedy, H., '"Libertarian" groupthink not helping mentally ill', *Irish Times*, 2012, 12 September.

'paternalism is incompatible with such a rights-based approach and accordingly the Act should be refocused away from "best interests" in order to enhance patient autonomy'.[294]

Overall, there is substantially more evidence of paternalism in Irish mental health law than there is in England, primarily attributable to Ireland's requirement that the 'best interests of the person shall be the principal consideration' in all decisions made under the 2001 Act.[295] Moreover, while certain aspects of England's legislation are somewhat paternalistic, recent moves in England appear to be away from paternalism: the Mental Health Act 2007, for example, repealed the 1983 Act's provision to make a renewal order on the grounds that 'the patient, if discharged, is unlikely to be able to care for himself, to obtain the care which he needs or to guard himself against serious exploitation'.[296]

Overall Assessment

Overall, England's Mental Health Act 2007 introduced several reforms with clear potential to advance dignity and human rights, albeit with certain limitations and caveats. These reforms include revising the definition of 'mental disorder' (although it is a broad definition)[297] and repealing the previous categorisations of mental disorder (although explicit exclusions for 'promiscuity or other immoral conduct, sexual deviancy' were repealed).[298] The replacement of the 'treatability test' with the requirement that 'appropriate medical treatment is available'[299] was also progressive in terms of access to treatment, but it is concerning that it is no longer necessary to demonstrate that treatment is 'likely' to help, only that it has the 'purpose' of helping (regardless of likely efficacy).

In addition, the precise consequences of widening the role of the 'responsible clinician'[300] have not yet been determined,[301] and it remains unclear whether or not renewal orders made out without the involvement of medical doctors will meet the ECHR requirement for objective medical evidence if liberty is lawfully to be denied on the grounds of 'unsound mind'.[302] On a positive note, the

---

294 Steering Group on the Review of the Mental Health Act 2001, 2012; p. 11.

295 Mental Health Act 2001, section 4(1).

296 Section 20(4) of the Mental Health Act 1983; Mental Health Act 2007, section 4(4)(c).

297 Mental Health Act 2007, section 1(2).

298 Mental Health Act 2007, section 1(3).

299 Mental Health Act 2007, section 4(2)(b).

300 Mental Health Act 2007, sections 9–17.

301 Bowen, 2007; p. 55.

302 *Winterwerp v Netherlands* (1979) 2 EHRR 387; Bowen, 2007: p. 134; ECHR, article 5(1).

2007 Act permits a patient's civil partner to be the 'nearest relative' and allows the patient to apply to displace their 'nearest relative', both of which support patient autonomy. It is concerning, however, that the court must be of the opinion that the patient's nominee for 'nearest relative' is 'a suitable person to act as such'.[303]

It is also broadly welcome that England's 2007 Act revises and simplifies 'supervised community treatment' procedures,[304] although the Tribunal's power over such orders is still limited and their clinical usefulness not established. The 2007 Act also introduces important new safeguards for detained patients in relation to ECT and further restricts the grounds on which emergency ECT can be administered, both of which are protective of patient's rights including their reasonable expectation to medical care when detained (the principle of reciprocity).[305] Also for detained patients, the 2007 Act introduced automatic referral to the Tribunal for patients admitted for assessment (albeit after six months)[306] and required the creation of a system of 'independent mental health advocates'.[307]

These changes, with their mix of better protections of human rights and occasionally concerning caveats, were received with a mixture of welcome and concern when the 2007 Act was introduced.[308] Interestingly, the King's Fund, an independent charity focusing on health policy and practice, highlighted that 'the amended Act does, as it intended, break the link between compulsory treatment and hospital by extending compulsion to certain patients in the community' through new supervised community treatment orders.[309] While there were specific concerns about various others matters, the legislation was generally seen as striking a reasonable balance between autonomy and paternalism.

Specific concerns were, however, raised about the 2007 Act's replacement of 'approved social workers' with 'approved mental health professionals',[310] owing to the possibly different ethical approaches of health workers and

---

303   Mental Health Act 2007, section 23(3); amending Mental Health Act 1983, section 29(1A).

304   Mental Health Act 2007, sections 32–36.

305   Universal Declaration of Human Rights, article 25(1).

306   Mental Health Act 1983, section 2.

307   Mental Health Act 2007, section 30(2); amending Mental Health Act 1983, section 130A(1).

308   Brindle, D., 'A new act, but mental health battles remain', *Guardian*, 2007, 11 July; Bhugra & Appleby, 2008; Mental Health Alliance, 2006.

309   King's Fund, *Briefing: Mental Health Act 2007*, London: The King's Fund, 2008; p. 7.

310   Mental Health Act 2007, section 18.

social workers to the use of compulsion.[311] The Mental Health Foundation, a mental health charity, expressed concern that the legislation increased stigma through its focus on risk of violence,[312] and both the Mental Health Alliance[313] and King's Fund noted that 'in redefining mental disorder and removing the "treatability" test, the new legislation allows clinicians to detain certain people' who might not have been detained under the 1983 Act as it previously stood.[314]

Ultimately, the lasting impact of the 2007 Act will be shaped by both the responses of mental health service-providers to the new legislation and the attitude of the courts in interpreting it in the context of the Human Rights Act 1998 and ECHR, as well as the growing European and international influences on mental health law and policy throughout the EU.[315] Current evidence suggests that the pace of change is slow: in 2012, the Department of Health reported that it did not know how many approved clinicians there are who are not doctors;[316] and the first non-doctor 'responsible clinician' in London, a consultant clinical psychologist, was only approved in May 2013.[317] The pace of change appears similarly slow with regard to 'approved mental health professionals'.[318]

In Ireland, as in England, it is apparent that the most recent legislative change (the Mental Health Act 2001) introduced several potentially positive and progressive reforms, albeit that the Irish reforms are, as in England, accompanied by certain limitations and caveats. The most progressive changes in Ireland relate to revised involuntary admission procedures and independent reviews of detention orders, and a strong majority of stakeholders agree that these kinds of provisions in the 2001 Act help protect human rights.[319] Other key changes include the removal of indefinite detention orders that existed under the Mental Treatment Act 1945; free legal representation and independent psychiatric

---

311 Rapaport, J., Manthorpe, J., 'Family matters: Developments concerning the role of the nearest relative and social worker under mental health law in England and Wales', *British Journal of Social Work*, 2008, 38, 1115–1131; p. 1126.

312 Batty, D., 'Law "reinforced mental health stereotypes"', *Guardian*, 2008, 18 February.

313 Mental Health Alliance, 2006; p. 6.

314 King's Fund, 2008; p. 7.

315 Kelly, B.D., 'The emerging mental health strategy of the European Union', *Health Policy*, 2008, 85, 60–70.

316 Department of Health, Post-Legislative Assessment of the Mental Health Act 2007 (Cm 8408), London: The Stationery Office, 2012; p. 7.

317 http://www.oxleas.nhs.uk/news/2013/5/londons-first-non-medical-appr/.

318 Department of Health. Post-Legislative Assessment of the Mental Health Act 2007 (Cm 8408), London: The Stationery Office, 2012; p. 7.

319 Mental Health Commission, 2008; p. 69; O'Donoghue and Moran, 2009; p. 24.

opinions for patients prior to tribunals; and establishment of the Mental Health Commission to oversee implementation of the Act and standards of care.

Notwithstanding these positive developments, emergent concerns centre on the absence of systematic data-collection about decisions of mental health tribunals; restrictions on acceptable grounds for civil proceedings in the Circuit and High Courts; the fact that the burden of proof lies with the patient in the Circuit Court; the legal definition of voluntary patient, which does not include a requirement for capacity;[320] and evidence of paternalism in the implementation and interpretation of the 2001 Act by psychiatric services and courts. It is not clear whether or not this level of paternalism is proportionate to the strong welfare-based concerns outlined in the Irish Constitution.[321]

Other concerns centre on the opportunity costs associated with the legislation, including increased workloads for medical staff and decreased time spent with patients,[322] with the result that, while there is significant agreement that the Act has enhanced protections of the right to liberty,[323] there is some concern that is has eroded time and resources devoted to treatment.[324] While raising these kinds of issues about resourcing of mental health services has been described politically as 'a bit tiresome',[325] they are still important matters: under-resourcing of mental health services could fatally undermine the valuable potential of the 2001 Act to protect patient rights and enhance patient dignity in real and meaningful ways.

Moreover, the issue of resourcing is explicitly highlighted not only in Ireland's own 2006 mental health policy, A Vision for Change,[326] but also through Ireland's public commitment to the WHO's Mental Health Declaration

320   The Mental Health Act 2001 does not require that voluntary patients possess capacity: the Act states that 'voluntary patient' means 'a person receiving care and treatment in an approved centre who is not the subject of an admission order to a renewal order'; i.e., any patient who is not legally detained (section 2(1)).

321   Constitution of Ireland, article 40(1). See also: Hogan and Whyte, 2003.

322   Baker, 2009; Jabbar et al., 2010, 179, 291–294; McGuinness, I., 'More court appeals', *Irish Medical Times*, 2007, 24, 3.

323   O'Donoghue & Moran, 2009; p. 24.

324   Fitzsimons, K., 'Right to treatment should not be forgotten in psychiatry', *Irish Medical News*, 2007, 45, 4; Jabbar et al., 2010; O'Donoghue & Moran, 2009.

325   O'Malley, T. (Minister of State at the Department of Health and Children), 'Mental Health Services', *Dáil Éireann Debate*, 2005 (10 February), 597, 4.

326   Expert Group on Mental Health Policy, *A Vision for Change*, Dublin: The Stationery Office, 2006; Guruswamy, S., Kelly, B.D., 'A change of vision? Mental health policy', *Irish Medical Journal*, 2006, 99: 164–166.

for Europe[327] and Mental Health Action Plan for Europe,[328] both of which emphasise adequate resourcing.[329] The WHO has also made specific and robust recommendations in relation to mental health law in individual states,[330] placing particular emphasis on human rights in the provision of care.[331] The precise extent to which mental health legislation in England and Ireland meets these WHO standards is considered next.

327 WHO Ministerial Conference on Mental Health, *Mental Health Declaration for Europe*, Helsinki: WHO, 2005.

328 WHO Ministerial Conference on Mental Health, *Mental Health Action Declaration for Europe*, Helsinki: WHO, 2005.

329 Mudiwa, L., 'Ireland signs WHO declaration on mental health', *Medicine Weekly*, 2005, 3, 18.

330 WHO, Mental Health Law: Ten Basic Principles, Geneva: WHO, 1996.

331 WHO, 2005.

Chapter 3

Human Rights and Mental Health Law: International Human Rights Standards for National Mental Health Legislation

A human rights approach to mental health legislation is strongly supported and informed by the UN, which in 1991 adopted Resolution 46/119, Principles for the Protection of Persons with Mental Illness and the Improvement of Mental Health Care.[1] Key rights include rights to the best mental health care available and to be treated with humanity and respect (see Chapter 1). All people with mental illnesses have the right to live, work and receive treatment in the community, as far as possible. Mental health facilities shall be appropriately resourced and an impartial review body shall, in consultation with mental health practitioners, review the cases of involuntary patients.

The WHO, as the directing and coordinating authority for health within the UN system, developed this human rights-based approach further by publishing 'ten basic principles' of mental health law in 1996, stemming from a comparative analysis of mental health laws in over 40 countries worldwide,[2] as well as the UN Principles. The WHO's 'ten basic principles' state that everyone should have access to basic mental health care and benefit from the best measures feasible to promote mental well-being. Mental health care should be provided in the least restrictive fashion possible, and, for decisions affecting integrity (treatment) and/or liberty (hospitalisation) with a long-lasting impact, there should be an automatic periodical review mechanism.

These principles were underscored by the WHO's Guidelines for the Promotion of Human Rights of Persons with Mental Disorders (1996), which provided much-needed detail on the implementation of the 'ten basic principles' at national level.[3] At global policy level, these rights-based considerations were

---

1 UN, 1991.

2 Division of Mental Health and Prevention of Substance Abuse (WHO), *Mental Health Care Law: Ten Basic Principles*, Geneva: WHO, 1996; p. 7.

3 Division of Mental Health and Prevention of Substance Abuse (WHO), *Guidelines for the Promotion of Human Rights of Persons with Mental Disorders*, Geneva: WHO,

further emphasised in 2001, when the WHO devoted its World Health Report to 'Mental Health: New Understanding, New Hope'.[4]

Throughout these rights-based publications from the UN and WHO, the division between mental health law and policy is not always a crisp one, and the extent to which legislation, as opposed to policy, should govern some of these issues not always apparent. Other issues related to these publications centre on the WHO's acceptance of involuntary committal in the first instance, something to which the World Network of Survivors and Users of Psychiatry objects on principle.[5]

Some of these issues were clarified somewhat in 2005 in the WHO Resource Book on Mental Health, Human Rights and Legislation,[6] which presents a detailed statement of human rights issues which, according to the WHO, need to be addressed at the national level. More specifically, the Resource Book includes a detailed 'Checklist on Mental Health Legislation' based, in large part, on previous UN and WHO publications, and aiming to assist countries in reviewing existing legislation and drafting new laws.[7]

The checklist, although lengthy, detailed and explicitly informed by the Universal Declaration of Human Rights,[8] is not a set of absolute rules, and is not legally binding. There are no sanctions for states which fail to accord with its standards and, unlike the UN International Covenant on Civil and Political Rights, the UN Human Rights Committee does not review Member States' reports on their compliance with it.

The WHO checklist appears, rather, designed to work by influencing member states as they draft, redraft and implement national mental health laws. Given the checklist's close links with the Universal Declaration of Human Rights and various WHO documents outlining the rights of the mentally ill, the authors appear to make the assumption that the checklist standards will be accepted by the international community and deemed worth reflecting in national mental health law. It is still arguable, however, that some of the issues which the WHO appears to suggest should be covered by mental health legislation should be covered by public health or social policy instead. Indeed, the WHO explicitly states that some countries may address some or all of these mental health issues in general legislation (e.g., equality legislation), other forms

---

1996; p. 11.

4 WHO, *Mental Health: New Understanding, New Hope*, Geneva: WHO, 2001.

5 Perlin, M.L., Kanter, A.S., Treuthart, M.P., Szeli, E., Gledhill, K., *International Human Rights and Comparative Mental Disability Law*, Durham, NC: Carolina Academic Press, 2006; pp. 891–894.

6 WHO, 2005.

7 WHO, 2005; p. 120.

8 UN, 1948.

of (not legally binding) regulation, or mental health policy, rather than specific mental health legislation.[9]

The history of psychiatry, however, supports the unique importance of dedicated mental health legislation, rather than general law or non-binding regulation, for protecting the rights of the mentally ill: while there were substantial advances in the articulation of human rights standards for the general population throughout the early twentieth century,[10] the plight of the mentally ill remained bleak until much later in most jurisdictions,[11] suggesting a need for specific and dedicated measures to protect their rights.[12] The WHO implicitly acknowledges the centrality of law in this process when it presents its final checklist in the Resource Book as a 'Checklist for Mental Health *Legislation*' (italics added).

This is the key reason why the WHO checklist forms the focus of the human rights analysis presented in this book: the WHO checklist is the most detailed and comprehensive human rights-based framework developed to date for the analysis of national mental health legislation. There are no other detailed, specific and comparable statements of standards to which national mental health legislation (as opposed to disability legislation) might reasonably be expected to adhere, and so the WHO checklist provides the only comprehensive, coherent and relevant framework for this kind of analysis.[13]

In addition, WHO guidelines have been previously used, to good effect, to inform analysis of mental health legislation in diverse Commonwealth jurisdictions (not including Ireland, which is not part of the Commonwealth).[14] However, the full detailed comprehensive WHO checklist used in the present study has not previously been applied to current legislation in England and Ireland.[15]

The analysis of Commonwealth countries, however, which used various WHO guidelines in combination with other sources to develop the authors' own analytic framework, did highlight one of the key general strengths of the WHO approach to this topic – its close reliance on the Universal Declaration of

---

9   WHO, 2005; p. 120.

10   Hunt, 2007.

11   Robins, 1986; Shorter, 1997; Torrey & Miller, 2001; Walsh & Daly, 2004.

12   Gostin et al., 2010.

13   WHO, 2005; pp. 8–17. The relevance of the CRPD is discussed in Chapter 4.

14   Fistein, E.C., Holland, A.J., Clare, I.C.H., Gunn, M.J., 'A comparison of mental health legislation from diverse Commonwealth jurisdictions', *International Journal of Law and Psychiatry*, 2009, 32, 147–155.

15   This analysis was originally published as: Kelly B.D., 'Mental health legislation and human rights in England, Wales and the Republic of Ireland', *International Journal of Law and Psychiatry*, 2011, 34, 439–454.

Human Rights to inform its principles and statements of rights.[16] This reliance on the Universal Declaration adds to the relevance of the WHO guidelines, increasing both their usefulness and likely acceptability in diverse countries around the world.

This is also a key strength of the WHO checklist as used in the present analysis: the contents of the checklist are based on both a widely accepted general statement of rights (Universal Declaration of Human Rights) *and* the literature's most comprehensive documents focussing on the rights of the mentally ill, including the UN Principles for the Protection of Persons with Mental Illness and the Improvement of Mental Health Care,[17] the WHO's Mental Health Care Law (Ten Basic Principles),[18] the WHO's Guidelines for the Promotion of Human Rights of Persons with Mental Disorders,[19] and the WHO's World Health Report on 'Mental Health: New Understanding, New Hope'.[20] As a result, the WHO checklist reflects *both* general human rights standards *and* human rights issues of particular relevance to the mentally ill. Both England and Ireland are members of the UN and WHO, so it is reasonable to compare their national legislation with these standards.

The WHO checklist is not, however, perfect, and shares one of the key limitations of many WHO guidance documents: it is based largely on expert opinion and international consensus, rather than empirical evidence.[21] That is, the WHO checklist is not based on research fieldwork among the mentally ill to determine precisely which rights are most commonly infringed and what steps might best be taken to improve matters. The checklist is, however, based on widely accepted human rights standards (e.g., Universal Declaration of Human Rights) and, as a result, achieves certain legitimacy. This issue of empirical evidence is still an important one, however, and is further explored in Chapter 7, which highlights the potential usefulness of a 'realisation-focused understanding of justice' (based on the *real-life outcomes* of measures intended to protect rights) as opposed to 'an arrangement-focused view of justice' (based on verifying that current legislation and other arrangements *appear likely to* promote human rights).[22]

---

16 Fistein et al., 2009, p. 149.

17 UN, 1991.

18 Division of Mental Health and Prevention of Substance Abuse (WHO), *Mental Health Care Law: Ten Basic Principles*, Geneva: WHO, 1996.

19 Division of Mental Health and Prevention of Substance Abuse (WHO), *Guidelines for the Promotion of Human Rights of Persons with Mental Disorders*, Geneva: WHO, 1996.

20 WHO, *Mental Health: New Understanding, New Hope*, Geneva: WHO, 2001.

21 Hill, S., Pang, T., 'Leading by example', *Lancet*, 2007, 369, 1842–1844; Oxman, A.D., 'Use of evidence in WHO recommendations', *Lancet*, 2007, 369, 1883–1889.

22 Sen, A., *The Idea of Justice*, London: Allen Lane, 2009; p. 10.

The second key limitation of the WHO checklist stems from the fact that, despite being a 'Checklist for Mental Health *Legislation*' (italics added), the WHO states that certain rights may be better advanced through public mental health or social policy rather than dedicated mental health legislation.[23] Arguably, the analysis presented in this book illustrates this point by identifying economic and social rights as a key area in which national mental health legislation of both England and Ireland fails significantly to accord with WHO standards (see below). This borderline between law and policy remains an important matter and is explored in greater depth in Chapters 6 and 7. First however, the extent to which mental health legislation in England and Ireland complies with WHO human rights standards is considered in some detail.

To What Extent Does National Mental Health Legislation Comply with International Human Rights Standards?

The WHO checklist comprises 175 individual human rights standards, grouped into 27 categories (A–AZ). This book focuses on civil rather than criminal detention, so nine standards which relate solely to mentally ill offenders (E4, T1–6) are omitted. This analysis (and this book in general) also focuses on adults rather than children, so, against this background, Table 1 lists the 166 WHO standards relevant to this analysis and summarises the extent to which mental health legislation in England and Ireland meets them; further detail is provided in the text (below).[24]

Overall, legislation in England meets 92 (55.4%) of the 166 relevant standards set out by the WHO, while legislation in Ireland meets 81 (48.8%). Thematically, there are identifiable areas of high, medium and low compliance in both jurisdictions.[25] These are discussed in the following three sections, with the appropriate WHO standards indicated in parentheses following each point, for example, (B1). For ease of reference, the same letters are used in Table 1 to label each WHO standard, in order to facilitate use of the table in conjunction with this text.

---

23   WHO, 2005.

24   The WHO Resource Book recommends that ratings for each criterion should be detailed rather than binary, so while Table 1 in this book supplies ratings for each criterion in a 'yes' or 'no' fashion, the table is supplemented by the text, which examines criteria in greater detail.

25   Kelly B.D., 'Mental health legislation and human rights in England, Wales and the Republic of Ireland', *International Journal of Law and Psychiatry*, 2011, 34, 439–454.

Areas of High Compliance with WHO Human Rights Standards

Definition and determination of mental disorder

Legislation in England and Ireland includes 'clear definition[s] of mental disorder/mental illness' as required by the WHO (B1),[26] although in neither jurisdiction is it evident why these particular definitions were chosen (B2). Legislation in England[27] and Ireland[28] also meets WHO criteria in relation to 'determinations of mental disorder' (N), emphasising medical involvement in diagnosis.

Involuntary admission and treatment

Legislation in England meets most criteria regarding involuntary admission,[29] apart from requirements for provision of information (I7)[30] and 'periodic

---

26 England: B1: Mental Health Act 2007; section 1(2); B3, B4, B5: Mental Health Act 2007, sections 1 and 2. Ireland: B1: Mental Health Act 2001, sections 3(1) and (2); B3, B4, B5: Mental Health Act 2001; sections 3(1), 3(2) and 8(2).

27 Mental Health Act 1983, sections 2, 3, 7, 12(2); Mental Health Act 2007, sections 1(2); section 9(4)(b); amending Mental Health Act 1983, section 20(5A).

28 Mental Health Act 2001, part 2, section 2(1).

29 I1a: Mental Health Act 1983, part II; Mental Health Act 2007, sections 1–3. I1b: Mental Health Act 1983, section 2(2)(b); Mental Health Act 1983, section 2(2)(c); Mental Health Act 1983, section 4. I1c: Under sections 3, 37, 45A and 47 (Mental Health Acts 1983 and 2007); Mental Health Act 2007, section 4; amending Mental Health Act 1983, sections 3(2)(b); 3(4)(b); 37(2)(a)(i); 45A(2)(c); 47(1); Mental Health Act 2007, section 4(4); amending Mental Health Act 1983, section 20(4); Mental Health Act 2007, section 5(8); amending Mental Health Act 1983, section 72(1)(b)(ii). [This criterion does not apply to those detained under sections 2 ('admission for assessment'), 35 ('remand to hospital for report on accused's mental condition'), 135 ('warrant to search for and remove patients') or 136 ('mentally disordered persons found in public places')]. I2: Mental Health Act 1983, section 2, 3, 7, 12(2); Mental Health Act 2007, section 9(4)(b); amending Mental Health Act 1983, section 20(5A). I3: The work of the Care Quality Commission in investigating the treatment and care of patients detained under the Mental Health Act 1983, community patients and those subject to guardianship, and their role in protecting such patients, is expressly recognised in Mental Health Act 1983 (sections 120–120(D)), with 'the regulatory authority' in relation to England being expressly recognised as the Care Quality Commission in Mental Health Act 1983 (section 145(1)) (amendments introduced by the Health and Social Care Act 2008) (section 1(2)). I4: Mental Health Act 2007, section 8; amending Mental Health Act 1983, section 118(2B)(c). I5, I6 and I8: Mental Health Act 1983 (section 66) as amended by the Mental Health Act 2007 (chapter 5). I10: Mental Health Act 1983; section 16(2).

30 If an application for involuntary admission or guardianship is made by the approved social worker, 'that social worker shall take such steps as are practicable to inform the person (if any) appearing to be the nearest relative of the patient' (Mental

reviews' of long-term *voluntary* admissions (I9). Most criteria are met in Ireland, too,[31] apart from provision of information (I7)[32] and reviews of long-term *voluntary* admissions (I9). Specific standards in relation to 'police responsibilities' are met in both England[33] and Ireland.[34]

Legislation in England[35] and Ireland[36] meets most WHO requirements regarding involuntary *treatment* (J) too, apart from the requirement that a second

---

Health Act 1983; section 11(3)). The approved social worker should try (as far as is practicable) to consult such a relative before making the application and, if the relative objects, the social worker shall not make the application (Mental Health Act 1983, section 11(4)). There is no requirement that the patient be informed.

31 I1a: Mental Health Act 2001, sections 3 and 8(1); I1b: Mental Health Act 2001, section 3(1)(a) and (b)(i). I1c: Mental Health Act 2001, section 3(1)(b)(ii). I2: Mental Health Act 2001, part 2. I3: Mental Health Act 2001, sections 50 and 63(1). I4: Mental Health Act 2001, section 4(1). I5 and I6: Mental Health Act 2001, part 3, sections 18(2) and (4). I8: Mental Health Act 2001, part 3. I10: Mental Health Act 2001, sections 8(1) and 28(1).

32 The Mental Health Act 2001 requires that patients (but *not* 'families and legal representatives') be informed of the legal basis of detention, right to appeal and various other matters (Mental Health Act 2001, section 16).

33 S1and 2: Mental Health Act 1983, as amended by the Mental Health Act 2007, sections 135 and 136. S3: Part III. S4 and 5: Mental Health Act 1983, as amended by the Mental Health Act 2007, sections 137 and 138.

34 S1 and 2: Mental Health Act 2001, sections 12 and 13. S3: Criminal Law (Insanity) Act 2006 (Kennedy, 2007). S4: Mental Health Act 2001, section 13. S5: Mental Health Act 2001, section 27(1).

35 J1a: Mental Health Act 1983, as amended by the Mental Health Act 2007, part II. J1b and c: Mental Health Act 1983, as amended by Mental Health Act 2007, sets out such requirements for involuntary admission for assessment (section 2(2)(b)), admission for treatment (section 2(2)(c)), or emergency admission (section 4). J2: Mental Health Act 2007, section 9(9); amending Mental Health Act 1983, section 34(1); Mental Health Act 2007, section 12(7)(a); amending Mental Health Act 1983, section 64(1); Mental Health Act 2007, section 10; amending Mental Health Act 1983, section 34(1). J4: Mental Health Act 1983, as amended by Mental Health Act 2007, part V [mental health tribunals review involuntary admission and, by implication, involuntary treatment]. J5: Mental Health Act 1983, as amended by Mental Health Act 2007, section 20. J6 and 7: Mental Health Act 1983, section 66, as amended by Mental Health Act 2007, chapter 5.

36 J1a: Mental Health Act 2001, part 2. J1b and c: Mental Health Act 2001 permits involuntary admission and, therefore, treatment, only if there is 'serious likelihood' of 'immediate and serious harm' (section 3(1)(a)) or 'failure to admit the person to an approved centre would be likely to lead to a serious deterioration' (section 3(1)(b)(i)). J2: Mental Health Act 2001, sections 2(1) and 15(2). J4: Mental Health Act 2001, part 3 [mental health tribunals review involuntary admission and, by implication, involuntary treatment]. J5: Mental Health Act 2001, section 15. J6 and 7: Mental Health Act 2001, part 3.

practitioner agree the treatment plan (J3): the Mental Health Acts 1983 and 2007 (England) require two 'medical recommendations' to support applications for detention for 'assessment',[37] 'treatment'[38] or guardianship,[39] and the Mental Health Act 2001 (Ireland) has a similar requirement for involuntary admission,[40] but neither jurisdiction requires endorsement of *treatment* plans, although certain treatments attract additional safeguards (e.g., ECT).[41]

Both jurisdictions provide for involuntary community treatment (L1): in England, individuals undergoing supervised community treatment enjoy 'all the criteria and safeguards required for involuntary inpatient treatment' (L2),[42] while in Ireland a detained patient may be given leave 'subject to such conditions as [the consultant psychiatrist] considers appropriate'[43] (e.g., taking medication) and retains access to tribunals.[44]

Offences and penalties

Both jurisdictions are compliant with WHO requirements regarding 'offences and penalties' (AZ).[45] The Mental Health Act 2001 (Ireland) outlines offences in connection with many matters relating to involuntary admissions,[46] obstructing inspectors,[47] approved centres[48] and rules governing seclusion and restraint.[49] The legislation also outlines *sanctions* for violations related to involuntary admissions[50] and rules governing seclusion and restraint (AZ2),[51]

---

37 Mental Health Act 1983, section 2.

38 Mental Health Act 1983, section 3.

39 Mental Health Act 1983, section 7.

40 Mental Health Act 2001, part 2.

41 England: Mental Health Act 2007, section 27; Ireland: Mental Health Act 2001, section 59.

42 Mental Health Act 2007, sections 32–36.

43 Mental Health Act 2001, section 26. See also: Bainbridge, E., Byrne, F., Hallahan, B., McDonald, C., 'Clinical stability in the community associated with long-term approved leave under the Mental Health Act 2001', *Irish Journal of Psychological Medicine*, 2014, 31, 143–148.

44 Kelly, B.D., 'Community treatment orders under the Mental Health Act 2007 in England and Wales', *Medico-Legal Journal of Ireland*, 2009, 15, 43–48.

45 England: AZ1: Mental Health Act 2007, as amended by Mental Health Act 2007, part IX. AZ2: Mental Health Act 1983, section 127.

46 Mental Health Act 2001, section 32.

47 Mental Health Act 2001, section 53.

48 Mental Health Act 2001, section 68.

49 Mental Health Act 2001, section 69(3).

50 Mental Health Act 2001, section 32.

51 Mental Health Act 2001, section 69(3).

and provides specific guidance if such offences are committed by an individual or 'body corporate'.[52]

Areas of Medium Compliance with WHO Human Rights Standards

Competence, capacity and consent

Mental health legislation in England meets some but not all WHO requirements in relation to 'competence, capacity and guardianship' (F);[53] it does not meet requirements for 'periodic reviews of decisions' (F4) and 'systematic review of the need for a guardian' (F7); although an appeal mechanism exists, it is neither systematic nor automatic.[54] The situation in Ireland is similarly mixed: Ireland's 'Ward of Court' system (F1) does not 'define "competence" and "capacity"' (F2);[55] is un-responsive to changes in capacity;[56] makes unwieldy provisions for appointing decision-makers (F3);[57] and permits appeals in front of a High Court judge, but there is no right to a jury and insufficient provision for *periodic* reviews (F4).[58] The law lays down procedures for the appointment of a guardian

---

52   Mental Health Act 2001, section 74.

53   F1: Mental Capacity Act 2005, as amended by Mental Health Act 2007; Mental Health Act 1983, as amended by Mental Health Act 2007, sections 7–10; Department of Health, *Code of Practice: Mental Health Act 1983*, London: The Stationery Office, 2008; p. 256; F2: Mental Capacity Act 2005, as amended by Mental Health Act 2007, sections 2(1) ['criteria']; 5, 24–26 ['treatment decisions']; and 9–23 ['selection of a substitute decision-maker, making financial decisions']; F3: Mental Capacity Act 2005, as amended by Mental Health Act 2007, sections 2(1), 9–29; F5: Mental Health Act 1983, as amended by Mental Health Act 2007, sections 7–10; Department of Health, 2008; chapters 26 and 28; Mental Capacity Act 2005, as amended by Mental Health Act 2007, sections 9–29; F6: Mental Capacity Act 2005, as amended by Mental Health Act 2007, sections 19(8) and 20(1); F8: Mental Capacity Act 2005, as amended by Mental Health Act 2007, section 53.

54   Mental Capacity Act 2005, as amended by the Mental Health Act 2007, section 53; Department for Constitutional Affairs, *The Mental Capacity Act Code of Practice*, London: The Stationery Office, 2007; p. 197. Patients under 'guardianship' under the Mental Health Act 1983, as amended by Mental Health Act 2007, have access to mental health tribunals (section 66(1)(c)).

55   Lunacy Regulations (Ireland) Act 1871; Leonard, P., and McLaughlin, M., 'Capacity legislation for Ireland: filling the legislative gaps', *Irish Journal of Psychological Medicine*, 2009, 26, 165–168.

56   Law Reform Commission, *Vulnerable Adults and the Law (LRC 83–2006)*, Dublin: Law Reform Commission, 2006.

57   Lunacy Regulations (Ireland) Act 1871, section 6; Court Service, *Office of Wards of Court*, Dublin: The Courts Information Service, 2003; p. 4–6; Law Reform Commission, 2006.

58   Court Service, 2003; p. 6.

(F5) although the initial consequences are notably profound, as the Court gains jurisdiction over *all matters* in relation to the 'person and estate',[59] although it may later specify areas in which a 'personal guardian' may 'take decisions on behalf of a patient' (F6).[60]

Irish law does not, however, make sufficient 'provision for a systematic review of the need for a guardian' (F7), although there is (limited) possibility of appeal (F8).[61] It is hoped these deficits will be addressed in new legislation in the coming years (see Chapter 5).[62] Notwithstanding these deficits, legislation in England[63] and Ireland[64] meet WHO criteria in relation to 'proxy consent for treatment' (K).

Oversight and review

Legislation in England meets some but not all WHO requirements in relation to 'oversight and review' (R). Mental health review tribunals assess involuntary admissions (R1a(i))[65] and community treatment orders (R1);[66] entertain appeals (R1a(ii));[67] and review the cases of involuntary but *not* 'long-term voluntary

---

59 Lunacy Regulations (Ireland) Act 1871, section 103; Law Reform Commission, 2006; p. 29. See Chapter 5 for consideration of Ireland's Assisted Decision-Making (Capacity) Bill 2013.

60 Lunacy Regulations (Ireland) Act 1871, section 103; Court Service, 2003; pp. 7–11.

61 Court Service, 2003; p. 6.

62 The Mental Capacity and Guardianship Bill 2008 indicated intent to legislate in this area (Leonard & McLaughlin, 2009; p. 165). In March 2012, the Joint Committee on Justice, Defence and Equality published a *Report on Hearings in Relation to the Scheme of the Mental Capacity Bill*, but legislation is not yet in place (Joint Committee on Justice, Defence and Equality, *Report on Hearings in Relation to the Scheme of the Mental Capacity Bill*, Dublin: Houses of the Oireachtas, 2012). See Chapter 5 for consideration of Ireland's Assisted Decision-Making (Capacity) Bill 2013.

63 K1: Mental Capacity Act 2005, as amended by the Mental Health Act 2007, sections 9–29; Mental Health Act 1983, as amended by the Mental Health Act 2007, sections 7–10; Department of Health, 2008; chapters 26 and 28. K2: Mental Capacity Act 2005, as amended by the Mental Health Act 2007, section 53; Mental Health Act 1983, as amended by the Mental Health Act 2007, section 66(1)(c). K3: Mental Capacity Act 1983, as amended by the Mental Health Act 2007, sections 24–26.

64 K1: Lunacy Regulations (Ireland) Act 1871; Court Service, 2003; pp. 4–6; Law Reform Commission, 2006. K2: Court Service, 2003; p. 6. K3: Powers of Attorney Act 1996, section 2(1); Court Service, 2003; p. 6; Law Reform Commission, 2006; pp. 99–112.

65 Mental Health Act 1983, as amended by the Mental Health Act 2007, part V.

66 Mental Health Act 2007, section 37(3); amending Mental Health Act 1983, section 68(1).

67 Mental Health Act 1983, as amended by the Mental Health Act 2007, section 66.

patients' (R1a(iii)). Legislation affirms the importance of the Mental Health Act Commission, now replaced by the Care Quality Commission,[68] with similar regulatory functions (R1a(iv)).[69] Legislation also regulates psychosurgery[70] and ECT (R1a(v)),[71] and tribunals are appropriately structured by law.[72] The Care Quality Commission regularly inspects facilities (R2a(i));[73] maintains appropriate statistics (R2a(iii));[74] publishes findings regularly (R2a(vi));[75] makes recommendations appropriately (R2a(v)); is appropriately structured (R2b);[76] and has clear authority (R2c).[77] It does not 'provide guidance on minimising intrusive treatments' (R2a(ii)) and maintains a register of 'accredited facilities'[78] but not 'professionals', who are approved by local social services authorities (R2a(iv)).[79] While the Commission conducts 'inquiries',[80] 'reviews and investigations',[81] it does *not* outline detailed complaint procedures (R3a-R3b(vi)).

In Ireland, the Mental Health Commission establishes tribunals[82] to review involuntary admissions (R1, R1a(i)-(ii))[83] but *not* 'long-term voluntary patients' (R1a(iii)); appoints an Inspector of Mental Health Services;[84] monitors involuntary treatments (R1a(iv));[85] regulates 'intrusive and irreversible

---

68 Health and Social Care Act 2008, section 1(2).

69 Health and Social Care Act 2008, section 2(2)(c).

70 Mental Health Act 1983, as amended by the Mental Health Act 2007, section 57(1)(a).

71 Mental Health Act 1983, as amended by the Mental Health Act 2007, section 58.

72 R1b: Mental Health Act 1983, as amended by the Mental Health Act 2007, schedule 2, section 4. R1c: Decisions can be appealed to the High Court, commonly by way of judicial review (Fennell, 2007; pp. 225–227).

73 Health and Social Care Act 2008, sections 60, 61, 52(1)(i).

74 Health and Social Care Act 2008, sections 52(1)(c).

75 Health and Social Care Act 2008, sections 38, 49, 53, 58, 83, 84.

76 Health and Social Care Act 2008, section 5; schedule 1, section 3.

77 Health and Social Care Act 2008, sections 1, 2, 52.

78 Health and Social Care Act 2008, chapter 2.

79 Mental Health Act 1983, as amended by the Mental Health Act 2007, section 114.

80 Health and Social Care Act 2008, section 75.

81 Health and Social Care Act 2008, sections 46–51; Care Quality Commission, *How to Complain about a Health Care or Social Care Service*, Newcastle upon Tyne: Care Quality Commission, 2009.

82 Mental Health Act 2001, section 33(3).

83 Mental Health Act 2001, section 18.

84 Mental Health Act 2001, section 50(1).

85 Mental Health Act 2001, section 51.

treatments' (R1a(v));[86] and is appropriately composed (R1b).[87] A detained patient may appeal to the Circuit Court on the grounds that they dispute the fact that they have 'mental disorder';[88] to the High Court 'on a point of law';[89] or to the High Court under the Constitution of Ireland (R1c).[90]

Ireland's Mental Health Commission is a 'regulatory and oversight' body (R2)[91] which incorporates an Inspectorate (R2a(i));[92] provides 'guidance on minimising intrusive treatments' (R2a(ii));[93] maintains statistics (R2a(iii));[94] maintains a register of 'accredited facilities'[95] but *not* 'professionals' (R2a(iv));[96] reports and makes recommendations appropriately (R2a(v));[97] and publishes findings regularly (R2a(vi)).[98] It does not, however, include 'members representing families of people with mental disorders' (R2b)[99] and, although its authority is clearly stated (R2c),[100] does not outline detailed complaint procedures (R3a-R3b(vi)).

---

86 Mental Health Act, sections 58, 59; Mental Health Commission, *Rules Governing the Use of Electro-Convulsive Therapy*, Dublin: Mental Health Commission, 2009.

87 Mental Health Act 2001, section 35. The composition of mental health tribunals, although smaller, is similar, including one medical representative, one legal representative and one other person (section 48(2)).

88 Mental Health Act 2001, section 19(1); Mills, 2004.

89 Mental Health Act 2001, section 19(16).

90 Constitution of Ireland, article 40.

91 Mental Health Act 2001, section 32(1) and 33(1).

92 Mental Health Act 2001, sections 50–55.

93 Mental Health Act 2001 33(3)(e); Mental Health Commission, *Code of Practice on the Use of Physical Restraint in Approved Centres*, Dublin: Mental Health Commission, 2009. Mental Health Act 2001, section, 69(2); Mental Health Commission, *Rules Governing the Use of Seclusion and Mechanical Means of Bodily Restraint*, Dublin: Mental Health Commission, 2009. Mental Health Act 2001, section 59(2); Mental Health Commission, *Rules Governing the Use of Electro-Convulsive Therapy*, Dublin: Mental Health Commission, 2009.

94 The Mental Health Commission must prepare an annual report (Mental Health Act 2001, section 42(1)) and publish data relevant to service quality, including intrusive treatments, restraint, seclusion, etc.; e.g., Mental Health Commission, *Report on the Use of Seclusion, Mechanical Means of Bodily Restraint and Physical Restraint in Approved Centres in 2008*, Dublin: Mental Health Commission, 2009.

95 Mental Health Act 2001, section 64.

96 The Mental Health Act 2001 does not establish a register of accredited professionals but makes explicit use of the statutory registers maintained by the Medical Council of Ireland (section 2(1)).

97 Mental Health Act 2001, sections 33(3)(d), 42(1).

98 Mental Health Act 2001, section 42(1).

99 Mental Health Act 2001, section 35(2).

100 Mental Health Act 2001, parts 3 and 5.

Overall, WHO requirements regarding 'oversight and review' (R) are met in part in England and Ireland, with the greatest deficit in both jurisdictions relating to imperfect or absent 'procedures for submissions, investigations and resolutions of complaints' (R3a-R3b(vi)). The narrow grounds for Circuit Court appeal in Ireland present further cause for concern.[101]

Special treatments, seclusion and restraint

None of the three Mental Health Acts (1983 and 2007 in England, 2001 in Ireland) explicitly 'require informed consent for major medical and surgical procedures on persons with a mental disorder' (O2), but none dispense with this requirement either. Similarly, while none of the three Mental Health Acts explicitly 'allow medical and surgical procedures without informed consent, if waiting for informed consent would put the patient's life at risk' (O2a), none forbid it. In England, the Mental Capacity Act 2005 permits, 'in cases where inability to consent is likely to be long term', 'authorisation for medical and surgical procedures from an independent review body or by proxy consent of a guardian' (O2b).[102] In Ireland, the Ward of Court system makes similar provision (O2b).[103]

None of the three Mental Health Acts 'outlaw' all 'irreversible treatments' on involuntary patients, although the Mental Health Acts 2007 (England)[104] and 2001 (Ireland)[105] introduce various safeguards. Regarding psychosurgery in England, the doctor providing the second opinion and 'two other persons' involved in treatment must be satisfied the patient has capacity to consent (O3a).[106] In Ireland, there is no similar requirement, as the mental health tribunal prior to psychosurgery must only decide if psychosurgery 'is in the best interests of the health of the patient' and does not comment on capacity.[107] Regarding ECT, there is, in England, a requirement for informed consent

---

101 Mental Health Act 2001, section 19(1); Mills, 2004.

102 Mental Capacity Act 2005, as amended by the Mental Health Act 2007, section 5.

103 Lunacy Regulations (Ireland) Act 1871; Law Reform Commission, 2006; Leonard & McLaughlin, 2009.

104 Mental Health Act 1983, as amended by the Mental Health Act 2007, section 57; safeguards for involuntary patients include requirements for consent and a second opinion prior to psychosurgery, among other specified treatments. See: Bowen, 2007; p. 99.

105 Mental Health Act 2001, section 58; safeguards for involuntary patients include requirements for consent and endorsement by a mental health tribunal prior to psychosurgery.

106 Mental Health Act 1983, as amended by the Mental Health Act 2007, section 57(2).

107 Mental Health Act 2001, section 58(3)(a).

for involuntary patients except those who lack capacity, for whom a second opinion is required (O4).[108] There is a similar requirement for informed consent prior to ECT in Ireland and a second opinion needed if the patient is 'unable or unwilling' to consent.[109] None of the three Mental Health Acts prohibits unmodified ECT (i.e., without anaesthetic) (O5) or 'ECT in minors' (O6), and none make reference to sterilisation (O1, O1a).

None of the three Mental Health Acts provide detailed guidance regarding seclusion and restraint (P). In England, there is a Code of Practice which addresses seclusion and mechanical restraint,[110] but the Code is for 'guidance' purposes[111] and 'the Act does not impose a legal duty to comply' with it (although staff 'must have regard to the Code').[112]

The situation in Ireland is significantly more consistent with WHO requirements: the Mental Health Act 2001 states that seclusion and restraint can only be used in accordance with rules made under the Act, violation of which constitutes an offence (P1).[113] The rules meet many of the WHO requirements,[114] although they do permit 'one period of seclusion and restraint' to be 'followed immediately by another' (P4).[115] Such is the level of concordance between the Irish rules and WHO guidelines (in both meaning and words), it appears reasonable to hypothesise that the WHO guidelines influenced the development of the Irish rules.

---

108 Mental Health Act 1983, as amended by the Mental Health Act 2007, section 58A.

109 Mental Health Act 2001, section 59(1)(b). The inclusion of 'unwilling' suggests that involuntary patients with capacity who are 'unwilling' to agree to ECT are liable to be given ECT against their wishes; the College of Psychiatrists of Ireland has suggested deleting the word 'unwilling' so as to limit involuntary ECT to those lacking capacity (Mulholland, P., 'ECT amendment proposal sent to the government', *Irish Medical News*, 2010, 35, 3).

110 Department of Health, 2008.

111 Mental Health Act 1983, section 118.

112 Department of Health, 2008; p. 2. The Code meets many of the WHO requirements including P1 (pp. 120, 133), P2 (p. 114), P5 (pp. 112–116) and, in part, P6 (pp. 112–127).

113 Mental Health Act 2001, section 69(1).

114 P2: Mental Health Commission, *Rules Governing the Use of Seclusion and Mechanical Means of Bodily Restraint*, Dublin: Mental Health Commission, 2009; p. 15. P3: pp. 19, 27. P5 and 6: pp. 1–45.

115 Mental Health Commission, *Rules Governing the Use of Seclusion and Mechanical Means of Bodily Restraint*, Dublin: Mental Health Commission, 2009; pp. 22, 27.

Various other matters

Legislation in England meets many of the WHO requirements in relation to 'rights of families or other carers' (E)[116] except for encouraging 'family members or other primary carers ... to become involved in the formulation and implementation of the patient's individualised treatment plan' (E2). In Ireland, the Mental Health Act 2001 meets *none* of these requirements (E).

The position regarding research (Q) differs between the jurisdictions. Mental health legislation in England does not provide detailed guidance regarding 'clinical experimental research' (Q1) but, for those who lack capacity, the Mental Capacity Act 2005 permits research subject to certain safeguards,[117] including a requirement for 'proxy consent' (Q2a) from an appropriate source;[118] that 'research cannot be conducted if the same research could be conducted on people capable of consenting' (Q2b);[119] and it 'is necessary to promote the health of the individual and that of the population represented' (Q2b).[120] The Mental Health Act 2001 (Ireland) states that no detained patient can participate in a clinical trial but does not meet any of the WHO requirements.[121]

Areas of Low Compliance with WHO Human Rights Standards

Fundamental principles

The preambles to the Mental Health Acts 1983, 2007 (England) and 2001 (Ireland) do not mention human rights and therefore fail to accord with most WHO requirements in relation to 'preamble and objectives' (A). Both jurisdictions raise some of these issues in different ways, however, as the preamble to Ireland's Mental Health Act 2001 highlights some of the Act's human rights-*related* goals (e.g., 'to provide for the independent review of the involuntary admission of such persons ... ')[122] and the main text of the legislation states 'due regard shall be given to the need to respect the right of the person to dignity, bodily integrity, privacy and autonomy'.[123]

---

116 E1: Mental Health Act 1983, section 132(4); Mental Health Act 1983, section 132A(3), amended by Mental Health Act 2007, schedule 3, paragraph 30. E3: Mental Health Act 1983; section 11(4). E5: Mental Health Act 2007, section 8; amending Mental Health Act 1983, section 118(2B)).

117 Mental Capacity Act 2005, section 30–34. Bowen, 2007; p. 188.

118 Mental Capacity Act 2005, section 32.

119 Mental Capacity Act 2005, section 31(4).

120 Mental Capacity Act 2005, section 31(5).

121 Mental Health Act 2001, section 70.

122 Mental Health Act 2001, preamble.

123 Mental Health Act 2001, section 4(3).

In England, the revised Mental Health Act 1983 states that 'the Secretary of State shall prepare, and from time to time revise, a code of practice'[124] which 'shall include a statement of the principles which the Secretary of State thinks should inform decisions under this Act'.[125] The Mental Health Act 2007 articulates 'minimising restrictions on liberty' as one of the matters to be addressed in preparing the 'statement of principles' for the Code of Practice.[126] These principles, however, belong in the Code of Practice rather than the legislation itself, and the English legislation, like the Irish, still lacks overall commitment to the 'promotion and protection of the rights of people with mental disorders', suggested by the WHO (A2b).

The Mental Health Act 2007 (England) also includes 'avoidance of unlawful discrimination' as another matter to be addressed in preparing the 'statement of principles' for the Code of Practice, which goes some way towards meeting the WHO requirements (A2a).[127] In addition, while none of the three Mental Health Acts explicitly promote 'a community-based approach' (A2d), the Mental Health Act 2007 (England) includes 'minimising restrictions on liberty' as matter to be addressed in preparing the 'statement of principles' for the Code of Practice,[128] and the Mental Health Act 2001 (Ireland) states 'due regard' is to be given to the 'right of the person to ... autonomy'.[129]

Notwithstanding these expressions of selected principles, the absence of strong, rights-based preambles has, arguably, reduced emphasis on human rights in other parts of the Mental Health Acts. One example concerns the 'rights of users of mental health services' regarding information (D). Legislation in both jurisdictions articulates 'rights to respect, dignity and to be treated in a humane way' (D1),[130] but both jurisdictions fail to meet WHO requirements regarding access to information, although the Mental Health Act 2001 (Ireland) states 'due regard' is to be given to the 'right of the person to ... privacy'[131] (D2) and the Mental Health Act 2007 (England) specifies 'exceptional circumstances when confidentiality may be legally breached' (D2b).[132] Some of these issues

---

124 Mental Health Act 1983, section 118(1).

125 Mental Health Act 1983, section 118(2A).

126 Mental Health Act 2007, section 8; amending Mental Health Act 1983, section 118(2B)(c).

127 Mental Health Act 2007, section 8; amending Mental Health Act 1983, section 118(2B)(e).

128 Mental Health Act 2007, section 8; amending Mental Health Act 1983, section 118(2B)(c).

129 Mental Health Act 2001, section 4(3).

130 England: Mental Health Act 2007, section 8; amending Mental Health Act 1983, section 118(2B). Ireland: Mental Health Act 2001, section 4(3).

131 Mental Health Act 2001, section 4(3).

132 Department of Health, 2008; p. 148.

relating to legislation are covered by data protection legislation and/or freedom of information laws in each jurisdiction,[133] but they are not addressed in mental health legislation, as ostensibly suggested by the WHO.

Selected other issues related to human rights are addressed, at least in principle: 'cruel, inhuman and degrading treatment' (D4), for example, would be grossly inconsistent with the matters to be addressed in preparing the 'statement of principles' for the Code of Practice outlined in the Mental Health Act 2007 (England),[134] and the Mental Health Act 2001 (Ireland) states 'due regard shall be given to the need to respect the right of the person to dignity, bodily integrity, privacy and autonomy'.[135] None of the three Mental Health Acts, however, set out 'the minimal conditions to be maintained in mental health facilities for a safe, therapeutic and hygienic environment' (D5) or make explicit 'provision for educational activities; vocational training; leisure and recreational activities; and religious or cultural needs of people with mental disorders' (D8).

Voluntary patients

Legislation in England and Ireland promotes treatment in the least restrictive setting as an alternative to involuntary admission (G1): the Mental Health Act 2007 (England) includes 'minimising restrictions on liberty' as a matter to be addressed in preparing the 'statement of principles' for the Code of Practice,[136] and the Mental Health Act 2001 (Ireland) states 'due regard' is to be given to the 'right of the person to ... autonomy'.[137] Neither jurisdiction meets any of the other WHO criteria regarding 'voluntary treatment and admission'.

The Mental Health Act 1983 (England) has detailed provisions regarding consent to treatment, but these apply only to specific groups of detained patients (G2).[138] Similarly, the Mental Health Act 2001 (Ireland) states that 'the consent of a patient shall be required for treatment'[139] except under specific circumstances; again, however, the term 'patient' refers *only* to involuntary patients,[140] so Ireland's Mental Health Act 2001 does *not* require informed consent from voluntary patients. Indeed, the Mental Health Act 2001 does not

---

133   England: Carey, P., *Data Protection (Third Edition)*, Oxford: Oxford University Press, 2009. Ireland: Kelleher, D., *Privacy and Data Protection Law in Ireland*, Dublin: Tottel Publishing, 2006.

134   Mental Health Act 2007, section 8; amending Mental Health Act 1983, section 118(2B).

135   Mental Health Act 2001, section 4(3).

136   Mental Health Act 2007, section 8; amending Mental Health Act 1983, section 118(2B)(c).

137   Mental Health Act 2001, section 4(1).

138   Mental Health Act 1983, part IV.

139   Mental Health Act 2001, section 56(a).

140   Mental Health Act 2001, section 2(1).

even require that voluntary patients *possess* capacity: the Act states that 'voluntary patient' means 'a person receiving care and treatment in an approved centre who is not the subject of an admission order to a renewal order'.[141]

Compliance with WHO standards regarding non-protesting patients (H) differs between jurisdictions and in both is troubling. In England, the Mental Capacity Act 2005 makes provision for admission (H1) and treatment (H2) of incapacitated, non-protesting patients[142] but does not clearly state that patients who object must be discharged unless criteria for involuntary detention are met (H3). In Ireland, the Mental Health Act 2001 makes no specific provision for admission (H1) and treatment (H2) of incapacitated, non-protesting patients, probably because such patients are included under Ireland's distinctly paternalistic definition of 'voluntary patient' which does not require capacity.[143] The legislation does, however, specify that when a 'voluntary' patient (including incapacitated, non-protesting patients)[144] indicates a wish to leave, he or she must be assessed to see if criteria for involuntary detention are met.[145]

Vulnerable patient groups

In relation to minors, the Mental Health Act 2007 (England) includes 'minimising restrictions on liberty' as a matter to be addressed in preparing the 'statement of principles' for the Code of Practice (Z1, minors);[146] emphasises age-appropriate facilities (Z2b, minors);[147] and requires that services 'take the opinions of minors into consideration' (Z4, minors).[148] Legislation does not 'ban all irreversible treatments for children' (Z5, minors), although there are specific safeguards for certain treatments (e.g., ECT).[149]

The Mental Health Act 2001 (Ireland) states that a 'child' (aged under 18 years)[150] can be involuntarily admitted if, among other criteria, 'the child requires treatment which he or she is unlikely to receive unless an order is made under

---

141 Mental Health Act 2001, section 2(1).

142 Mental Capacity Act 2005, as amended by the Mental Health Act 2007, schedules A1 and 1A. These provisions are long, complex and bureaucratic.

143 Mental Health Act 2001, section 2(1).

144 Mental Health Act 2001, section 2(1).

145 Mental Health Act 2001, section 23.

146 Mental Health Act 2007, section 8; amending Mental Health Act 1983, section 118(2B)(c).

147 Mental Health Act 2007, section 31(3); amending Mental Health Act 1983, section 131.

148 Mental Health Act 1983, section 131(2); Department of Health, 2008: pp. 326–354; Bowen, 2007; pp. 160–163.

149 Mental Health Act 2007, section 58A, amending Mental Health Act 1983, section 58.

150 Mental Health Act 2001, section 2(1).

this section' (Z1, minors).[151] The remaining WHO requirements are addressed, in part, in the Mental Health Commission's Code of Practice Relating to Admission of Children under the Mental Health Act 2001,[152] but there is no 'legal duty on persons working in the mental health services to comply with codes of practice'.[153] The Mental Health Act 2001 does not 'ban all irreversible treatments for children' (Z5, minors), but psychosurgery[154] and ECT[155] require District Court approval.

Regarding women, the Mental Health Act 2007 (England) includes, as matters to be addressed in preparing the 'statement of principles' for the Code of Practice, 'respect for diversity generally including, in particular, diversity of religion, culture and sexual orientation'[156] and 'avoidance of unlawful discrimination' (Z1, women).[157] The Mental Health Act 2001 (Ireland) states 'due regard shall be given to the need to respect the right of the person to dignity, bodily integrity, privacy and autonomy' (Z1, women)[158] and the 'right of the person to ... privacy' (Z2a, women).[159] None of the three Mental Health Acts meet any of the other WHO requirements in relation to women.

Regarding minorities, the Mental Health Act 2007 (England) includes, as a matter to be addressed in preparing the 'statement of principles' for the Code of Practice, 'respect for diversity generally including, in particular, diversity of religion, culture and sexual orientation'[160] and 'avoidance of unlawful

---

151 Mental Health Act 2001, section 25(1)(b).

152 Z2a, minors: Mental Health Commission, *Code of Practice Relating to Admission of Children under the Mental Health Act 2001*, Dublin: Mental Health Commission, 2006; p. 12. Z2b, minors: pp. 12–13. Z3, minors: Certain protections are covered in the *Code of Practice* (pp. 22–23), but these do not include the WHO requirement that law 'ensure that all minors have an adult to represent them'. Z4, minors: Certain issues regarding the child's own views are mentioned in the *Code* in relation to voluntary child patients (p. 22), but the law does not fulfil the WHO requirement 'to take the opinions of minors into consideration on all issues affecting them'.

153 Mental Health Commission, 2006; p. 9.

154 Mental Health Act 2001, section 25(12).

155 Mental Health Act 2001, section 25(13).

156 Mental Health Act 2007, section 8; amending Mental Health Act 1983, section 118(2B)(b).

157 Mental Health Act 2007, section 8; amending Mental Health Act 1983, section 118(2B)(e).

158 Mental Health Act 2001, section 4(3).

159 Mental Health Act 2001, section 4(3).

160 Mental Health Act 2007, section 8; amending Mental Health Act 1983, section 118(2B)(b).

discrimination' (Z1, minorities).[161] While the Mental Health Act 2001 (Ireland) states 'due regard shall be given to the need to respect the right of the person to dignity, bodily integrity, privacy and autonomy',[162] none of the three Mental Health Acts meet any of the other WHO requirements in relation to minorities.

Overall, the level of special protection offered to 'vulnerable groups' as specified by the WHO varies significantly between jurisdictions and, in both, falls significantly short of WHO requirements.

Emergency treatment

Mental health legislation in England permits 'emergency treatment for patients lacking capacity or competence' if 'the treatment needs to be given in order to prevent harm' (M1);[163] outlines involuntary procedures 'for admission and treatment in emergency situations' (M2);[164] and provides considerable detail about the roles of mental health professionals including the 'responsible clinician' (M3).[165]

In Ireland, the Mental Health Act 2001 does not outline a separate procedure for 'emergency admission/treatment' (M1) and the standard involuntary admission/treatment process requires either a 'serious likelihood of the person concerned causing immediate and serious harm to himself or herself or to other persons'[166] or that 'failure to admit' would 'likely lead to a serious deterioration in his or her condition';[167] on this basis, the Irish legislation does *not* necessarily require 'high probability of immediate and imminent danger or harm' for emergency admission, although there is such a requirement if there is to be substantial police involvement.[168] Irish legislation does, however, outline involuntary procedures which can be used 'for admission and treatment in emergency situations' (M2)[169] (i.e., the standard procedure) and requires

---

161 Mental Health Act 2007, section 8; amending Mental Health Act 1983, section 118(2B)(e).

162 Mental Health Act 2001, section 4(3).

163 Mental Health Act 1983, as amended by the Mental Health Act 2007, part II; Mental Health Act 2007, section 35(1); amending Mental Health Act 1983, section 64G. Emergency admission is addressed in the Mental Health Act 1983, section 4.

164 Mental Health Act 1983, as amended by the Mental Health Act 2007, part II.

165 Mental Health Act 2007, section 9(9); amending Mental Health Act 1983, section 34(1), and section 12(7)(a); amending Mental Health Act 1983, section 64(1).

166 Mental Health Act 2001, section 3(1)(b)(i).

167 Mental Health Act 2001, section 3(1)(b)(ii).

168 Mental Health Act 2001, section 12(1).

169 Mental Health Act 2001, part 2.

there be a 'consultant psychiatrist responsible for the care and treatment of the patient' (M3).[170]

Both jurisdictions outline explicit procedures 'after the emergency situation has ended' (M5)[171] but neither jurisdiction meets other WHO requirements in relation to outlawing 'treatments such as ECT, psychosurgery and sterilisation, as well as participation in clinical or experimental trials … for people held as emergency cases' (M6);[172] or explicitly stating whether 'patients, family members and personal representatives have the right to appeal against emergency admission/treatment' (M7).[173] Regarding the 'time limit for emergency admission (usually no longer than 72 hours)' (M4), the Mental Health Act 1983 (England) permits emergency admission for 72 hours[174] but also permits admission for 'assessment' for up to 28 days,[175] while the Mental Health Act 2001 (Ireland) permits initial involuntary admission for 21 days, although orders can be revoked sooner if clinically indicated.[176]

Economic and social rights

The greatest single way in which mental health legislation in England and Ireland fails to comply with WHO requirements relates to economic and social rights. Regarding 'discrimination' (U), the Mental Health Act 2007 (England) includes 'avoidance of unlawful discrimination' as matters to be addressed in preparing the 'statement of principles' for the Code of Practice,[177] but the

---

170   Mental Health Act 2001, sections 2(1) and 15(2).

171   England: Mental Health Act 1983, section 4(4), Ireland: Mental Health Act 2001, section 15.

172   In Ireland, no detained patient can participate in a clinical trial (Mental Health Act 2001; section 70).

173   Under the Mental Health Act 1983, as amended by the Mental Health Act 2007, the patient's 'nearest relative' can prevent the making of an application detention for 'treatment' (sections 3 and 11(4)) or guardianship (sections 7 and 11(4)) by an 'approved social worker'; apply to a tribunal on the patient's behalf, under certain circumstances (section 66(1)(ii)); and make 'an order for discharge' from detention for assessment (section 23(2)(a)), treatment (section 23(2)(a) or guardianship (section 23(2)(b)), although such an order can be denied following a report from the 'responsible medical officer' (section 25(1)). These provisions apply to involuntary admission in general, as opposed specifically to emergency admission (Mental Health Act 1983, section 4).

174   Mental Health Act 1983, section 4(4).

175   Mental Health Act 1983, section 2(2)(a).

176   Mental Health Act 2001, section 15(1).

177   Mental Health Act 2007, section 8; amending Mental Health Act 1983, section 118(2B)(d).

Mental Health Act 2001 (Ireland) does *not* 'include provisions aimed at stopping discrimination against people with mental disorders' (U1). The positions regarding housing (V) and employment (W) are similar: in England, 'avoidance of unlawful discrimination' is specified as a matter to be addressed in preparing the 'statement of principles' for the Code of Practice[178] and is relevant but vague, while in Ireland the Mental Health Act 2001 does not include *any* relevant measures.

None of the three Mental Health Acts meet WHO requirements relating to 'social security' (X1) or civil issues (Y), notwithstanding the inclusion of 'avoidance of unlawful discrimination' as a matter to be addressed in preparing the 'statement of principles' for the Code of Practice in England.[179] Some of these issues are addressed in a general sense, for all citizens, through equality legislation in England[180] and Ireland[181] but are not explicitly addressed in the Mental Health Acts.

While issues such as housing, employment and social security might, arguably, be better addressed through government policy rather than mental health law, the failure of Mental Health Acts in both jurisdictions to comply with many WHO standards regarding 'access to mental health care' (C) is, arguably, a more pointed problem. Regarding 'allocation of resources to underserved populations and specify[ing] that these services should be culturally appropriate' (C3), the Mental Health Act 2007 (England) emphasises 'equitable distribution of services'[182] and includes 'respect for diversity' as a matter to be addressed in preparing the 'statement of principles' for the Code of Practice.[183] Irish legislation makes no reference to these matters. Similarly, while Mental Health Acts in England[184] and Ireland[185] all emphasise treatment in the least restrictive setting, none of the Mental Health Acts explicitly 'promote community care and deinstitutionalisation' (C8) at policy level.

---

178 Mental Health Act 2007, section 8; amending Mental Health Act 1983, section 118(2B)(d).

179 Mental Health Act 2007, section 8; amending Mental Health Act 1983, section 118(2B)(d).

180 Wadham, J., Ruebain, D., Robinson, A., Uppal, S., *Blackstone's Guide to the Equality Act 2010*, Oxford: Oxford University Press, 2010.

181 Hughes, I., Clancy, P., Harris, C., Beetham, D., *Power to the People*, Dublin: TASC, 2007; p. 199.

182 Mental Health Act 2007, section 8; amending Mental Health Act 1983, section 118(2C)(b).

183 Mental Health Act 2007, section 8, amending Mental Health Act 1983, section 118(2B)(b).

184 Mental Health Act 2007, section 8; amending Mental Health Act 1983, section 118(2B)(c).

185 Mental Health Act 2001, section 4(1).

Summary: Areas of High, Medium and Low Compliance with WHO Standards

Mental health legislation in England meets 92 (55.4%) of the 166 relevant human rights standards set out by the WHO while mental health legislation in Ireland meets 81 (48.8%). The higher compliance rate in England compared to Ireland is chiefly attributable to the Mental Capacity Act 2005 in England; in Ireland, dedicated capacity legislation is currently being developed but has not yet been introduced into law.[186]

Looking across both jurisdictions, areas of high compliance include clear definitions of mental disorder, relatively robust procedures for involuntary treatment (although provision of information remains suboptimal) and clarity regarding offences and penalties. These issues, primarily relating to compulsion and coercion, are issues of long-standing concern in asylum-based mental healthcare, since the eighteenth century and even earlier.[187] It is therefore reasonable that these matters are highlighted in the WHO checklist, and the high level of compliance in England and Ireland is both reassuring and historically significant, albeit that they tend to focus on the right to liberty alone, and in a broadly paternalistic fashion, and fail to engage more widely with other rights, especially for non-detained patients.

Areas of medium compliance relate to competence, capacity and consent, oversight and review procedures (which exclude long-term voluntary patients and require more robust complaints procedures), and rules governing special treatments, seclusion and restraint, as well as other, more specific matters (the rights of families, research). Many of the WHO standards in these areas relate, again, to areas of traditional concern in mental health (e.g., seclusion, restraint) but some also date from more recent decades (e.g., research). The medium level of compliance in England and Ireland again reflects a growing awareness of the human rights of the mentally ill, especially as reflected through the ECHR and related case law. There also are, however, areas of notable deficit including the lack of reasonable and responsive capacity legislation in Ireland. The ongoing relevance of European influences in the context of these changes and deficits is explored further in Chapter 6.

Areas of low compliance relate to overall commitments in mental health legislation to promoting the rights of the mentally ill (impacting on other areas within legislation, such as information management), definition and treatment of voluntary patients (especially non-protesting incapacitated patients in Ireland), protection of vulnerable patient groups and emergency treatment.

---

186 See Chapter 5 for consideration of Ireland's Assisted Decision-Making (Capacity) Bill 2013.

187 Shorter, 1997; Porter, 2002.

The greatest single deficit in both jurisdictions relates to economic and social rights which the WHO suggests should be explicitly protected in mental health provisions but which are not addressed in any detailed or substantive fashion in mental health legislation in England or Ireland.

Overall, compliance with WHO standards is highest in areas of traditional concern in asylum-based mental health services (involuntary detention and treatment) and lowest in areas of growing relevance to modern community-based mental health services (e.g., rights of voluntary patients, economic and social rights, rights to a minimum standard of care). This is a key conclusion from the present analysis: mental health legislation in both jurisdictions focuses on specific rights (e.g., the right to liberty) to the exclusion of certain others and does so in a fashion shaped largely by paternalism.

In England this situation stems primarily from the emphasis on public safety during the recent revision of legislation, and in Ireland it stems from a strongly welfare-based or paternalistic tradition in mental health law. If mental health legislation focussed more broadly on economic and social rights, as the WHO suggests, it might well remedy this situation by affording greater protection of dignity and facilitating patients to exercise their own capabilities in areas other than strictly defined mental health care (e.g., housing, employment and social participation).

These conclusions stem from this analysis of legislation based on the WHO checklist, and it should be remembered that the WHO checklist, while it is both comprehensive and explicitly based on human rights standards (e.g., Universal Declaration of Human Rights), is not necessarily perfect. For example, while the WHO checklist places considerable emphasis on economic and social rights, it is not clear whether or not such rights belong in a 'Checklist for Mental Health *Legislation*' (italics added)[188] or might be best addressed through other forms of legislation or governmental mental health policy (see Chapters 6 and 7).

This issue is an important one, because in practice the WHO checklist may well achieve some of its aims by influencing mechanisms other than dedicated mental health *legislation*. In Ireland, for example, the level of concordance between the statutory Rules Governing the Use of Seclusion and Mechanical Means of Bodily Restraint[189] and relevant WHO standards (Table 1, Section P) is such that it appears reasonable to conclude that the WHO standards were taken into consideration in the development of the Rules: not only do the two documents overlap in meaning, but the same phrases are used throughout both. This is consistent with the influence of other WHO documents, such as the

---

188   WHO, 2005.

189   Mental Health Commission, *Rules Governing the Use of Seclusion and Mechanical Means of Bodily Restraint*, Dublin: Mental Health Commission, 2009.

ICD-10 Guide for Mental Retardation,[190] which is also reflected, at least in part, in revised national mental health legislation (see Chapter 2).

Overall, then, the human rights-based analysis of mental health legislation presented in this chapter and the previous one articulates clearly the substantial influence of international human rights documents[191] (e.g., UN/WHO publications) and the ECHR (and related case law) in shaping mental health law. This is evidenced through both a growing *overall* emphasis on human rights and more specific instances, such as the apparent influence of the WHO guidance on the Irish rules for seclusion and restraint.

Notwithstanding these developments, there are still clear areas of high, medium and low compliance with WHO human rights standards across the two jurisdictions. However, while these WHO standards are certainly the most detailed human rights standards specific to mental health legislation formulated to date, they are not the only standards with which such legislation can be compared. Chapter 4, examines the relevance of the CRPD,[192] which is arguably the most significant development in the field of mental disability, mental disorder and human rights in recent years, and has considerable relevance to mental health legislation in England, Ireland and elsewhere.

More specifically, Chapter 4 explores the precise implications of the CRPD for mental health legislation in England and Ireland, and concludes that the CRPD strongly discourages, if not precludes, *any* deprivation of liberty based on mental disorder. This is a dramatic change in the human rights landscape for people with mental disorder in England and Ireland, and will likely have far-reaching implications for current and future revisions of mental health legislation in both jurisdictions. These matters are considered next.

---

190   WHO, *ICD-10 Guide for Mental Retardation*, Geneva: WHO, 1996.

191   McSherry, B., Weller, P., 'Rethinking rights-based mental health laws', in McSherry, B. and Weller, P. (eds), *Rethinking Rights-Based Mental Health Laws* (pp. 3–10), Oxford and Portland, Oregon: Hart Publishing, 2010; p. 10.

192   UN, 2006.

Chapter 4

United Nations Convention on the Rights of Persons with Disabilities

Introduction

The human rights landscape in which capacity and mental health legislation is developed and operates has been significantly re-shaped with the emergence of the CRPD (Convention on the Rights of Persons with Disabilities), adopted by the UN General Assembly in December 2006.[1] The CRPD came into effect in May 2008 and by June 2014 had 158 signatories and was ratified by 147 'states parties', as well as the EU.

The UK signed the CRPD in 2007 and ratified it in 2009, albeit with specific reservations (unrelated to mental disorder). The CRPD is not, however, incorporated into UK domestic law by legislation and therefore is not part of domestic law and not binding in domestic courts. It can, nonetheless, be referred to by UK courts and used in the interpretation of domestic law.[2] Ireland signed the CRPD in 2007 but has not yet ratified it owing in part to the absence of up-to-date capacity legislation, which is currently being formulated.[3]

Overall, the CRPD represents a long-overdue articulation of the rights of people with disabilities. In the specific context of psychiatry, the CRPD raises several important issues, most notably in relation to its definition of disability and its apparent incompatibility with legislation that uses mental disorder or mental illness as part of criteria for deprivation of liberty and involuntary treatment. There are also significant issues regarding the CRPD's implications for systems of supported decision-making in national mental health legislation, among other areas. This chapter examines relevant aspects of the CRPD in the context of mental health and capacity legislation, with particular focus on human rights.

---

1 UN, 2006; Bartlett et al., 2007.

2 Szmukler, G., Daw, R., Callard, F., 'Mental health law and the UN Convention on the rights of persons with disabilities', *International Journal of Law and Psychiatry*, 2014, 37, 245–252.

3 Kelly, B.D., 'The Assisted Decision-Making (Capacity) Bill 2013: content, commentary, controversy', *Irish Journal of Medical Science*, 2015, 184, 31–46. See also Chapter 5.

Purpose and Purview of the CRPD

The CRPD is clearly located within the pre-existing UN human rights framework and reaffirms 'the universality, indivisibility, interdependence and interrelatedness of all human rights and fundamental freedoms and the need for persons with disabilities to be guaranteed their full enjoyment without discrimination'.[4] It emphasises 'the importance of mainstreaming disability issues as an integral part of relevant strategies of sustainable development';[5] recognises 'that discrimination against any person on the basis of disability is a violation of the human person';[6] and recognises 'the importance for persons with disabilities of their individual autonomy and independence, including the freedom to make their own choices'.[7] Most importantly, the CRPD acknowledges the social context of disability, highlighting 'the fact that the majority of persons with disabilities live in conditions of poverty' and recognising the 'critical need to address the negative impact of poverty on persons with disabilities'.[8]

Against this background, states parties to the CRPD must be convinced 'that a comprehensive and integral international convention to promote and protect the rights and dignity of persons with disabilities will make a significant contribution to redressing the profound social disadvantage of persons with disabilities and promote their participation in the civil, political, economic, social and cultural spheres with equal opportunities, in both developing and developed countries'.[9] Consistent with this, the CRPD's over-arching purpose is 'to promote, protect and ensure the full and equal enjoyment of all human rights and fundamental freedoms by all persons with disabilities, and to promote respect for their inherent dignity'.[10] To this significant extent, the CRPD re-states many rights outlined in the Universal Declaration of Human Rights,[11] re-emphasising and re-framing them within a disability framework.

Definition of 'Disability' in the CRPD

Regarding its definition of 'disability', the CRPD states that 'persons with disabilities include those who have long-term physical, mental, intellectual or sensory impairments which in interaction with various barriers may hinder their

---

4 CRPD, preamble (c).
5 CRPD, preamble (g).
6 CRPD, preamble (h).
7 CRPD, preamble (n).
8 CRPD, preamble (t).
9 CRPD, preamble (y).
10 CRPD, article 1.
11 UN, 1948.

full and effective participation in society on an equal basis with others'.[12] From the point of view of psychiatry, it appears relatively clear that this definition does not include all people with mental disorder, because many mental disorders (e.g., adjustment disorder) are not 'long-term'. The CRPD does not, however, present its definition of 'persons with disabilities' as a comprehensive one but states that the term 'persons with disabilities' *includes* people with 'long-term' impairments; others, presumably, may also fit the definition, at least at certain times.[13]

On this basis, it appears likely that some people with mental disorder meet the definition at least some of the time (e.g., a person with chronic schizophrenia) but others do not (e.g., a person with a single phobia). Moreover, the CRPD states 'that disability is an evolving concept and that disability results from the interaction between persons with impairments and attitudinal and environmental barriers that hinders their full and effective participation in society on an equal basis with others'.[14] Unlike the CRPD's definition of '*persons* with disabilities' (italics added), this conceptualisation of 'disability' holds particularly strong resonance for psychiatry, because the stigma commonly associated with mental disorder stems largely from such 'attitudinal and environmental barriers' that hinder 'full and effective participation in society', often resulting in social exclusion and denial of rights among certain people with mental disorders.[15]

The CRPD goes on to define 'discrimination on the basis of disability' as 'any distinction, exclusion or restriction on the basis of disability which has the purpose or effect of impairing or nullifying the recognition, enjoyment or exercise, on an equal basis with others, of all human rights and fundamental freedoms in the political, economic, social, cultural, civil or any other field'.[16] This 'includes all forms of discrimination, including denial of reasonable accommodation'. This refers to 'accommodation' as in 'adjustments' (similar to the 'adjustments' in the Equality Act 2010,[17] in England, Wales and Scotland) and extends into all areas covered by the CRPD, albeit that the nature of the adjustments required is likely to vary significantly from person to person, rendering observance of this right especially challenging[18] – and important.

---

12 CRPD, article 1.

13 Kelly, B.D., 'An end to psychiatric detention? Implications of the United Nations Convention on the Rights of Persons with Disabilities', *British Journal of Psychiatry*, 2014, 204, 174–175.

14 CRPD, preamble (e).

15 Kelly, 2005.

16 CRPD, article 2.

17 Equality Act 2010, sections 20–22.

18 Bartlett, P., 'The United Nations Convention on the Rights of Persons with Disabilities and mental health law', *Modern Law Review*, 2012, 75, 752–778.

General Principles

The CRPD's broad definition of 'discrimination on the basis of disability' is consistent with its 'general principles', the first of which is 'respect for inherent dignity, individual autonomy including the freedom to make one's own choices, and independence of persons' (Box 1).[19] States parties must not only 'take into account the protection and promotion of the human rights of persons with disabilities in all policies and programmes'[20] but also 'refrain from engaging in any act or practice that is inconsistent with the present Convention' and 'ensure that public authorities and institutions act in conformity with the present Convention'.[21]

General principles of the *United Nations Convention on the Rights of Persons with Disabilities*

- Respect for dignity, autonomy (including the freedom to make one's own choices) and independence
- Non-discrimination
- Full and effective inclusion and participation in society
- Respect for difference and acceptance of persons with disabilities as part of humanity and human diversity
- Equality of opportunity for all
- Accessibility
- Equality between women and men
- Respect for the right of children with disabilities to preserve their identities and respect for the evolving capacities of children with disabilities.

Box 1   Adapted from article 3 of: *United Nations, Convention on the Rights of Persons with Disabilities*, Geneva: United Nations, 2006.

Although the CRPD does not have the status of primary legislation in the UK jurisdictions or Ireland, these measures still appear to articulate a positive obligation to protect rights that is similar in magnitude to the Human Rights Act 1998 in the UK, which makes it 'unlawful for a public authority to act in a way which is incompatible with a convention right'.[22] Similarly in Ireland, the European Convention on Human Rights Act 2003 states that, 'subject to any

---

19 CRPD, article 3(a).
20 CRPD, article 4(c).
21 CRPD, article 4(1)(d).
22 Human Rights Act, section 6(1).

statutory provision (other than this Act) or rule of law, every organ of the State shall perform its functions in a manner compatible with the State's obligations under the Convention provisions'.[23] These legal arrangements create positive obligations for public bodies, including public mental health services, in both the UK[24] and Ireland[25] to act in ways consistent with human rights.

As already noted, this positive obligation appears to be quite extensive.[26] In 2010, the case of *Savage versus South Essex Partnership National Health Service (NHS) Foundation Trust* centred on an individual who had been detained in a psychiatric facility, but then absconded and died by suicide.[27] In its judgment, the House of Lords found that the NHS trust had an obligation, under the ECHR, to reasonably protect psychiatry patients from taking their own lives and concluded that, in this case, the trust had failed to meet this obligation to protect the patient's right to life.[28]

In 2012, a similar judgment was made in the case of *Rabone and Anor versus Pennine Care NHS Trust*.[29] This case cenered on a 24-year-old woman who was an 'informal' inpatient in a psychiatric hospital (i.e., not detained under mental health legislation) and was on two days' home leave when she ended her life. In this case, the relevant NHS trust settled a negligence claim but then faced a further claim that it had failed to meet its obligation to protect the woman's right to life under the ECHR.[30]

As in the earlier case, the English Supreme Court found that the trust had failed to meet its obligation to protect the patient's right to life and awarded further compensation to the family. In this case, the court noted in particular that the woman had been originally admitted owing to risk of suicide and the trust had 'failed to do all that could reasonably have been expected to prevent the real and immediate risk of [her] suicide'. Clearly, this positive obligation to protect rights under the ECHR, as incorporated into national legislation, is, then, a substantial one, further underscored by the CRPD.

---

23   European Convention on Human Rights Act 2003, section 3(1).

24   Szmukler, G., Richardson, G., Owen, G., '"Rabone" and four unresolved problems in mental health law', *Psychiatric Bulletin*, 2013, 37, 297–301.

25   Kelly, B.D., 'Human rights and the obligation to prevent suicide', *Irish Times*, 2012, 23 July.

26   Rahman, M.S., Wolferstan, N., 'A human right to be detained? Mental healthcare after "Savage" and "Rabone"', *The Psychiatrist*, 2013, 37, 294–296.

27   *Savage v South Essex Partnership NHS Foundation Trust* [2008] UKHL 74; *Savage v South Essex Partnership NHS Foundation Trust* [2010] EWHC 865 (QB).

28   'Everyone's right to life shall be protected by law' (ECHR, Article 2(1)).

29   *Rabone and Anor v Pennine Care NHS Trust* [2012] UKSC 2.

30   Bowcott, O., 'Hospital breached duty of care to psychiatric patient, supreme court rules', *Guardian*, 2012, 8 February; Madden, E., 'Important UK Supreme Court decision on human rights', *Irish Medical Times*, 2012, 18, 26.

Equality and Non-Discrimination

The CRPD requires that states parties recognise 'that all persons are equal before and under the law and are entitled without any discrimination to the equal protection and equal benefit of the law'.[31] They must also recognise 'that women and girls with disabilities are subject to multiple discrimination, and in this regard shall take measures to ensure the full and equal enjoyment by them of all human rights and fundamental freedoms'.[32]

In the case of children, 'the best interests of the child shall be a primary consideration' in 'all actions concerning children with disabilities'[33] and states parties 'shall ensure that children with disabilities have the right to express their views freely on all matters affecting them, their views being given due weight in accordance with their age and maturity, on an equal basis with other children, and to be provided with disability and age-appropriate assistance to realise that right'.[34]

This emphasis on the 'best interests' of children is consistent with that in Ireland's Mental Health Act 2001, which states that 'in making a decision under this Act concerning the care or treatment of a person (including a decision to make an admission order in relation to a person), the best interests of the person shall be the principal consideration with due regard being given to the interests of other persons who may be at risk of serious harm if the decision is not made'.[35] By way of contrast with the CRPD, however, Ireland's legislation states that 'the best interests of the person shall be the principal consideration' for *all* detained patients, not just children.

In similar fashion, the Mental Capacity Act 2005 in England and Wales states that 'an act done, or decision made, under this Act for or on behalf of a person who lacks capacity must be done, or made, in his best interests';[36] the Mental Health (Care and Treatment) (Scotland) Act 2003 includes 'the importance of providing the maximum benefit to the patient' as a principle;[37] and in Northern Ireland, the Mental Capacity Bill (2014) (which incorporates both mental health and capacity legislation into one bill, and is still in development) states that every 'act or decision must be done, or made, in the best interests of the person who lacks capacity';[38] this application of 'best interests' to children and adults alike

---

31 CRPD, article 5(1).
32 CRPD, article 6(1).
33 CRPD, article 7(2).
34 CRPD, article 7(3).
35 Mental Health Act 2001, section 4(1).
36 Mental Capacity Act 2005, section 1(5).
37 Mental Health (Care and Treatment) (Scotland) Act 2003, section 1(3)(f).
38 Mental Capacity Bill (2014), section 1(7).

contrasts sharply with the CRPD's application of 'best interests' to children but *not* adults.

The CRPD also requires that states' parties take specific steps 'to raise awareness throughout society, including at the family level, regarding persons with disabilities, and to foster respect for the rights and dignity of persons with disabilities',[39] and 'promote awareness of the capabilities and contributions of persons with disabilities'.[40] There are extensive and welcome requirements to ensure equal access 'to the physical environment, to transportation, to information and communications, including information and communications technologies and systems, and to other facilities and services open or provided to the public, both in urban and in rural areas'.[41]

Access to Justice and the Law

The CRPD requires that states parties 'reaffirm that persons with disabilities have the right to recognition everywhere as persons before the law';[42] 'recognise that persons with disabilities enjoy legal capacity on an equal basis with others in all aspects of life';[43] and 'take appropriate measures to provide access by persons with disabilities to the support they may require in exercising their legal capacity'.[44] Such safeguards must 'ensure that measures relating to the exercise of legal capacity respect the rights, will and preferences of the person, are free of conflict of interest and undue influence, are proportional and tailored to the person's circumstances, apply for the shortest time possible and are subject to regular review by a competent, independent and impartial authority or judicial body'.[45]

These measures are extensive and important, but the requirement 'that persons with disabilities enjoy legal capacity on an equal basis with others in *all* aspects of life'[46] (italics added) contrasts sharply with specific aspects of legislation enacted or proposed in certain jurisdictions. In Ireland, for example, the Assisted Decision-Making (Capacity) Bill 2013 (which is still in development) outlines a range of decision-making supports for persons with reduced mental capacit, but also states that, 'nothing in this Act shall be construed as altering or amending the law in force on the coming into operation of this section relating

---

39 CRPD, article 8(1)(a).
40 CRPD, article 8(1)(c).
41 CRPD, article 9(1).
42 CRPD, article 12(1).
43 CRPD, article 12(2).
44 CRPD, article 12(3).
45 CRPD, article 12(4).
46 CRPD, article 12(2).

to the capacity or consent required as respects a person in relation to any of the following: (a) marriage; (b) civil partnership; (c) judicial separation, divorce or a non-judicial separation agreement; (d) the dissolution of a civil partnership; (e) the placing of a child for adoption; (f) the making of an adoption order; (g) guardianship; (h) sexual relations; (i) voting at an election or at a referendum; (j) serving as a member of a jury'.[47]

While it is exceedingly difficult to envisage a form of decision-making support that would support an individual with substantially impaired capacity to, for example, make subtle decisions regarding sexual relations, it is nonetheless the case that this provision of the Irish bill is inconsistent with the CRPD requirement that 'persons with disabilities enjoy legal capacity on an equal basis with others in *all* aspects of life'[48] (italics added). In England and Wales, there are similar exclusions for certain decisions relating to family relationships,[49] Mental Health Act matters[50] and voting rights;[51] while in Northern Ireland the Mental Capacity Bill (2014) has exclusions for certain decisions relating to family relationships[52] and voting rights.[53]

There are two other concerning issues regarding this section of the CRPD as it relates to mental capacity legislation. First, the requirement that 'appropriate measures' taken by states parties 'to provide access by persons with disabilities to the support they may require in exercising their legal capacity'[54] are 'free of conflict of interest and undue influence'[55] is generally not met in national legislation. Ireland's Assisted Decision-Making (Capacity) Bill 2013, for example, makes minimal reference to such matters, while, in England and Wales, the Mental Capacity Act 2005 does not prohibit conflicts of interest.[56] While this situation likely reflects the reality of most decision-making arrangements, which are often within-family arrangements in which multiple interests coincide and conflict, it nonetheless represents a point of significant inconsistency with the CRPD.

Second, with regard to access to justice and the law more broadly, while Ireland's Mental Health Act 2001 provides for free legal presentation for persons detained in psychiatric facilities,[57] the Assisted Decision-Making (Capacity) Bill

---

47 Assisted Decision-Making (Capacity) Bill 2013, section 106. See Chapter 5.
48 CRPD, article 12(2).
49 Mental Capacity Act 2005, section 27.
50 Mental Capacity Act 2005, section 28.
51 Mental Capacity Act 2005, section 29.
52 Mental Capacity Bill (2014), section 149.
53 Mental Capacity Bill (2014), section 150.
54 CRPD, article 12(3).
55 CRPD, article 12(4).
56 Bartlett, 2012.
57 Mental Health Act 2001, section 33(3)(c).

2013 makes no such provision, simply stating that those who would qualify financially for free legal aid in any case can avail of it.[58] In England, Wales, Scotland and Northern Ireland, free legal aid is available when appealing detention orders under the Mental Health Act 1983, and the Mental Health Act 2007 also requires that the 'appropriate national authority shall make such arrangements as it considers reasonable to enable persons ("independent mental health advocates") to be available to help qualifying patients', although not all patients qualify.[59] These measures are important in ensuring detained persons access to justice and the law, as required by the CRPD, although the lack of automatic legal representation under Ireland's Assisted Decision-Making (Capacity) Bill 2013 is a concern and a further point of inconsistency with the CRPD (see Chapter 5 also).

Liberty and Security of Person

The CRPD's provisions relating to liberty and disability are among the most important and controversial in the convention. The CRPD requires that states parties 'shall ensure that persons with disabilities, on an equal basis with others: (a) enjoy the right to liberty and security of person; (b) are not deprived of their liberty unlawfully or arbitrarily, and that any deprivation of liberty is in conformity with the law, and that the existence of a disability shall in no case justify a deprivation of liberty'.[60]

These measures, especially the statement that 'that the existence of a disability shall in no case justify a deprivation of liberty', are notably inconsistent with mental health legislation as it currently exists in the UK jurisdictions and Ireland. In England and Wales, the Mental Health Act 1983 (as amended by the Mental Health Act 2007) includes both 'mental disorder' and risk to self or others in the criteria for detention.[61] 'Mental disorder' is defined as 'any disorder or disability of the mind',[62] although persons with a learning disability 'shall not be considered by reason of that disability' to be suffering from mental disorder 'unless that disability is associated with abnormally aggressive or seriously irresponsible conduct on his part'.[63] If, however, 'mental disorder' fulfils the CRPD definition of 'disability', then this provision of the Mental Health Act 1983 is in direct contradiction with the requirements of the CRPD.

---

58   Assisted Decision-Making (Capacity) Bill 2013, section 32.
59   Mental Health Act 2007, section 30(2), amending Mental Health Act 1983, section 130A(1).
60   CRPD, article 14(1)(b).
61   Mental Health Act 1983, sections 2–5.
62   Mental Health Act 1983, section 1(2).
63   Mental Health Act 1983, section 1(2A).

Similarly in Scotland, criteria for 'short-term detention in hospital', for example, include 'that the patient has a mental disorder';[64] 'because of the mental disorder, the patient's ability to make decisions about the provision of medical treatment is significantly impaired';[65] detention is necessary for treatment;[66] 'if the patient were not detained in hospital there would be a significant risk' to self or others;[67] and detention is necessary.[68] In Scotland, 'mental disorder' means 'any (a) mental illness; (b) personality disorder; or (c) learning disability, however caused or manifested',[69] although 'a person is not mentally disordered by reason only of any of the following (a) sexual orientation; (b) sexual deviancy; (c) transsexualism; (d) transvestism; (e) dependence on, or use of, alcohol or drugs; (f) behaviour that causes, or is likely to cause, harassment, alarm or distress to any other person; (g) acting as no prudent person would act'.[70]

In Northern Ireland, the Mental Health (Northern Ireland) Order 1986 states that 'admission for assessment' can occur if an individual 'is suffering from mental disorder of a nature or degree which warrants his detention in a hospital for assessment'[71] and 'failure to so detain him would create a substantial likelihood of serious physical harm to himself or to other persons'.[72] 'Detention for treatment' can occur if 'the patient is suffering from mental illness or severe mental impairment of a nature or degree which warrants his detention in hospital for medical treatment'[73] and 'failure to so detain the patient would create a substantial likelihood of serious physical harm to himself or to other persons'.[74] 'Mental disorder' means 'mental illness, mental handicap and any other disorder or disability of mind' and 'mental illness' means 'a state of mind which affects a person's thinking, perceiving, emotion or judgment to the extent that he requires care or medical treatment in his own interests or the interests of other persons'.[75] In addition, 'no person shall be treated ... as suffering from mental disorder, or from any form of mental disorder, by reason only of personality disorder, promiscuity or other immoral conduct, sexual deviancy or dependence on alcohol or drugs'.[76]

---

64 Mental Health (Care and Treatment) (Scotland) Act 2003, Section 44(4)(a).
65 Mental Health (Care and Treatment) (Scotland) Act 2003, Section 44(4)(b).
66 Mental Health (Care and Treatment) (Scotland) Act 2003, Section 44(4)(c).
67 Mental Health (Care and Treatment) (Scotland) Act 2003, Section 44(4)(d).
68 Mental Health (Care and Treatment) (Scotland) Act 2003, Section 44(4)(e).
69 Mental Health (Care and Treatment) (Scotland) Act 2003, Section 328(1).
70 Mental Health (Care and Treatment) (Scotland) Act 2003, Section 32892).
71 Mental Health (Northern Ireland) Order 1986, section 4(2)(a).
72 Mental Health (Northern Ireland) Order 1986, section 4(2)(b).
73 Mental Health (Northern Ireland) Order 1986, section 12(1)(a).
74 Mental Health (Northern Ireland) Order 1986, section 12(1)(b).
75 Mental Health (Northern Ireland) Order 1986, section 3(1).
76 Mental Health (Northern Ireland) Order 1986, section 3(2).

A similar situation pertains in Ireland, where a person can be detained under mental health legislation if he or she has 'mental disorder' which is 'mental illness, severe dementia or significant intellectual disability where (a) because of the illness, disability or dementia, there is a serious likelihood of the person concerned causing immediate and serious harm to himself or herself or to other persons, or (b) (i) because of the severity of the illness, disability or dementia, the judgment of the person concerned is so impaired that failure to admit the person to an approved centre would be likely to lead to a serious deterioration in his or her condition or would prevent the administration of appropriate treatment that could be given only by such admission, and (ii) the reception, detention and treatment of the person concerned in an approved centre would be likely to benefit or alleviate the condition of that person to a material extent'.[77] Involuntary admission cannot, however, be authorised 'by reason only of the fact that the person (a) is suffering from a personality disorder, (b) is socially deviant, or (c) is addicted to drugs or intoxicants'.[78]

Unlike the UK, however, Ireland has not yet ratified the CRPD, so it has less effect in Ireland than in the UK jurisdictions. Nonetheless, legislative positions in Ireland, England, Wales, Scotland and Northern Ireland are all inconsistent with the CRPD requirement 'that the existence of a disability shall in no case justify a deprivation of liberty',[79] if 'mental disorder' or 'mental illness' (as defined in the various jurisdictions) come within the CRPD definition of 'disability'.

In 2009, the UN High Commissioner for Human Rights appeared to clarify this matter by objecting especially strongly to any link between 'preventive detention' and risk to self or others stemming from 'mental illness':

Legislation authorising the institutionalisation of persons with disabilities on the grounds of their disability without their free and informed consent must be abolished. This must include the repeal of provisions authorising institutionalisation of persons with disabilities for their care and treatment without their free and informed consent, as well as provisions authorising the preventive detention of persons with disabilities on grounds such as the likelihood of them posing a danger to themselves or others, in all cases in which such grounds of care, treatment and public security are linked in legislation to an apparent or diagnosed mental illness. This should not be interpreted to say that persons with disabilities cannot be lawfully subject to detention for care and treatment or to preventive detention, but that the legal grounds upon which

---

77 Mental Health Act 2001, section 3(1).

78 Mental Health Act 2001, section 8(2).

79 CRPD, article 14(1)(b).

restriction of liberty is determined must be de-linked from the disability and neutrally defined so as to apply to all persons on an equal basis.[80]

Notwithstanding this apparent clarification, the UK government, in its first report on implementing the CRPD, stated that 'no one in the UK can be deprived of his or her liberty because he or she is disabled'.[81] Although it is true that no one in the UK jurisdictions can be detained *solely* because he or she has a mental disorder (other criteria must be fulfilled), the UN High Commissioner for Human Rights is clear that 'disability' must not be linked *in any way* with deprivation of liberty.

The view of the UN High Commissioner is supported by the Committee on the Rights of Persons with Disabilities, which monitors implementation of the CRPD. In its 2011 report on Spain, the Committee recommended that Spain 'review its laws that allow for the deprivation of liberty on the basis of disability, including mental, psychosocial or intellectual disabilities; repeal provisions that authorise involuntary internment linked to an apparent or diagnosed disability; and adopt measures to ensure that health-care services, including all mental-health-care services, are based on the informed consent of the person concerned'.[82]

The link that the Mental Health Act 1983 in England and Wales draws between detention, risk and mental disorder,[83] and which appear to violate the CRPD, were retained in legislation only following very careful deliberation. The 'Expert Committee' charged with advising the government on reforming the legislation noted that a 'small minority' believed that 'a mental health act should authorise treatment in the absence of consent only for those who lack capacity' and 'if a person with a mental disorder who refused treatment was thought to pose a serious risk to others then he or she should be dealt with through the criminal justice system, not through a health provision'.[84]

There was, however, 'a much larger body of opinion which was prepared to accept the overriding of a capable refusal in a health provision on grounds

---

80   UN High Commissioner for Human Rights, *Annual Report of the United Nations High Commissioner for Human Rights and Reports of the Office of the High Commissioner and the Secretary General: Thematic Study by the Office of the United Nations High Commissioner for Human Rights on Enhancing Awareness and Understanding of the Convention on the Rights of Persons with Disabilities*, Geneva: UN, 2009 (paragraph 49).

81   Office for Disability Issues, *UK Initial Report on the UN Convention on the Rights of Persons with Disabilities*, London: HM Government, 2009 (paragraph 133).

82   Committee on the Rights of Persons with Disabilities, *Concluding Observations of the Committee on the Rights of Persons with Disabilities: Spain*, Geneva: UN, 2011 (paragraph 36).

83   Mental Health Act 1983, sections 2–5.

84   Expert Committee, 1999; p. 19.

of public safety in certain circumstances'. The Committee inclined towards the latter view:

> The reasons given were in part pragmatic and in part driven by principle. Essentially most of those who commented accepted that the safety of the public must be allowed to outweigh individual autonomy where the risk is sufficiently great and, if the risk is related to the presence of a mental disorder for which a health intervention of likely benefit to the individual is available, then it is appropriate that such intervention should be authorised as part of a health provision. Mental disorder unlike most physical health problems may occasionally have wider consequences for the individual's family and carer, and very occasionally for unconnected members of the public affected by the individual's behaviour, acts and omissions. The Committee supports this reasoning and in what follows we seek to describe a framework which adequately reflects it.[85]

Whether or not the legislative provisions in England and Wales, as well as Scotland, Northern Ireland and Ireland (all of which link mental disorder, risk and detention), represent violations of the CRPD depends critically on whether or not the CRPD's definition of disability includes mental disorder. All the indications from the UN to date are that it does, but this needs clarification. If mental disorder is indeed included within the definition, this will have the positive effect of affording the protections and supports of the CRPD to persons with mental disorder, but will also result in significant pressure on ratifying countries to revise mental health legislation so as to de-link psychiatric detention from mental disorder and the risks associated with it in certain cases.[86]

The CRPD also states that 'if persons with disabilities are deprived of their liberty through any process, they are, on an equal basis with others, entitled to guarantees in accordance with international human rights law and shall be treated in compliance with the objectives and principles of the present Convention, including by provision of reasonable accommodation'.[87] In terms of procedures for review of involuntary detention orders, there is now substantial compliance with Article 5(4) of the European Convention on Human Rights, that 'everyone who is deprived of his liberty by arrest or detention shall be entitled to take proceedings by which the lawfulness of his detention shall be decided speedily by a court and his release ordered if the detention is not lawful' (see Chapter

---

85 Expert Committee, 1999; p. 19.

86 Kelly, B.D., 'An end to psychiatric detention? Implications of the United Nations Convention on the Rights of Persons with Disabilities', *British Journal of Psychiatry*, 2014, 204, 174–175.

87 CRPD, article 14(2).

3).[88] In addition, the quality of accommodation is subject to inspection in all the UK jurisdictions and Ireland, although there is, of course, always room for improvement of inspection and complaints processes.

Other CRPD Provisions

Consistent with previous UN declarations of rights, especially the Universal Declaration of Human Rights,[89] the CRPD emphasises that no one should be 'subjected to torture or to cruel, inhuman or degrading treatment or punishment' and adds that no one shall be 'subjected without his or her free consent to medical or scientific experimentation'.[90] Consistent with this, Ireland's Mental Health Act 2001 specifies that 'a person suffering from a mental disorder who has been admitted to an approved centre under this Act shall not be a participant in a clinical trial'[91] and the Assisted Decision-Making (Capacity) Bill 2013 states that 'nothing in this Act shall be construed as authorising any person to give consent on behalf of a person who lacks capacity to be a participant in a clinical trial'.[92] By way of contrast, there are explicit and quite detailed legislative frameworks whereby people with reduced capacity can participate in research, subject to certain conditions, in the Mental Capacity Act 2005 in England and Wales,[93] the Adults with Incapacity (Scotland) Act 2000,[94] and the Mental Capacity Bill (2014) in Northern Ireland.[95]

The CRPD requires that states parties must 'take all appropriate legislative, administrative, social, educational and other measures to protect persons with disabilities, both within and outside the home, from all forms of exploitation, violence and abuse, including their gender-based aspects'.[96] To this end, 'all facilities and programmes designed to serve persons with disabilities' must be 'effectively monitored by independent authorities'.[97]

In addition, the CRPD outlines rights to respect for 'physical and mental integrity on an equal basis with others',[98] 'liberty of movement and nationality'[99]

---

88 Kelly, 2011.
89 UN, 1948.
90 CRPD, article 15(1).
91 Mental Health Act 2001, section 70.
92 Assisted Decision-Making (Capacity) Bill 2013, section 103.
93 Mental Capacity Act 2005, sections 30–34.
94 Adults with Incapacity (Scotland) Act 2000, part 5.
95 Mental Capacity Bill (2014), part 8.
96 CRPD, article 16(1).
97 CRPD, article 16(3).
98 CRPD, article 17.
99 CRPD, article 18.

and to 'live in the community, with choices equal to others',[100] including that persons with disabilities have 'the opportunity to choose their place of residence and where and with whom they live on an equal basis with others'.[101] There are also extensive rights to 'effective measures to ensure personal mobility',[102] 'freedom of expression and opinion, and access to information',[103] 'privacy',[104] education[105] and 'respect for home and the family' including the right to marry[106] and assurance that 'in no case shall a child be separated from parents on the basis of a disability of either the child or one or both of the parents'.[107]

In relation to health, there are rights to the 'enjoyment of the highest attainable standard of health'[108] and 'comprehensive habilitation and rehabilitation services and programmes, particularly in the areas of health, employment, education and social services'.[109] These are key issues for many people with mental disorder. In relation to employment, for example, 3% of people attending secondary mental health services in the UK are employed for 16 hours or more per week, compared to 72.5% of the population as a whole.[110] According to the CRPD, however, people with disabilities have the right 'to work, on an equal basis with others';[111] the right to an 'adequate standard of living and social protection';[112] 'political rights and the opportunity to enjoy them on an equal basis with others',[113] including accessible voting procedures;[114] and rights of 'participation in cultural life, recreation, leisure and sport'.[115]

Throughout the CRPD, these statements of rights are accompanied by explicit requirements that states parties support *meaningful realisation* of these rights in the lives of people with disabilities. In relation to 'living independently and being included in the community', for example, the CRPD outlines a right

---

100 CRPD, article 19.
101 CRPD, article 19(a).
102 CRPD, article 20.
103 CRPD, article 21.
104 CRPD, article 22.
105 CRPD, article 24.
106 CRPD, article 23(1)(a).
107 CRPD, article 23(4).
108 CRPD, article 25.
109 CRPD, article 26(1).
110 National Mental Health Development Unit, *Work, Recovery and Inclusion*, London: National Mental Health Development Unit, 2009.
111 CRPD, article 27(1).
112 CRPD, article 28.
113 CRPD, article 29.
114 CRPD, article 29(a)(i).
115 CRPD, article 30.

'to live in the community, with choices equal to others'[116] including that people with disabilities have 'the opportunity to choose their place of residence and where and with whom they live on an equal basis with others'.[117] The CPRD goes on to emphasise this further by stating that states parties must ensure that 'persons with disabilities have access to a range of in-home, residential and other community support services, including personal assistance necessary to support living and inclusion in the community, and to prevent isolation or segregation from the community',[118] and that 'community services and facilities for the general population are available on an equal basis to persons with disabilities and are responsive to their needs.[119]

Moreover, the CRPD sees the protection and promotion of these rights as benefiting not only people with disabilities but *everyone* in society. For example, in relation to rights of 'participation in cultural life, recreation, leisure and sport',[120] the CRPD requires that states parties 'shall take appropriate measures to enable persons with disabilities to have the opportunity to develop and utilise their creative, artistic and intellectual potential, not only for their own benefit, but also *for the enrichment of society*'[121] (italics added). Promoting the rights of persons with disabilities is of benefit and importance to *all*.

At national level, the CRPD imposes quite extensive responsibilities on states parties in relation to 'statistics and data collection' in order to 'formulate and implement policies to give effect' to the CRPD;[122] 'international cooperation' in promoting realisation of the 'purpose and objectives' of the CRPD;[123] and 'national reporting and monitoring', with involvement of 'civil society, in particular persons with disabilities and their representative organisations'.[124] States parties must also participate in a new 'Committee on the Rights of Persons with Disabilities'[125] and provide the Committee with 'a comprehensive report on measures taken to give effect to its obligations under the present Convention and on the progress made in that regard, within two years after the entry into force of the present Convention for the State Party concerned'.[126]

---

116 CRPD, article 19.
117 CRPD, article 19(a).
118 CRPD, article 19(b).
119 CRPD, article 19(c).
120 CRPD, article 30.
121 CRPD, article 30(2).
122 CRPD, article 31(1).
123 CRPD, article 32(1).
124 CRPD, article 33(3).
125 CRPD, articles 34–39.
126 CRPD, article 35(1).

The Committee requires reports every four years thereafter[127] and 'each report shall be considered by the Committee, which shall make such suggestions and general recommendations on the report as it may consider appropriate and shall forward these to the State Party concerned'.[128] The Committee cannot legally enforce its recommendations or the provision of an overdue report, but reports are to be made public[129] and 'if a State Party is significantly overdue in the submission of a report, the Committee may notify the State Party concerned of the need to examine the implementation' of the CRPD.[130]

Moreover, 'the Committee shall report every two years to the General Assembly and to the Economic and Social Council on its activities, and may make suggestions and general recommendations based on the examination of reports and information received from the States Parties. Such suggestions and general recommendations shall be included in the report of the Committee together with comments, if any, from States Parties'.[131]

The Optional Protocol: Communication of Alleged Violations of the CRPD

The CRPD has an Optional Protocol which can be signed and ratified separately to the CRPD itself. The Optional Protocol provides that the UN Committee on the Rights of Persons with Disabilities can 'receive and consider communications from or on behalf of individuals or groups of individuals subject to its jurisdiction who claim to be victims of a violation by that State Party of the provisions of the Convention'.[132] It is, therefore, a supra-national complaints mechanism for persons who reside in ratifying states and believe that their rights, as outlined in the CRPD, are being violated.

Such a communication to the Committee is inadmissible if it is anonymous;[133] 'all available domestic remedies have not been exhausted' (unless the application of such 'remedies is unreasonably prolonged or unlikely to bring effective relief');[134] or the communication 'is manifestly ill-founded or not sufficiently substantiated';[135] among other circumstances. On receiving a valid communication, the Committee shall submit it confidentially to the

---

127 CRPD, article 35(2).
128 CRPD, article 36(1).
129 CRPD, article 36(4).
130 CRPD, article 36(2).
131 CRPD, article 39.
132 CRPD Optional Protocol, article 1(1).
133 CRPD Optional Protocol, article 2(a).
134 CRPD Optional Protocol, article 2(d).
135 CRPD Optional Protocol, article 2(e).

relevant state party and, 'within six months, the receiving State shall submit to the Committee written explanations or statements clarifying the matter and the remedy, if any, that may have been taken by that State'.[136] Prior to any final determination on the matter, the Committee 'may transmit to the State Party concerned for its urgent consideration a request that the State Party take such interim measures as may be necessary to avoid possible irreparable damage to the victim or victims of the alleged violation'.[137]

The Committee shall hold closed meetings to consider such communications and will forward its suggestions and recommendations to the state party concerned and the petitioner.[138] If there is 'reliable information indicating grave or systematic violations by a State Party of rights set forth in the Convention, the Committee shall invite that State Party to cooperate in the examination of the information and to this end submit observations with regard to the information concerned'.[139] One or more Committee members may be designated to conduct an enquiry which may involve visiting the country in question[140] and, following the Committee's consideration of the matter, the Committee shall convey its findings, comments and recommendations to the state party.[141]

The state party is expected to respond within six months[142] and the Committee may, if necessary, at the end of that period, 'invite the State Party concerned to inform it of the measures taken in response to such an inquiry'.[143] In addition, the Committee 'may invite the State Party concerned to include in its report under article 35 of the Convention [i.e., its four-yearly report to the Committee] details of any measures taken in response to an inquiry conducted under article 6 of the present Protocol'.[144]

The Committee's inquiries will be conducted confidentially and with the co-operation of the state party at all stages,[145] although 'each State Party may, at the time of signature or ratification of the present Protocol or accession thereto, declare it does not recognise the competence of the Committee provided for in articles 6 and 7' (i.e., in relation to these inquiries).[146] This is, therefore, an *optional* part of the CRPD architecture, but one which appears important in providing another avenue of appeal for persons who reside in ratifying states

---

136 CRPD Optional Protocol, article 3.
137 CRPD Optional Protocol, article 4(1).
138 CRPD Optional Protocol, article 5.
139 CRPD Optional Protocol, article 6(1).
140 CRPD Optional Protocol, article 6(2).
141 CRPD Optional Protocol, article 6(3).
142 CRPD Optional Protocol, article 6(4).
143 CRPD Optional Protocol, article 7(2).
144 CRPD Optional Protocol, article 7(1).
145 CRPD Optional Protocol, article 6(5).
146 CRPD Optional Protocol, article 8.

and believe that their rights, as outlined in the CRPD, are being violated. The UK signed and ratified the protocol in 2009; Ireland has neither signed nor ratified it.

Overall Assessment: The CRPD and Mental Health Legislation

The CRPD provides a strong articulation of the rights of persons with disabilities. While the rights of all human beings were already articulated in previous UN documents, especially the Universal Declaration of Human Rights,[147] the CRPD provides an important and specific articulation of the rights of persons with disabilities, with particular regard for the challenges people with disabilities face in attaining observance of these rights.[148]

The CRPD contains an especially welcome acknowledgement of the social context of disability, recognising that 'the majority of persons with disabilities live in conditions of poverty'.[149] The CRPD also underscores the positive obligation on public authorities to protect rights, an obligation already outlined in the UK in Human Rights Act 1998[150] and, in Ireland, in the European Convention on Human Rights Act 2003.[151] This positive obligation has yet to be characterised in detail but appears to be extensive, at least in relation to the right to life;[152] its precise extent in relation to economic and social rights has also yet to be clarified, and it is in this domain that the provisions of the CRPD may well prove most helpful to persons with disabilities and their representative organisations.

Certain provisions of the CRPD appear to be incompatible with certain aspects of mental health legislation in England, Wales, Scotland, Northern Ireland and Ireland, and certain other provisions are, at best, unclear. There are, in the first instance, several areas in which national mental health laws in the UK and Ireland diverge clearly and significantly from the CRPD. In terms of principles, the CRPD applies the principle of 'best interests' to children[153] but not adults, and this contrasts sharply with the Mental Capacity Act 2005 in England and Wales, which applies 'best interests' to all persons with reduced capacity;[154] the Mental Health Act 2001 in Ireland, which applies 'best interests'

---

147 UN, 1948.
148 Bartlett et al., 2007; Bartlett, 2012.
149 CRPD, preamble (t).
150 Human Rights Act 1998, section 6(1).
151 European Convention on Human Rights Act 2003, section 3(1).
152 Rahman & Wolferstan, 2013.
153 CRPD, article 7(2).
154 Mental Capacity Act 2005, section 1(5).

to all detained persons;[155] the Mental Health (Care and Treatment) (Scotland) Act 2003, which includes 'the importance of providing the maximum benefit to the patient' as a principle;[156] and the Mental Capacity Bill (2014) in Northern Ireland, which states that any 'act or decision must be done, or made, in the best interests of the person who lacks capacity'.[157] This is a significant point of divergence between the CRPD and national legislation in the UK and Ireland.

Perhaps the most controversial areas of divergence, however, relate to involuntary psychiatric detention and treatment. Minkowitz, a chairperson of the World Network of Users and Survivors of Psychiatry and member of the UN Working Group that produced the first draft of the CRPD, argues that *all* forced psychiatric interventions are *by their very nature* violations of the CRPD, requiring that perpetrators (i.e., mental health professionals) be criminalised and victims receive reparations.[158] Minkowitz bases this argument on alleged violations of Articles 12 ('equal recognition before the law'), 15 ('freedom from torture or cruel, inhuman or degrading treatment or punishment'), 17 ('protecting the integrity of the person') and 25 ('health', especially the requirement for 'free and informed consent' for care). Current mental health legislation may also violate Article 4 (no 'discrimination of any kind on the basis of disability').[159] In the UK jurisdictions and Ireland, however, there are national laws permitting involuntary psychiatric detention and treatment under certain circumstances and, provided such laws are observed, it appears unlikely that mental health professionals can be labelled as criminal.

Moreover, from a definitional perspective, it is not at all clear what proportion of persons with mental disorder or mental illness actually fit the UN definition of 'persons with disabilities'.[160] For persons with mental disorder who do fulfil the UN definition of 'persons with disabilities' (e.g., certain persons with chronic schizophrenia), however, mental health legislation in the UK jurisdictions and Ireland does appear to violate Article 14(1)(b) of the CRPD ('the existence of a disability shall in no case justify a deprivation of liberty') by plainly and strongly linking mental disorder or mental illness and risk with involuntary detention.[161] Involuntary treatment of individuals with mental disorder may

---

155 Mental Health Act 2001, section 4(1).

156 Mental Health (Care and Treatment) (Scotland) Act 2003, section 1(3)(f).

157 Mental Capacity Bill (2014), section 1(7).

158 Minkowitz, T., 'The United Nations Convention on the Rights of Persons with Disabilities and the right to be free from non-consensual psychiatric interventions', *Syracuse Journal of International Law and Commerce*, 2007, 34, 405–428.

159 Szmukler et al., 2014.

160 CRPD, article 1.

161 Kelly, B.D., 'An end to psychiatric detention? Implications of the United Nations Convention on the Rights of Persons with Disabilities', *British Journal of Psychiatry*, 2014, 204, 174–175.

also be inconsistent with Article 25(d) which requires 'health professionals to provide care of the same quality to persons with disabilities as to others' on 'the basis of free and informed consent'.

While the CRPD states 'that persons with disabilities enjoy legal capacity on an equal basis with others in *all* aspects of life'[162] (italics added), Ireland's Assisted Decision-Making (Capacity) Bill 2013 excludes certain areas from the remit of its decision-making supports (e.g. marriage, voting).[163] There are similar exclusions in England and Wales, relating to family relationships,[164] Mental Health Act matters[165] and voting rights,[166] while in Northern Ireland the Mental Capacity Bill (2014) has exclusions relating to family relationships[167] and voting rights.[168] These arrangements support the idea that mental capacity legislation in these jurisdictions violate Article 12 of the CRPD ('equal recognition before the law'),[169] as, possibly, does mental health legislation by permitting compulsory treatment of mental but not (most) physical illness.[170]

These issues are made more acute by the fact that earlier references to 'substitute decision-making' were dropped from the CRPD during its development, suggesting that *all* forms of 'substitute decision-making' violate the CRPD. Consistent with this, the Netherlands, Canada and various Arab states entered reservations to the CRPD in order to ensure their models of substitute decision-making were protected, suggesting that they view the CRPD as requiring changes in this regard.[171] As Szmukler and colleagues point out, however, it is not at all clear that the CRPD out-rules all forms of substitute decision-making;[172] Article 12(4) states that:

> States Parties shall ensure that all measures that relate to the exercise of legal capacity provide for appropriate and effective safeguards to prevent abuse in accordance with international human rights law. Such safeguards shall ensure that measures relating to the exercise of legal capacity respect the rights, will and preferences of the person, are free of conflict of interest and undue influence, are proportional and tailored to the person's circumstances, apply for the shortest time possible and are subject to regular review by a competent, independent and

---

162 CRPD, article 12(2).
163 Assisted Decision-Making (Capacity) Bill 2013, section 106.
164 Mental Capacity Act 2005, section 27.
165 Mental Capacity Act 2005, section 28.
166 Mental Capacity Act 2005, section 29.
167 Mental Capacity Bill (2014), section 149.
168 Mental Capacity Bill (2014), section 150.
169 Minkowitz, 2007.
170 Bartlett, 2012.
171 Bartlett, 2012.
172 Szmukler et al., 2014.

impartial authority or judicial body. The safeguards shall be proportional to the degree to which such measures affect the person's rights and interests.[173]

This passage appears to reflect an acceptance of substitute decision-making in certain circumstances, although it was a much-contested text.[174] To resolve this matter, Szmukler and colleagues return to the definition of 'disability' in Article 1 of the CRPD ('persons with disabilities include those who have long-term physical, mental, intellectual or sensory impairments') and argue that there is a significant difference between reduced decision-making capacity in relation to a specific matter for a period of time and 'disability'.[175] They go on to propose a 'fusion law' which would cover all persons whether they have a mental or physical illness, and only allows involuntary treatment where supported decision-making has failed and the person's decision-making capacity for a specific treatment decision is impaired. This moves away from an approach based on 'disability' to one based on decision-making capacity; places greatest emphasis on the person's own values and perspective, as best as they can be ascertained; and, to this extent, appears more complaint with the CRPD than current laws in the UK jurisdictions and Ireland.

In addition to these apparent inconsistencies between national laws and the CRPD, however, there are various other possible violations of the CRPD across the UK jurisdictions and Ireland. Some of these violations appear readily remediable, such as the failure of Ireland's Assisted Decision-Making (Capacity) Bill 2013 to introduce free legal aid for all who come under its provisions.[176] This appears to be a violation of CRPD Article 13 ('access to justice') but is one which appears relatively easy to remedy; there already is a well-developed free legal aid scheme for all who are detained under Ireland's Mental Health Act 2001[177] and there is no apparent reason (other than financial constraints) why this should not be extended to persons coming under the Assisted Decision-Making (Capacity) Bill 2013.

There are also potential inconsistencies with the CRPD in relation to research in the UK jurisdictions, although the CRPD itself is arguably inconsistent in this regard. On the one hand, the CRPD states that no one shall be 'subjected without his or her free consent to medical or scientific experimentation',[178]

---

173 CRPD, article 12(4).

174 Dhanda, A., 'Legal capacity in the disability rights convention: stranglehold of the past or lodestar for the future?', *Syracuse Journal of International Law and Commerce*, 2007, 34, 429–461.

175 Szmukler et al., 2014.

176 Assisted Decision-Making (Capacity) Bill 2013, section 32.

177 Mental Health Act 2001, section 33(3)(c).

178 CRPD, article 15(1).

although there are legislative frameworks whereby individuals with reduced capacity can participate in research, subject to certain conditions, in England and Wales,[179] Scotland,[180] and Northern Ireland.[181] On the other hand, excluding persons with disabilities from research, as is the case for individuals under Ireland's mental health and proposed capacity laws,[182] may deny them access to certain treatments (e.g., experimental cancer therapies) and, arguably, represents a violation of Article 25(a) which requires states parties to 'provide persons with disabilities with the same range, quality and standard of free or affordable health care and programmes as provided to other persons'. Clearly a balance needs to be reached in this area, and, arguably, it is the provisions of the Mental Capacity Act 2005 in England and Wales,[183] rather than the CRPD, that achieve an optimal balance in this regard.

Key Unresolved Issues

Clarity is needed on the relationship between the CRPD and various specific aspects of national mental health and capacity legislation in the UK jurisdictions and Ireland; these areas include the following:

- Clarification is needed on the CRPD's articulation of a positive obligation on states parties to protect human rights;[184] this provision appears to underscore similar obligations under the Human Rights Act 1998 in the UK[185] and European Convention on Human Rights Act 2003 in Ireland,[186] but the precise extent of this obligation remains unclear, especially in relation to social, economic and cultural rights.
- Clarity is also needed on the divergence between the CRPD and national legislation in relation to the principle of 'best interests' which the CRPD applies only to children[187] but which also applies to adults under Ireland's Mental Health Act 2001,[188] the Mental Capacity Act 2005 in England and

---

179 Mental Capacity Act 2005, sections 30–34.

180 Adults with Incapacity (Scotland) Act 2000, section 51.

181 Mental Capacity Bill (2014), part 8.

182 Kelly, B.D., 'Mental capacity and participation in research', *Irish Medical Times*, 2014, 18, 20.

183 Mental Capacity Act, sections 30–34.

184 CRPD, article 4(1)(d).

185 Human Rights Act 1998, section 6(1).

186 European Convention on Human Rights Act 2003, section 3(1).

187 CRPD, article 7(2).

188 Mental Health Act 2001, section 4(1).

Wales,[189] the Mental Health (Care and Treatment) (Scotland) Act 2003,[190] and the Mental Capacity Bill (2014) in Northern Ireland.[191]

- National legislations also diverge significantly from the CRPD requirement that 'persons with disabilities enjoy legal capacity on an equal basis with others in all aspects of life';[192] not only are certain 'aspects of life' excluded from schemes of supported decision making in Ireland,[193] England and Wales,[194] and Northern Ireland,[195] but there is a general failure to meet the CRPD requirement that measures to support persons with disabilities are 'free of conflict of interest and undue influence';[196] the lack of automatic legal representation under Ireland's Assisted Decision-Making (Capacity) Bill 2013 is a further point of inconsistency, as is the possibility that the CRPD out-rules all forms of substitute decision-making, although this appears substantially less likely owing to its apparent acceptance of substitute decision-making under certain circumstances and subject to certain conditions.[197]

- National mental health legislation in England, Wales, Northern Ireland and Ireland is inconsistent with the CRPD requirement 'that the existence of a disability shall in no case justify a deprivation of liberty',[198] if persons with mental disorder are considered within the UN definition of 'persons with disabilities';[199] while at least some individuals with mental disorder (especially those likely to be detained) may fulfil this definition, others do not;[200] this is a key, unresolved issue.

- Participation in research is another area in need of clarity: while the CRPD states that no one shall be 'subjected without his or her free consent to medical or scientific experimentation',[201] there are legislative frameworks whereby individuals with reduced capacity can participate in research, subject to certain conditions, in the Mental Capacity Act

---

189 Mental Capacity Act 2005, section 1(5).

190 Mental Health (Care and Treatment) (Scotland) Act 2003, section 1(3)(f).

191 Mental Capacity Bill (2014), section 1(7).

192 CRPD, article 12(2).

193 Assisted Decision-Making (Capacity) Bill 2013, section 106.

194 Mental Capacity Act 2005, sections 27–29.

195 Mental Capacity Bill (2014), sections 149–150.

196 CRPD, article 12(4).

197 CRPD, article 12(4).

198 CRPD, article 14(1)(b).

199 CRPD, article 1.

200 Kelly, B.D., 'An end to psychiatric detention? Implications of the United Nations Convention on the Rights of Persons with Disabilities', *British Journal of Psychiatry*, 2014, 204, 174–175.

201 CRPD, article 15(1).

2005 in England and Wales,[202] the Adults with Incapacity (Scotland) Act 2000,[203] and the Mental Capacity Bill (2014) in Northern Ireland;[204] moreover, denying persons with disabilities equal access to experimental treatments would appear to violate Article 25 ('health') and would seem generally inconsistent with the spirit and purpose of the CRPD.

- The issue of capacity in criminal proceedings also remains unresolved in the CRPD, especially in relation to Article 12 concerning 'equal recognition before the law'; despite this provision, it would appear counter-intuitive to remove capacity-based defences on the grounds that they violate Article 12 if it meant that even more persons with disabilities or mental disorders end up in prison,[205] with ever-diminishing chances of community reintegration; this, again would appear profoundly contrary to the spirit and purpose of the CRPD.[206]

- Finally, in terms of specific rights, Bartlett points out that the language of the CRPD is rather sparse in places,[207] as in Article 17 which concerns 'protecting the integrity of the person' and comprises a total of 23 words: 'Every person with disabilities has a right to respect for his or her physical and mental integrity on an equal basis with others'. It was not possible to agree on a more specific wording during the drafting process, with the result that the details of this right are open to a particularly wide array of possible interpretations, and possible violations will be difficult to identify, let alone remedy.

All of the above issues, although important, are chiefly of relevance to specific sub-groups, such as patients detained under mental health legislation. From a broader, societal perspective, there are likely to be other, more readily identifiable violations of the CRPD which concern far greater numbers of persons with disabilities, if not the majority. These relate to social and economic rights such as rights regarding place and nature of residence,[208] personal mobility,[209] 'habilitation and rehabilitation programmes',[210] social

---

202 Mental Capacity Act 2005, sections 30–34.

203 Adults with Incapacity (Scotland) Act 2000, part 5.

204 Mental Capacity Bill (2014), part 8.

205 Fazel, S., Seewald, K., 'Severe mental illness in 33,588 prisoners worldwide: systematic review and meta-regression analysis', *British Journal of Psychiatry*, 2012, 200, 364–373.

206 Bartlett, 2012.

207 Bartlett, 2012.

208 CRPD, article 19.

209 CRPD, article 20.

210 CRPD, article 26.

protection[211] and 'participation in cultural life, recreation, leisure and sport'.[212] There is already strong evidence of systematic violation of the CRPD in many of areas including, for example, employment rights[213] and the right to an 'adequate standard of living and social protection';[214] the latter is of particular relevance to persons with mental disorder, who are commonly at increased risk of homelessness.[215]

The right to 'freedom from exploitation, violence and abuse'[216] is another important and, arguably, new right with far-reaching implications.[217] Implementation is clearly critical in this area, as certain countries have, for example, strong laws in relation to employment of persons with disabilities but limited implementation, with the result that potential benefits are not realised in practice,[218] sometimes to the point where exploitative and abusive situations can develop. Clearly, laws guaranteeing rights need to be accompanied by programmes of implementation if they are to have meaning[219] and if they are to advance one of the CRPD's most central and, arguably, revolutionary proposals, which is to place the 'inherent dignity'[220] of persons with disabilities at the heart of its mission.

This broader dimension of rights, especially their pragmatic observance in the lives of persons with disability, is possibly the most crucial issue raised by the CRPD, and it is the single area in which the CRPD can make the greatest difference. In this context, Perlin correctly identifies not only the lack of legislative provision as a core issue, but also lack of access to counsel and judicial review for persons with disabilities, a failure to provide humane care to those who need it, systematic deficits in community as opposed to institutional

---

211 CRPD, article 28.

212 CRPD, article 30; see also: Lawson, A., 'The United Nations Convention on the Rights of Persons with Disabilities: new era or false dawn?', *Syracuse Journal of International Law and Commerce*, 2007, 34, 563–619.

213 CRPD, articles 26(1) and 27; National Mental Health Development Unit, 2009.

214 CRPD, article 28.

215 Whitley, R., Henwood, B.F., 'Life, liberty, and the pursuit of happiness: reframing inequities experienced by people with severe mental illness', *Psychiatric Rehabilitation Journal*, 2014, 37, 68–70.

216 CRPD, article 16.

217 Bartlett, 2012.

218 Kanter, A.S., 'The promise and challenge of the United Nations Convention on the Rights of Persons with Disabilities', *Syracuse Journal of International Law and Commerce*, 2007, 34, 287–321.

219 Sen, A., *The Idea of Justice*, London: Allen Lane, 2009.

220 CRPD, article 1.

provision, and a particular failure to provide humane care for forensic patients.[221] Many of these deficits relate not to the *content* of declarations of rights (such as the CRPD) or to the *specific provisions* of legislation (such as mental health and capacity legislation), but to a profound failure to *observe* laws, *implement* policy and *realise* agreed principles in the day-to-day lives of persons with disabilities and mental disorder, resulting in systematic denial of rights, social exclusion and political disempowerment.[222]

While remedying these matters involves much more than simply reforming mental health and capacity laws, legislative reform still has a key role to play. The next chapter, Chapter 5, examines ways in which legislative reform can be used to address at least some of the issues raised by the CRPD by examining the current process of reform of Ireland's mental capacity legislation, which is ongoing. Chapter 6 then explores key international influences on law and policy other than the CRPD (e.g., EU initiatives), and examines key values underpinning human rights in mental health, as well as more recent developments. Following this, the final chapter, Chapter 7, summarises key arguments presented throughout the book, placing particular emphasis on the centrality of human dignity and necessity to integrate mental health policy with legislation in order to provide meaningful protection and promotion of rights in practice. Chapter 7 also presents overall conclusions stemming from the book, and outlines useful areas for future research.

---

221   Perlin, M.L., 'International human rights law and comparative mental disability law: the universal factors', *Syracuse Journal of International Law and Commerce*, 2007, 34, 333–357.

222   Kelly, 2005.

Chapter 5
Changing the Law: The Example of Ireland

Introduction

Against the background of the human rights-based analyses presented in Chapters 1, 2 and 3, and the exploration of the CRPD in Chapter 4, this chapter examines how these and various other issues can shape legislative reform, by examining the reform of mental capacity legislation currently underway in Ireland. In 2013, the Irish government published the Assisted Decision-Making (Capacity) Bill 2013, which proposes an entirely new legislative framework to govern decision-making by persons with impaired mental capacity. This process of reform is interesting not only in relation to Ireland but also for the lessons it potentially holds for other jurisdictions contemplating similar legislative reform, especially in the context of evolving interpretations of the CRPD.

The Assisted Decision-Making (Capacity) Bill 2013

The primary purpose of Ireland's Assisted Decision-Making (Capacity) Bill 2013, which was published in 2013 but is still in development, is 'to provide for the reform of the law relating to persons who require or may require assistance in exercising their decision-making capacity, whether immediately or in the future'.[1] The Explanatory Memorandum published alongside the Bill clarifies its primary aim:

> The purpose of the Bill is to reform the law and to provide a modern statutory framework that supports decision-making by adults and enables them to retain the greatest amount of autonomy possible in situations where they lack or may shortly lack capacity. The Bill changes the existing law on capacity, shifting from the current all or nothing status approach to a flexible functional one, whereby capacity is assessed on an issue- and time-specific basis. The Bill replaces the

---

1   Assisted Decision-Making (Capacity) Bill 2013, preamble. See also: Kelly, B.D., 'The Assisted Decision-Making (Capacity) Bill 2013: content, commentary, controversy', *Irish Journal of Medical Science*, 2015, 184, 31–46.

Wards of Court system with a modern statutory framework to assist persons in exercising their decision-making capacity.[2]

In the years leading up to the 2014 Bill, many commentators had highlighted a need for reform of Ireland's Ward of Court system,[3] not least because the consequences of becoming a ward are currently notably profound, as the wardship court gains jurisdiction over *all* matters in relation to the 'person and estate' of the individual.[4] In addition, the ward of court framework does not adequately define capacity; is poorly responsive to changes in capacity; makes unwieldy provision for appointing decision-makers; and has insufficient provision for periodic review.[5]

Against this background, the Assisted Decision-Making (Capacity) Bill 2013 aims to introduce new models of assisted decision-making and establish an Office of the Public Guardian to oversee an entirely new legislative framework. The Bill's Explanatory Memorandum clarifies that 'reform of the law on decision-making capacity is one of the actions required to enable the State to ratify the United Nations Convention on the Rights of Persons with Disabilities'.[6]

The CRPD is discussed in depth in Chapter 4, but for the present discussion it is important to note that the CRPD does not equate disability with lack of mental capacity; that is, while certain individuals may have specific disabilities, this does not mean that they lack mental capacity. Consistent with this, Ireland's new Bill does not equate a lack of capacity with having a disability, and Ireland's Bill is primarily concerned with capacity (as opposed to disability) while the CRPD is primarily concerned with disability (as opposed to capacity).

Ireland signed the CRPD in 2007 but has yet to ratify it. One of the key barriers to ratification has been Ireland's outdated capacity legislation, some of which dates from the Lunacy Regulation (Ireland) Act 1871. Shortly after the Assisted Decision-Making (Capacity) Bill was published in 2013, the Minister of State for Disability, Equality and Mental Health described the new Bill as 'a key stepping stone towards ratification' of the CRPD.[7] The specific contents of the Bill and its implications in the context of the CRPD and other matters are considered next.

---

2 Assisted Decision-Making (Capacity) Bill 2013: Explanatory Memorandum; p. 1.

3 Leonard, P., McLaughlin, M., 'Capacity legislation for Ireland: filling the legislative gaps', *Irish Journal of Psychological Medicine*, 2009, 26, 165–168.

4 Lunacy Regulation (Ireland) Act 1871, section 103.

5 Kelly, 2011.

6 Assisted Decision-Making (Capacity) Bill 2013: Explanatory Memorandum; p. 2.

7 Lynch, K., 'Balancing the scales of justice', *Irish Examiner*, 2013, 24 September.

Capacity

'Capacity' is defined in Ireland's 2013 Bill as 'mental capacity'[8] and is to be 'construed functionally'; that is, 'a person's capacity shall be assessed on the basis of his or her ability to understand the nature and consequences of a decision to be made by him or her in the context of the available choices at the time the decision is made'.[9] 'A person lacks capacity to make a decision if he or she is unable:

a. To understand the information relevant to the decision;
b. To retain that information;
c. To use or weigh up that information as part of the process of making the decision; or
d. To communicate his or her decision (whether by talking, writing, using sign language, assisted technology, or any other means) or, if the implementation of the decision requires the act of a third party, to communicate by any means with that third party'.[10]

'A person is not to be regarded as unable to understand the information relevant to a decision if he or she is able to understand an explanation of it given to him or her in a way that is appropriate to his or her circumstances',[11] and 'the fact that a person is able to retain the information relevant to a decision for a short period only does not prevent him or her from being regarded as having the capacity to make the decision';[12] that is, the decision can be made during the 'short period' during which the individual 'is able to retain the information'.

In addition, 'any question as to whether a person lacks capacity shall be decided on the balance of probabilities'.[13] The Circuit Court has 'exclusive jurisdiction'[14] under this legislation except for certain matters which are within the remit of the High Court, including '(a) non-therapeutic sterilisation, (b) withdrawal of artificial life-sustaining treatment, or (c) the donation of an organ'.[15]

---

8   Assisted Decision-Making (Capacity) Bill 2013, section 2(1).
9   Assisted Decision-Making (Capacity) Bill 2013, section 3(1).
10   Assisted Decision-Making (Capacity) Bill 2013, section 3(2).
11   Assisted Decision-Making (Capacity) Bill 2013, section 3(3).
12   Assisted Decision-Making (Capacity) Bill 2013, section 3(4).
13   Assisted Decision-Making (Capacity) Bill 2013, section 3(6).
14   Assisted Decision-Making (Capacity) Bill 2013, section 4(1).
15   Assisted Decision-Making (Capacity) Bill 2013, section 4(2).

Principles

The Bill outlines 'guiding principles' which include a presumption of capacity: 'It shall be presumed that a relevant person ... has capacity in respect of the matter concerned unless the contrary is shown in accordance with the provisions of this Act'.[16] A person 'shall not be considered as unable to make a decision in respect of the matter concerned unless all practicable steps have been taken, without success, to help him or her to do so'.[17] A person 'shall not be considered as unable to make a decision in respect of the matter concerned merely by reason of making, having made, or being likely to make, an unwise decision'.[18]

Interventions under this Act shall not occur 'unless it is necessary to do so having regard to the individual circumstances of the relevant person',[19] and any intervention 'shall: (a) be made in a manner that minimises (i) the restriction of the relevant person's rights, and (ii) the restriction of the relevant person's freedom of action, and (b) have due regard to the need to respect the right of the relevant person to his or her dignity, bodily integrity, privacy and autonomy'.[20] The 'intervener' must encourage participation and 'give effect, in so far as is practicable, to the past and present will and preferences of the relevant person, in so far as that will and those preferences are reasonably ascertainable'.[21]

As part of this process, the intervener 'may consider the views of (a) any person engaged in caring for the relevant person, (b) any person who has a bona fide interest in the welfare of the relevant person, or (c) healthcare professionals'.[22] Regard shall also 'be had to (a) the likelihood of the recovery of the relevant person's capacity in respect of the matter concerned, and (b) the urgency of making the intervention prior to such recovery';[23] that is, a non-urgent decision may be deferred if capacity is likely to improve.

Assisted Decision-Making

The first level of decision-making support outlined in the Bill is 'assisted decision-making', whereby an individual aged 18 years or over 'who considers that his or her capacity is in question or may shortly be in question may appoint another person who has also attained that age to assist the first-mentioned

---

16 Assisted Decision-Making (Capacity) Bill 2013, section 8(2).
17 Assisted Decision-Making (Capacity) Bill 2013, section 8(3).
18 Assisted Decision-Making (Capacity) Bill 2013, section 8(4).
19 Assisted Decision-Making (Capacity) Bill 2013, section 8(5).
20 Assisted Decision-Making (Capacity) Bill 2013, section 8(6).
21 Assisted Decision-Making (Capacity) Bill 2013, section 8(7).
22 Assisted Decision-Making (Capacity) Bill 2013, section 8(8).
23 Assisted Decision-Making (Capacity) Bill 2013, section 8(9).

person in making one or more than one decision on the first-mentioned person's personal welfare or property and affairs, or both'.[24] The functions of a decision-making assistant are:

a. To advise the appointer by explaining relevant information and considerations relating to a relevant decision,
b. To ascertain the will and preferences of the appointer on a matter the subject or to be the subject of a relevant decision and to assist the appointer to communicate them,
c. To assist the appointer to obtain any information or personal records … that the appointer is entitled to and that is or are required in relation to a relevant decision,
d. To assist the appointer to make and express a relevant decision, and
e. To endeavour to ensure that the appointer's relevant decisions are implemented.[25]

The Explanatory Memorandum published alongside the Bill emphasises that 'decision-making authority remains with the appointer who will be actively assisted, typically by family members, relatives and carers, in accessing information, in understanding the information, in making and expressing decisions on matters specified in the agreement, and in implementing decisions made'.[26] The appointer can revoke the decision-making assistance agreement at any time.[27]

Co-Decision-Maker

This part of the Bill concerns applications to the Circuit Court in respect of 'relevant persons' (i.e., persons whose decision-making capacity may be in question). Various parties, including the 'relevant person', must be notified of such an application,[28] and an application may only occur if 'the person making the application has received the consent of the court to the making of the application, which consent may be sought by way of an ex parte application'.[29]

The Circuit Court application shall specify 'the benefit to the relevant person sought to be achieved by the application'[30] and why this benefit 'has failed to be

---

24 Assisted Decision-Making (Capacity) Bill 2013, section 10(1).
25 Assisted Decision-Making (Capacity) Bill 2013, section 11(1).
26 Explanatory Memorandum; p. 4.
27 Assisted Decision-Making (Capacity) Bill 2013, section 10(11).
28 Assisted Decision-Making (Capacity) Bill 2013, section 14(1).
29 Assisted Decision-Making (Capacity) Bill 2013, section 14(2).
30 Assisted Decision-Making (Capacity) Bill 2013, section 14(4)(b).

achieved in any other appropriate and practicable manner'.[31] The hearing 'shall (a) be conducted with the least amount of formality consistent with the proper administration of justice, and (b) be heard and determined otherwise than in public'.[32] Following the hearing, the Court may declare that the relevant person 'lacks capacity, unless the assistance of a suitable person as a co-decision-maker is made available',[33] or 'lacks capacity, even if the assistance of a suitable person as a co-decision-maker were made available'.[34] In addition, the Court 'may make a declaration as to the lawfulness of an intervention proposed to be made in respect of the relevant person'.[35]

The co-decision-making agreement, if one is indicated,[36] can be initiated by a person 'who considers that his or her capacity is in question or may shortly be in question' and that person 'may appoint a suitable person who has also attained that age to jointly make … one or more than one decision on the first-mentioned person's personal welfare or property and affairs, or both'.[37]

The co-decision-maker must be 'a relative or friend of the proposed appointer who has had such personal contact with the proposed appointer over such period of time that a relationship of trust exists between them',[38] and must not be 'the owner, or the registered provider, of a nursing home … a mental health facility, or a residential facility for persons with disabilities, in which the relevant person resides, or a person residing with, or an employee or agent of, such owner or registered provider'.[39]

The chief role of the co-decision-maker is 'to jointly make with the appointer decisions on the appointer's personal welfare or property and affairs, or both'.[40] The court 'shall review a co-decision-making order (a) not earlier than 3 months before and not later than 3 months after the first anniversary of the making of the order, and (b) thereafter, at intervals such that there is no gap greater than 3 years between one review of the order and the next review'.[41] The Circuit Court may also vary or revoke the co-decision-making order under certain conditions,[42] including if the relevant person's capacity 'has improved to

---

31 Assisted Decision-Making (Capacity) Bill 2013, section 14(4)(c)(i).
32 Assisted Decision-Making (Capacity) Bill 2013, section 14(10).
33 Assisted Decision-Making (Capacity) Bill 2013, section 15(1)(a).
34 Assisted Decision-Making (Capacity) Bill 2013, section 15(1)(b).
35 Assisted Decision-Making (Capacity) Bill 2013, section 15(3).
36 Assisted Decision-Making (Capacity) Bill 2013, section 17(1).
37 Assisted Decision-Making (Capacity) Bill 2013, section 18(1).
38 Assisted Decision-Making (Capacity) Bill 2013, section 18(2).
39 Assisted Decision-Making (Capacity) Bill 2013, section 20(1)(g).
40 Assisted Decision-Making (Capacity) Bill 2013, section 16.
41 Assisted Decision-Making (Capacity) Bill 2013, section 17(7).
42 Assisted Decision-Making (Capacity) Bill 2013, sections 17(9)–(11).

the extent that he or she no longer requires the assistance of the co-decision-maker for that relevant decision'.[43]

Decision-Making Representative

If the Circuit Court declares that the relevant person 'lacks capacity, even if the assistance of a suitable person as a co-decision-maker were made available',[44] the court may either make 'an order making the decision or decisions concerned on behalf of the relevant person where it is satisfied that the matter is urgent or that it is otherwise expedient for it to do so' or appoint 'a decision-making representative for the relevant person for the purposes of making one or more than one decision specified in the order on behalf of the relevant person'.[45] A decision-making order or decision-making representative order may authorise decisions relating to the relevant person's 'personal welfare' or 'property or affairs'. There are various limits on the actions of the decision-making representative; for example, the decision-making representative 'shall not refuse consent to the carrying out or continuation of life-sustaining treatment for the relevant person'.[46]

In addition, a decision-making representative 'shall not do an act that is intended to restrain the relevant person unless':

a. The relevant person lacks capacity in relation to the matter in question or the decision-making representative reasonably believes that the relevant person lacks such capacity,
b. The decision-making representative reasonably believes that it is necessary to do the act in order to prevent harm to the relevant person or to another person, and
c. The act is a proportionate response to the likelihood of the harm referred to in paragraph (b) and to the seriousness of such harm'.[47]

A decision-making representative uses 'restraint' if he or she '(a) uses, or indicates an intention to use, force to secure the doing of an act which the relevant person resists, (b) restricts the relevant person's liberty of movement, whether or not the relevant person resists, or (c) authorises another person to do any of the things referred to in paragraph (a) or (b)'.[48] The decision-

---

43 Assisted Decision-Making (Capacity) Bill 2013, section 17(10)(a).
44 Assisted Decision-Making (Capacity) Bill 2013, section 15(1)(b).
45 Assisted Decision-Making (Capacity) Bill 2013, section 23(2).
46 Assisted Decision-Making (Capacity) Bill 2013, section 27(4).
47 Assisted Decision-Making (Capacity) Bill 2013, section 27(5).
48 Assisted Decision-Making (Capacity) Bill 2013, section 27(6).

making representative 'does more than restrain the relevant person if he or she deprives the relevant person of the relevant person's liberty within the meaning of Article 5(1) of the European Convention on Human Rights'.[49] This Part of the Bill 'shall not be construed to prejudice the generality of section 69 of the Mental Health Act 2001 or of rules made under that section'.[50]

The decision-making representative 'shall at least once every 12 months, or within such shorter period as the court may direct, prepare and submit to the Public Guardian[51] a report as to the performance of his or her functions,'[52] and the Circuit Court has the power to review a court 'declaration as respects capacity'.[53] Such a review must occur at intervals of 'not more than 12 months'[54] or 'not more than 3 years if the court is satisfied that the relevant person is unlikely to recover his or her capacity'.[55] In making or reviewing declarations or orders, the court can direct that 'reports as the court considers necessary be furnished to it'; for example, medical reports ('including reports relating to the cognitive ability of that person'), 'reports relating to the circumstances of the relevant person (including financial reports and valuations of property)', and 'reports from healthcare professionals'.[56] The Public Guardian will be notified of all declarations and orders.[57]

---

49   Assisted Decision-Making (Capacity) Bill 2013, section 27(7). For relevant case law relating to deprivation of liberty, see: *HL v UK (Bournewood)* (2004) 40 EHRR 761; *DD v Lithuania* (2012) ECHR 254; *Stanev v Bulgaria* (2012) EHRR 46.

50   Assisted Decision-Making (Capacity) Bill 2013, section 27(8). Section 69 of the Mental Health Act 2001 outlines legally binding rules governing seclusion and 'mechanical means of bodily restraint'.

51   The Assisted Decision-Making (Capacity) Bill 2013 states that the 'Courts Service shall appoint a person to perform the functions conferred on the Public Guardian by this Act' (section 55(1)); the Public Guardian will have a range of roles including promoting public awareness of relevant international conventions and the provisions of the 2013 Bill (section 56(2)); the Public Guardian may also publish codes of practice (section 63(2)) and 'a person concerned shall have regard to a code of practice ... when performing any function under this Act in respect of which the code provides guidance' (section 63(13)).

52   Assisted Decision-Making (Capacity) Bill 2013, section 24(7)(a).

53   Assisted Decision-Making (Capacity) Bill 2013, section 29.

54   Assisted Decision-Making (Capacity) Bill 2013, section 29(2)(a).

55   Assisted Decision-Making (Capacity) Bill 2013, section 29(2)(b).

56   Assisted Decision-Making (Capacity) Bill 2013, section 30(2).

57   Assisted Decision-Making (Capacity) Bill 2013, section 31.

Enduring Power of Attorney

This part of the Bill concerns 'enduring power of attorney' as outlined in the Powers of Attorney Act 1996 and states that 'no enduring power of attorney shall be created under the Act of 1996 from the commencement of this section'.[58] A power of attorney is defined as an 'an enduring power of attorney' if it contains a statement 'that the donor intends the power to be effective at any subsequent time when the donor lacks or shortly may lack (i) capacity to look after his or her personal welfare, (ii) capacity to manage his or her property and affairs, or (iii) both' and is in compliance with relevant regulations.[59]

The enduring power 'may confer authority on an attorney for a donor to make any decisions about the donor's personal welfare'[60] including 'giving or refusing treatment by a person providing healthcare for the donor other than refusing life-sustaining treatment'.[61] Powers in relation to 'restraint'[62] are similar to those for decision-making representatives.[63] The enduring power may confer general authority on an attorney 'to act on the donor's behalf in relation to all or a specified part of the property and affairs of the donor' or 'to do on the donor's behalf specified things or make decisions on specified matters'.[64]

In order to activate the enduring power, a certificate stating that 'the donor lacks or shortly may lack capacity to look after his or her personal welfare', 'property and affairs', or both, and 'purporting to be signed by a registered medical practitioner (or other healthcare professional whom the High Court considers suitable to assess a person's capacity) may be accepted as evidence'.[65]

Once the power of attorney is in place, the attorney 'shall at least once every 12 months prepare and submit to the Public Guardian a report as to the performance of his or her functions as such attorney'.[66] The High Court may cancel the registration of the instrument under specific circumstances including 'being satisfied that the donor has, and is likely to continue to have, capacity'.[67] The donor may also revoke the enduring power 'if the donor has capacity to do so', subject to certain regulations.[68]

---

58   Assisted Decision-Making (Capacity) Bill 2013, section 39(4).
59   Assisted Decision-Making (Capacity) Bill 2013, section 40(1).
60   Assisted Decision-Making (Capacity) Bill 2013, section 41(1).
61   Assisted Decision-Making (Capacity) Bill 2013, section 41(2)(b).
62   Assisted Decision-Making (Capacity) Bill 2013, section 41(4–7).
63   Assisted Decision-Making (Capacity) Bill 2013, section 27(5–8).
64   Assisted Decision-Making (Capacity) Bill 2013, section 42(1).
65   Assisted Decision-Making (Capacity) Bill 2013, section 45(4).
66   Assisted Decision-Making (Capacity) Bill 2013, section 48(4)(a).
67   Assisted Decision-Making (Capacity) Bill 2013, section 49(5)(b).
68   Assisted Decision-Making (Capacity) Bill 2013, section 50(1–2).

Various Other Matters

The Bill introduces a new term, 'informal decision-maker', and states that an 'informal decision-maker may take or authorise the taking of an action in respect of the personal welfare (including healthcare and treatment) of the relevant person where the provisions of this section are complied with' and the action does not involve, and is not closely connected with, non-therapeutic sterilisation, withdrawal of artificial life-sustaining treatment or organ donation.[69] Once the 'informal decision-maker ... acts in compliance with the provisions of this Act [he or she] shall not incur any legal liability which he or she would not have incurred if the relevant person (a) had the capacity to consent in relation to the action, and (b) had given consent to the informal decision-maker to take or authorise the taking of the action'.[70] Powers in relation to 'restraint' for informal decision-makers[71] are similar to those outlined for decision-making representatives.[72]

Part 11 of the Bill makes a range of provisions in relation to a variety of other issues. It states, for example, that 'nothing in this Act shall be construed as authorising any person to give consent on behalf of a person who lacks capacity to be a participant in a clinical trial'.[73] In addition, 'nothing in this Act authorises a person' to give a patient treatment for mental disorder 'if, at the time when it is proposed to treat the patient, his or her treatment is regulated by Part 4' of the Mental Health Act 2001 (which primarily governs treatment of individuals detained under the 2001 Act).[74]

Part 11 also states that, 'unless otherwise expressly provided, nothing in this Act shall be construed as altering or amending the law in force on the coming into operation of this section relating to the capacity or consent required as respects a person in relation to any of the following: (a) marriage; (b) civil partnership; (c) judicial separation, divorce or a non-judicial separation agreement; (d) the dissolution of a civil partnership; (e) the placing of a child for adoption; (f) the making of an adoption order; (g) guardianship; (h) sexual relations; (i) voting at an election or at a referendum; (j) serving as a member of a jury'.[75] In addition, 'nothing in this Act shall be construed as altering or amending the law relating to the capacity of a person to make a will'.[76]

---

69 Assisted Decision-Making (Capacity) Bill 2013, section 53(1).
70 Assisted Decision-Making (Capacity) Bill 2013, section 53(2).
71 Assisted Decision-Making (Capacity) Bill 2013, section 53(6).
72 Assisted Decision-Making (Capacity) Bill 2013, section 27(5–8).
73 Assisted Decision-Making (Capacity) Bill 2013, section 103.
74 Assisted Decision-Making (Capacity) Bill 2013, section 104.
75 Assisted Decision-Making (Capacity) Bill 2013, section 106.
76 Assisted Decision-Making (Capacity) Bill 2013, section 108(1).

Regarding the courts, the Bill amends the Courts (Supplemental Provisions) Act 1961 'to allow Specialist Judges to perform and exercise the functions, powers and jurisdiction conferred on the Circuit Court by this Bill in relation to capacity matters'.[77] More generally, applications to the Circuit or High Courts should, for the most part, be heard in the presence of the relevant individual, except in specific circumstances,[78] and appeal is to the High or Supreme Court, as indicated, but 'on a point of law only'.[79]

Key Issues Arising from the Assisted Decision-Making (Capacity) Bill 2013

Two of the key purposes of the Assisted Decision-Making (Capacity) Bill 2013 were to provide a range of decision-making supports for people whose mental capacity is, or may soon be, compromised, and to bring Ireland into greater accordance with the CRPD. While the Bill takes demonstrable steps in both of these directions, especially by introducing a range of decision-making supports to replace the outdated 'ward of court' system, various specific issues would benefit from clarification.

First, however, it is to be noted and welcomed that the proposed legislation takes an explicitly functional approach to capacity[80] and provides a relatively clear definition of incapacity.[81] The requirement for appropriate information to support decision-making is also welcome,[82] not least because it moves some way towards meeting CRPD requirements regarding provision of information to persons with disabilities.[83] The provisions regarding *retention* of information are less clear: section 3(4) of the 2013 Bill specifies that 'the fact that a person is able to retain the information relevant to a decision for a short period only does not prevent him or her from being regarded as having the capacity to make the decision'. It is not clear, however, for how long the person must retain the information, and there may be a dilemma if a decision is made when the person 'is able to retain the information' but later appears no longer to agree with their earlier decision (when he or she can no longer retain the information).

---

77 Explanatory Memorandum; p. 30.
78 Assisted Decision-Making (Capacity) Bill 2013, section 107.
79 Assisted Decision-Making (Capacity) Bill 2013, section 109.
80 Assisted Decision-Making (Capacity) Bill 2013, section 3(1).
81 Assisted Decision-Making (Capacity) Bill 2013, section 3(2).
82 Assisted Decision-Making (Capacity) Bill 2013, section 3(3).
83 CRPD, article 21.

With regard to principles, the presumption of capacity[84] is welcome, not least because it emphasises the capacity (rather than any proposed *in*capacity) of the individual, and is consistent with the Medical Council's Guide to Professional Conduct and Ethics for Registered Practitioners, which outlines a similar presumption of capacity.[85] Also consistent with this, the Bill states that a person 'shall not be considered as unable to make a decision ... merely by reason of making, having made, or being likely to make, an unwise decision'.[86] This, too, is welcome.

This Part of the Bill also usefully emphasises the right to 'dignity, bodily integrity, privacy and autonomy'[87] and prioritises 'will and preferences'.[88] The emphasis on 'will and preferences' rather than 'best interests' contrasts with the Mental Capacity Act 2005 in England and Wales which states that 'an act done, or decision made, under this Act for or on behalf of a person who lacks capacity must be done, or made, in his best interests'.[89] This places 'best interests' firmly at the heart of the legislation in England and Wales, where the relevant code of practice also presents what is known as a 'best interests checklist' which includes paying due attention to the person's own views.[90]

The Mental Capacity Act 2005 in England and Wales also includes provisions to appoint a 'deputy' to manage the affairs of a person who has impaired capacity[91] and establishment of an Independent Mental Capacity Advocate (IMCA) Service.[92] Somewhat like the decision-making assistant in Ireland, the IMCA's central role is to support and represent a person who lacks capacity in making a specific decision (when the person has nobody else to support them) by 'ascertaining what [the person's] wishes and feelings would be likely to be, and the beliefs and values that would be likely to influence [the person], if he had capacity'.[93]

---

84   Assisted Decision-Making (Capacity) Bill 2013, section 8(2).

85   Medical Council, *Guide to Professional Conduct and Ethics for Registered Practitioners (Seventh Edition)*, Dublin: Medical Council, 2009; p. 34.

86   Assisted Decision-Making (Capacity) Bill 2013, section 8(4).

87   Assisted Decision-Making (Capacity) Bill 2013, section 8(6).

88   Assisted Decision-Making (Capacity) Bill 2013, section 8(7)(b).

89   Mental Capacity Act 2005, section 1(5).

90   Hughes, J.C., 'Best interests', in Jacob, R., Gunn, N., and Holland, A. (eds), *Mental Capacity Legislation: Principles and Practice* (pp. 33–53), London: RCPsych Publications, 2013.

91   Mental Capacity Act 2005, section 16(2).

92   Mental Capacity Act 2005, sections 35 and 36.

93   Mental Capacity Act 2005, section 36(2)(c).

A more detailed account of the Mental Capacity Act 2005 in England and Wales is provided by Bartlett.[94] While certain elements of the 2005 Act have been welcomed,[95] certain other provisions, including its Deprivation of Liberty Safeguards,[96] have generated significant concern; further detail on the operation of these and other aspects of the Mental Capacity Act 2005 are also provided by Bartlett.[97] Overall, however, while there are certain similarities and dissimilarities between Ireland and England and Wales, the most striking dissimilarity remains the centrality of 'best interests' in England and Wales, and the proposed move away from 'best interests' in Ireland.

Ireland's move away from 'best interests' is not quite absolute, however, as the Circuit Court can consider the 'interests' of the individual under certain circumstances; for example, 'where the court is satisfied that a co-decision-maker for a relevant person has behaved, is behaving or is proposing to behave in a manner outside the scope of the authority conferred on him or her'.[98] Despite such caveats, however, the Bill still marks a significant move away from 'best interests' as an over-arching principle and towards 'will and preferences'.[99] This shift is further underlined by the provision that a 'relevant person … shall not be considered as unable to make a decision in respect of the matter concerned merely by reason of making, having made, or being likely to make, an unwise decision'.[100] While the use of subjective terminology ('unwise') may not be especially helpful, these changes are strongly consistent with both the CRPD's emphasis on dignity[101] and its requirement 'that measures relating to the exercise of legal capacity respect the rights, will and preferences of the person'.[102]

---

94   Bartlett, P., *Blackstone's Guide to the Mental Capacity Act 2005*, Oxford: Oxford University Press, 2005.

95   Samsi, K., Manthorpe, J., Nagendran, T., Heath, H., 'Challenges and expectations of the Mental Capacity Act 2005: an interview-based study of community-based specialist nurses working in dementia care', *Journal of Clinical Nursing*, 2012, 21, 1697–1705.

96   Mental Capacity Act 2005, schedule A1.

97   Bartlett, P., 'Informal admissions and deprivation of liberty under the Mental Capacity Act 2005', in Gostin, L., McHale, J., Fennell, P., Mackay, R.D., and Bartlett, P. (eds), *Principles of Mental Health Law and Policy* (pp. 385–412), Oxford: Oxford University Press, Oxford, 2010.

98   Assisted Decision-Making (Capacity) Bill 2013, section 17(9).

99   Shannon, J., 'New capacity Bill has gaps in human rights protection', *Irish Medical News*, 2013, 34, 4.

100   Assisted Decision-Making (Capacity) Bill 2013, section 8(4).

101   CRPD, preamble.

102   CRPD, article 12(4).

Part 3 ('Assisted Decision-Making') provides a structure for decision-making assistants and outlines their functions, making it clear that the ultimate decision still lies with the 'appointer'.[103] An assisted decision-making agreement is a voluntary arrangement, and whether or not an individual makes such an arrangement will depend on his or her awareness that his or her 'capacity is in question or may shortly be in question',[104] and his or her willingness to take appropriate action. Prior to finalisation and implementation of the legislation, it is not possible to predict how much use will be made of these provisions.

Part 4 ('Applications to Court in respect of Relevant Persons and Related Matters') presents the Bill's central provisions in relation to 'co-decision-making'[105] and 'decision-making representatives'.[106] In the first instance, it is noteworthy that these processes both involve the Circuit Court, possibly sitting with a 'specialist judge'.[107] As a result, if these provisions are widely used, they are likely to place significant pressure on Circuit Court resources; again, extent of use is impossible to estimate prior to implementation, but enhanced court resources are likely to be needed to ensure timely hearings.

In addition, the Circuit Court hearings will clearly require complex, subtle decision-making by the court, which can declare that the relevant person 'lacks capacity, unless the assistance of a suitable person as a co-decision-maker is made available'[108] or 'lacks capacity, even if the assistance of a suitable person as a co-decision-maker were made available'.[109] These distinctions are exceptionally difficult to make in clinical practice, and it appears likely the court will rely heavily on expert evidence for the clinical element of its decision.[110]

If the court decides that the relevant person 'lacks capacity, unless the assistance of a suitable person as a co-decision-maker is made available',[111] the person may initiate a co-decision-making agreement, likely to be a 'a relative or friend of the proposed appointer who has had such personal contact with the proposed appointer over such period of time that a relationship of trust exists

---

103 Assisted Decision-Making (Capacity) Bill 2013, Explanatory Memorandum; p. 4.

104 Assisted Decision-Making (Capacity) Bill 2013, section 10(1).

105 Assisted Decision-Making (Capacity) Bill 2013, chapter 4.

106 Assisted Decision-Making (Capacity) Bill 2013, chapter 5.

107 Assisted Decision-Making (Capacity) Bill 2013, section 111.

108 Assisted Decision-Making (Capacity) Bill 2013, section 15(1)(a).

109 Assisted Decision-Making (Capacity) Bill 2013, section 15(1)(a).

110 Hotopf, M., 'The assessment of mental capacity', in Jacob, R., Gunn, N. and Holland, A. (eds), *Mental Capacity Legislation: Principles and Practice* (pp. 15–32), London: RCPsych Publications, 2013; Jacob, R., Fistein. E., 'Clinical ambiguities in the assessment of capacity', in Jacob, R., Gunn, N. and Holland, A. (eds), *Mental Capacity Legislation: Principles and Practice* (pp. 96–108), London: RCPsych Publications, 2013.

111 Assisted Decision-Making (Capacity) Bill 2013, section 15(1)(a).

between them'.[112] The exclusion criteria here seem reasonable,[113] but much of the detail of these arrangements will depend on the regulations yet to be introduced by the Minister for Justice and Equality.[114]

Unlike the decision-making assistance agreement which will likely be notified to the Public Guardian,[115] a co-decision-making agreement must be approved by the Circuit Court, once the court is satisfied it is in accordance with the law and 'the will and preferences of the relevant person'.[116] Once that occurs, the roles of the co-decision-maker may be broad so the requirement for annual reports to the Public Guardian will be of critical importance[117] as will the three-yearly reviews by the Circuit Court.[118]

The next level of assisted decision-making is the decision-making representative agreement which can approved by the Circuit Court if it declares that the relevant person 'lacks capacity, even if the assistance of a suitable person as a co-decision-maker were made available',[119] or if a co-decision-making agreement was deemed sufficient by the court but the court is unable to make a co-decision-making order;[120] for example, if the 'relevant person' does not consent to the creation of a co-decision-making agreement.[121] As with a co-decision-making agreement order, a decision-making representative order may authorise a decision-making representative to make decisions relating to a broad range of issues relating to 'personal welfare' or 'property or affairs', so the requirement for annual reports to the Public Guardian will be of critical importance,[122] as will be the annual[123] or three-yearly reviews by the court.[124]

It is important that the Bill outlines limits on 'restraint';[125] specifies that the decision-making representative 'does more than restrain the relevant person if he or she deprives the relevant person of the relevant person's liberty within the meaning of Article 5(1) of the European Convention on Human Rights';[126] and specifies that this part of the Bill 'shall not be construed to prejudice the

---

112 Assisted Decision-Making (Capacity) Bill 2013, section 18(2).
113 Assisted Decision-Making (Capacity) Bill 2013, section 20(1).
114 Assisted Decision-Making (Capacity) Bill 2013, section 18(4).
115 Assisted Decision-Making (Capacity) Bill 2013, section 10(2)(g)(i).
116 Assisted Decision-Making (Capacity) Bill 2013, section 17(2).
117 Assisted Decision-Making (Capacity) Bill 2013, section 21(7)(a).
118 Assisted Decision-Making (Capacity) Bill 2013, section 17(7).
119 Assisted Decision-Making (Capacity) Bill 2013, section 15(1)(b).
120 Assisted Decision-Making (Capacity) Bill 2013, section 23(1)(a).
121 Assisted Decision-Making (Capacity) Bill 2013, section 17(5).
122 Assisted Decision-Making (Capacity) Bill 2013, section 24(7)(a).
123 Assisted Decision-Making (Capacity) Bill 2013, section 29(2)(a).
124 Assisted Decision-Making (Capacity) Bill 2013, section 29(2)(b).
125 Assisted Decision-Making (Capacity) Bill 2013, section 27(5–6).
126 Assisted Decision-Making (Capacity) Bill 2013, section 27(7).

generality of section 69 of the Mental Health Act 2001 [governing seclusion and "mechanical means of bodily restraint"] or of rules made under that section';[127] It is not entirely clear, however, under what circumstances the decision-making representative would be using 'restraint' in the first instance; this requires clarification.

Part 6 ('Enduring Power of Attorney') contains the measures regarding enduring power of attorney, although how these will work in practice will depend greatly on regulations to be made by the Minister for Justice and Equality.[128] In terms of powers, 'an enduring power may confer authority on an attorney for a donor to make any decisions about the donor's personal welfare',[129] including 'giving or refusing treatment by a person providing healthcare for the donor other than refusing life-sustaining treatment.[130] The issue of life-saving treatment may yet be addressed in greater detail within the new legislative framework as advanced medical directives may be introduced to the legislation at a later date, possibly along the lines of the relevant provisions in the Mental Capacity Act 2005 in England and Wales.[131]

The attorney's potential powers in relation to 'restraint'[132] are similar to those outlined for decision-making representatives,[133] so similar caveats apply; that is, it is not clear when, if ever, an attorney would be authorising 'restraint' of any description.

Part 7 concerns 'informal decision-making on personal welfare matters' apart from issues closely connected with non-therapeutic sterilisation, withdrawal of artificial life-sustaining treatment or organ donation.[134] These provisions appear, on the face of them, to mandate much of the day-to-day informal decision-making that is performed by family members and carers of, for example, individuals with intellectual disability. In her commentary on this Part, the Minister of State for Disability, Equality and Mental Health stated that this provision was designed to meet a particular need among families and healthcare workers who often have to make decisions in situations of crisis.[135]

---

127 Assisted Decision-Making (Capacity) Bill 2013, section 27(8).
128 Assisted Decision-Making (Capacity) Bill 2013, section 40(3).
129 Assisted Decision-Making (Capacity) Bill 2013, section 41(1).
130 Assisted Decision-Making (Capacity) Bill 2013, section 41(2)(b).
131 Jacob, R., Holland, A., 'Introduction', in Jacob, R., Gunn, N. and Holland, A. (eds), *Mental Capacity Legislation: Principles and Practice* (pp. 1–14), London: RCPsych Publications, 2013; Welsh, S.F., 'Provisions of the Mental Capacity Act 2005', in Jacob, R., Gunn, N. and Holland, A. (eds), *Mental Capacity Legislation: Principles and Practice* (pp. 54–77), London: RCPsych Publications, 2013.
132 Assisted Decision-Making (Capacity) Bill 2013, section 41(4–7).
133 Assisted Decision-Making (Capacity) Bill 2013, section 27(5–8).
134 Assisted Decision-Making (Capacity) Bill 2013, section 53(1).
135 Lynch, K., 'Balancing the scales of justice', *Irish Examiner*, 2013, 24 September.

There is, however, a remarkable lack of oversight of this provision,[136] possibly stemming from a desire to avoid the kind of complexity associated with the Deprivation of Liberty Safeguards under the Mental Capacity Act 2005 in England and Wales.[137] Given this lack of oversight, it is reasonable that powers in relation to 'restraint' for informal decision-makers[138] must not result in a deprivation of liberty that meets or exceeds the threshold outlined in Article 5(1) of the European Convention on Human Rights. As a result, however, this provision fails to address some of the key issues faced by informal decision-makers, such as carers, who seek, for example, to lock the door if a confused individual with dementia repeatedly tries to wander outside at night. The provisions of this legislation do not address this relatively common dilemma, in contrast to the Deprivation of Liberty Safeguards in England and Wales which, although cumbersome, at least provide a framework that both addresses this clinical need and ensures accountability.[139]

Part 8 ('Public Guardian') sets up the office of the Public Guardian which will have many critical roles, including producing codes of practice.[140] Much will depend on the nature and contents of these codes of practice and, while such codes will not be legally binding, 'a person concerned shall have regard to a code of practice … when performing any function under this Act in respect of which the code provides guidance'.[141]

Part 11 ('Miscellaneous') makes a range of provisions in relation to a variety of issues, most notably stating that this Bill will not alter or amend existing laws regarding marriage, civil partnership and various other specific areas.[142] As a result, this Bill arguably fails to promote the 'legal capacity' of individuals with disability to marry, but it also means that a decision-making representative cannot agree to a marriage on behalf of an individual with reduced mental capacity, thus hopefully preventing the forced marriage of individuals with disabilities, as has been reported in other jurisdictions.[143]

---

136 Shannon, 2013.

137   Welsh, S.F., Keeling, A., 'The Deprivation of Liberty Safeguards', in Jacob, R., Gunn, N., and Holland, A. (eds), *Mental Capacity Legislation: Principles and Practice* (pp. 78–95), London: RCPsych Publications, 2013.

138 Assisted Decision-Making (Capacity) Bill 2013, section 53(6).

139 Bartlett, 2005.

140 Assisted Decision-Making (Capacity) Bill 2013, section 63(2).

141 Assisted Decision-Making (Capacity) Bill 2013, section 63(13).

142 Assisted Decision-Making (Capacity) Bill 2013, section 106.

143 Pidd, H., 'Grim tip of a forced marriage iceberg', *Guardian*, 2013, 10 August.

Challenges for the Future

The Assisted Decision-Making (Capacity) Bill 2013 is an important step forward in protecting and promoting the rights of people with disabilities. There are, however, several areas in need of clarification. These areas stem from specific issues in the Bill, the Bill's interaction with the Mental Health Act 2001, and the Bill's relationship to international human rights standards, most notably the CRPD. More specifically, the following issues require clarification either at a later stage in the development of the legislation or in codes of practice:

- The issue of 'restraint' requires a great deal of clarification since is it not at all clear from the Bill when, if ever, decision-making representatives[144] or attorneys[145] might authorise 'restraint' of any description. The 'restraint' provisions regarding informal decision-makers are even more concerning: co-decision-makers,[146] decision-making representatives[147] and attorneys[148] must, at least, report to the Public Guardian annually; informal decision-makers, however, are subject to no such oversight and their powers in relation to 'restraint'[149] appear similar to those of decision-making representatives,[150] suggesting that this Bill mandates restraint by informal decision-makers almost to the level outlined in Article 5(1) of the European Convention on Human Rights, without apparent oversight. This is deeply concerning from a human rights perspective, and also from the perspective of families and carers who seek to ensure the safety of individuals with disabilities and deserve clear, protective regulations when doing so.
- In Section 3(4), it is not clear for how long a person must retain the information in order to make a valid decision, and there will be a dilemma if a decision is made when the person 'is able to retain the information' but some time later the person appears no longer to agree with the chosen course of action; such a decision should be regarded as no longer valid.
- In Part 4, applications to the Circuit Court in respect of 'co-decision-making' and 'decision-making representatives' are likely to place significant demands on court resources; and while the possibility of

---

144 Assisted Decision-Making (Capacity) Bill 2013, section 27(7).
145 Assisted Decision-Making (Capacity) Bill 2013, section 41(4–7).
146 Assisted Decision-Making (Capacity) Bill 2013, section 21(7)(a).
147 Assisted Decision-Making (Capacity) Bill 2013, section 24(7)(a).
148 Assisted Decision-Making (Capacity) Bill 2013, section 48(4)(a).
149 Assisted Decision-Making (Capacity) Bill 2013, section 53(6).
150 Assisted Decision-Making (Capacity) Bill 2013, section 27(5–8).

- specialist judges[151] is welcome, increased resourcing for the Circuit Court should be confirmed in order to ensure efficiency.
- Also in Part 4, it is stated that applications to the Circuit Court shall 'be heard and determined otherwise than in public',[152] and this raises concerns about the extent to which there will be consistent decision-making by the court and establishment of consistent principles of interpretation; publication of anonymised outlines of cases or anonymised accounts of decisions would help address such concerns, if this is possible.
- In Part 11 there is a welcome requirement that applications to the Circuit or High Courts should, for the most part, be heard in the presence of the relevant individual,[153] but appeal is to the High or Supreme Court 'on a point of law only';[154] this appears restrictive.

In addition to the above-mentioned, it is vitally important that the Assisted Decision-Making (Capacity) Bill 2013 interacts in a logical fashion with the Mental Health Act 2001. There are three key issues here.

First, there is a need for clarity as to whether a person whom the Circuit Court has declared to be of reduced mental capacity[155] can be a voluntary psychiatry inpatient. At present the Mental Health Act 2001 defines 'voluntary patient' as 'a person receiving care and treatment in an approved centre who is not the subject of an admission order or a renewal order';[156] that is, there is no requirement for capacity. In 2012 the *Interim Report of the Steering Group on the Review of the Mental Health Act 2001* suggested that this 'definition of voluntary patient should be amended such that a voluntary patient is a person who consents on his own behalf or with the support of others to admission to an approved centre for the purposes of care and treatment for mental illness, or on whose behalf a Personal Guardian appointed under the proposed Capacity legislation consents to such admission'.[157] If, however, an individual with reduced mental capacity becomes a 'voluntary' psychiatry inpatient solely at the direction of a 'decision-making representative', it could be argued that this constitutes a deprivation of liberty under Article 5(1) of the European Convention on Human Rights and is thus not permitted under the Assisted Decision-Making (Capacity) Bill 2013.[158] Moreover,

---

151 Assisted Decision-Making (Capacity) Bill 2013, section 111.
152 Assisted Decision-Making (Capacity) Bill 2013, section 14(10)(b).
153 Assisted Decision-Making (Capacity) Bill 2013, section 107.
154 Assisted Decision-Making (Capacity) Bill 2013, section 109.
155 Assisted Decision-Making (Capacity) Bill 2013, section 15(1).
156 Mental Health Act, section 2(1).
157 Steering Group on the Review of the Mental Health Act 2001, 2012; p. 21.
158 Assisted Decision-Making (Capacity) Bill 2013, section 27(7).

the proposed review process for decision-making representatives is likely to be inadequate.

Second, the Bill notes that 'nothing in this Act authorises a person' to give a patient treatment for a mental disorder 'if, at the time when it is proposed to treat the patient, his or her treatment is regulated by Part 4' of the Mental Health Act 2001.[159] This provision ensures a certain amount of consistency with the 2001 Act with regard to involuntary psychiatry inpatients, but issues relating to voluntary psychiatry inpatients remain unresolved by this provision.

Third, it is important that any further measures introduced as the capacity legislation develops (e.g., advanced medical directives) are compatible with the Mental Health Act 2001 and any legislative change which may result from the current review of the 2001 Act (which is also ongoing).

From an international perspective, the 2013 Bill goes some way towards meeting certain international human rights standards, of which the CRPD is the most notable. In particular, the Bill's shift in emphasis from a 'bests interests' approach to one based on 'will and preferences'[160] has been welcomed in this regard[161] and interpreted as a significant move away from 'paternalism'.[162] In a similar vein, the *Interim Report of the Steering Group on the Review of the Mental Health Act 2001* asserted in 2012 that 'paternalism is incompatible with ... a rights-based approach and accordingly the [Mental Health Act 2001] should be refocused away from "best interests" in order to enhance patient autonomy'.[163] A similar approach has clearly been taken with the Assisted Decision-Making (Capacity) Bill 2013, presumably in the belief that this will increase compliance with the first principle of the CRPD, which is 'respect for inherent dignity, individual autonomy including the freedom to make one's own choices, and independence of persons'.[164]

The Irish proposals contrast sharply, however, with recent developments in neighbouring jurisdictions. In Northern Ireland, for example, the Mental Capacity Bill 2014 (which fuses mental health legislation and capacity legislation into a single bill) proposes, as a principle, that every 'act or decision must be done, or made, in the best interests of the person'.[165]

Section 6 of the Northern Irish bill goes on to provide detailed guidelines to prevent over-paternalistic interpretation of 'best interests', including a legal

---

159 Mental Health Act 2001, section 104.

160 Assisted Decision-Making (Capacity) Bill 2013, section 8(7)(b).

161 Shannon, 2013.

162 Costello, J., 'Bill on assisted decision-making will support the vulnerable', *Irish Times*, 2013, 29 July.

163 Steering Group on the Review of the Mental Health Act 2001, 2012; p. 11.

164 CRPD, article 3(a).

165 Mental Capacity Bill 2014, section 1(7).

requirement to 'take into account' the patient's (P's) 'past and present wishes and feelings (and, in particular, any relevant written statement made by P when P had capacity); (b) the beliefs and values that would be likely to influence P's decision if P had capacity; and (c) the other factors that P would be likely to consider if able to do so'. There is also a legal requirement to 'consult the relevant people about what would be in P's best interests' and 'take into account the views of those people' (if practicable).[166]

In England and Wales, the Mental Health Act 2007 introduced 'patient wellbeing and safety' as a principle[167] and the Mental Health (Care and Treatment) (Scotland) Act 2003 includes 'the importance of providing the maximum benefit to the patient' in its principles.[168] Scotland's Mental Health (Scotland) Bill 2014 does not propose changing this. By comparison, the Irish recommendations accord relatively little importance to the idea that acts taken under proposed mental health or capacity legislation must be reciprocated by a requirement that the best interests of the patient be central to all treatment and management decisions.

This is a regrettable omission, and it is not a minor issue. The history of psychiatry is replete with examples of various actors (state, private, medical) taking actions which were societally convenient and ostensibly in the interests of the mentally ill, but ultimately proved to be of questionable benefit or even harmful.[169] A clear requirement for benefit to the patient is a critical element in any mental health legislation that seeks genuinely to protect rights and, in the broader scheme, focus public, professional and political attention on the need for services that are effective and empowering for the mentally ill and those with impaired capacity.

This proposed shift also contrasts strongly with the apparently paternalistic provisions of the Irish Constitution,[170] which, arguably, serve as a means to ensure that the executive meets its welfare obligations towards citizens, including the mentally ill or incapacitated.[171] On this basis, the principle of 'best interests', if interpreted with care, is an important, empowering concept, especially for patients, families and carers who struggle daily with complex dilemmas.[172]

---

166 Mental Capacity Bill 2014, section 6(7).

167 Mental Health Act 2007, section 8.

168 Mental Health (Care and Treatment) (Scotland) Act 2003, section 1(3)(f).

169 Scull, 2005; Shorter, 1997; El-Hai, 2005.

170 Constitution of Ireland, article 40(3).

171 Kennedy, H., '"Libertarian" groupthink not helping mentally ill', *Irish Times*, 2012, 12 September.

172 Kelly, B.D., 'Progressive Bill on assisted decision-making offers real hope for families and carers', *Irish Times*, 2013, 28 October.

Ultimately, it is likely that, even following ratification of the CRPD, detailed observance of specific measures in it will vary significantly among signatory countries,[173] including Ireland. In her commentary on the 2013 Bill, the Minister of State for Disability, Equality and Mental Health emphasised that the Bill has the potential to bring about a culture change and facilitate greater independence in terms of decision-making capacity.[174] These are laudable goals, and the 2013 Bill certainly goes a considerable way towards achieving them. However, addressing the issues highlighted in this chapter, paying close attention to rigorous implementation, and a robust review of operation after five years would go even further to ensuring these potential benefits are realised in practice.

From a broader perspective, Ireland's Assisted Decision-Making (Capacity) Bill 2013 demonstrates not only the overall complexities and opportunities inherent in revising national legislation to increase accordance with the CRPD, but also the necessity to ensure that mental capacity legislation and mental health legislation interact in a logical fashion, and the importance of fundamental principles in the formulation and interpretation of legislation. The most dramatic feature of both reform processes in Ireland is the proposed omission of the 'best interests' principle from both the Mental Health Act 2001 and the new capacity legislation; this is attributable to both the arguably over-paternalistic interpretation of 'best interests' by the Irish courts (Chapter 2) and growing international influences on mental health law and policy in Ireland and elsewhere, especially the CRPD.

The CRPD was already explored in some detail in Chapter 4, so now other key international influences on law and policy will be explored in greater depth in the next chapter (e.g., EU, UN, WHO), which will examine key values underpinning human rights in mental health (with particular emphases on human dignity and human capabilities theory) and the relevance of the 'third wave'[175] of human rights in mental health law and policy. Following this, the final chapter, Chapter 7, summarises key arguments presented throughout the book, placing particular emphasis on the centrality of human dignity and the necessity to integrate mental health policy with legislation in order to provide meaningful protection and promotion of rights in practice. The closing chapter also presents overall conclusions stemming from the book, and outlines useful areas for future research.

---

173 Lewis, O., 'The expressive, educational and proactive roles of human rights', in McSherry, B., and Weller, P. (eds), *Rethinking Rights-Based Mental Health Laws* (pp. 97–128), Oxford and Portland, Oregon: Hart Publishing, 2010.

174 Lynch, 2013.

175 Klug, 2000; 2001.

Chapter 6
Human Rights and Mental Health Law: An Evolving Relationship

The European Dimension and Mental Health Policy

There is a diverse range of mental health traditions, policies and laws across Europe.[1] This diversity may account for the fact that the EU has become involved in mental health policy only relatively recently and, even then, in a gradual, incremental fashion.[2] The first significant EU involvement in this area to date occurred in 2005, when the Health and Consumer Protectorate Director-General of the European Commission published a Green Paper on mental health and launched a consultation process.[3] This led to the establishment of an EU 'Consultative Platform'[4] and, in 2008, the European Pact for Mental Health and Well-being, published by the EU with the WHO.[5]

The issue of human rights emerged as an especially important concern throughout this process, owing to both the existence of legal mechanisms whereby people with mental disorder may be detained in psychiatric facilities and evidence of social exclusion of the mentally ill.[6] The strong emphasis on human rights is consistent with the EU's involvement in others areas of law

---

1 Conrady, J., Roeder, T., 'The legal point of view', in Kallert, T.W., and Torres-González, F. (eds), *Legislation on Coercive Mental Health Care in Europe* (pp. 349–374), Frankfurt: Peter Lang, 2006.

2 Kelly, B.D., 'The emerging mental health strategy of the European Union', *Health Policy*, 2008, 85, 60–70.

3 Health and Consumer Protectorate Director-General. *Improving the Mental Health of the Population: Towards a Strategy on Mental Health for the European Union*, Brussels: European Commission, 2005.

4 Kelly, B.D., 'The emerging mental health strategy of the European Union', *Health Policy*, 2008, 85, 60–70.

5 EU, *European Pact for Mental Health and Well-Being*, Brussels: EU, 2008.

6 Gillon, R., *Philosophical Medical Ethics*, London: Wiley, 1997; Kelly, 2005; Pilgrim, D., 'New "mental health" legislation for England and Wales', *Journal of Social Policy*, 2007, 36, 79–95.

making,[7] including health law,[8] and the EU Charter of Fundamental Rights (2000). Against this background, the EU's European Pact for Mental Health and Well-Being places especially strong emphases on promoting social inclusion of the mentally ill and protecting human rights, including economic and social, as well as civil and political, rights.[9]

The EU's emphasis on human rights in mental health policy has remained consistent in the years since the European Pact for Mental Health and Well-Being was published in 2008. In September 2011, the EU published a paper presenting outcomes of the implementation of the European Pact for Mental Health and Well-Being, titled Mental Well-Being: For a Smart, Inclusive and Sustainable Europe.[10] This reported on the proceedings of five thematic conferences in each of the priority areas identified by the EU, between 2009 and 2011. The EU priority areas were depression and suicide (conference in Budapest, 2009), mental health of young people (Stockholm, 2009), mental health in work-places (Berlin, 2011), mental health of older people (Madrid, 2010) and social inclusion (Lisbon, 2010). These conferences all maintained the EU's emphasis on human rights as a key element in mental health policy and law in all of these contexts.[11] This emphasis has been clearly sustained and deepened since then.[12]

This emphasis on human rights in the context of health is consistent with the Universal Declaration of Human Rights which outlines a 'right to a standard of living adequate for … health and well-being … including food, clothing, housing and medical care and necessary social services'.[13] Similarly, article 12 of the UN's International Covenant on Economic, Social and Cultural Rights outlines a right to 'the enjoyment of the highest attainable standard of physical and mental health', to be advanced progressively.[14] The ECHR, by contrast, does not outline *any* rights to health or health-care, although, like the Universal

---

7 Hervey, T.K., McHale, J.V., *Health Law and the European Union*, Cambridge: Cambridge University Press, 2004; Jans, J.H., De Lange, R., Prechal, S., Widdershoven, R., *Europeanisation of Public Law*, Groningen: Europa Law Publishing, 2006.

8 Hervey & McHale (2004) identify rights as a key concern in the EU's involvement in health law (pp. 391–392) in relation to access to healthcare (p. 156) and health information privacy (pp. 163–166), among other areas.

9 EU, 2008.

10 EU, *Mental Well-Being: For a Smart, Inclusive and Sustainable Europe*, Brussels: EU, 2011.

11 EU, 2011; p. 13.

12 http://ec.europa.eu/health/mental_health/portal/index_en.htm (website verified, 30 May 2015).

13 Universal Declaration of Human Rights, article 25(1).

14 This text was drafted in the 1960s (Ishay, 2004; p. 224).

Declaration,[15] it does articulate certain other rights of particular relevance to *mental* health-care, including the right to liberty.[16] The emphasis on human rights in recent revisions of mental health law in England and Ireland is demonstrably consistent with both the ECHR and the EU's emphasis on rights. In England, this emphasis on rights finds particularly strong roots in the Human Rights Act 1998, implemented explicitly in order to give further effect to the ECHR,[17] and the Richardson Committee's emphasis on protecting and promoting rights through the Mental Health Act 2007, as well as public safety (Chapter 2).[18]

In Ireland, human rights were the *sole* key driver of reform, as reflected in the Human Rights Commission Act 2000 and European Convention on Human Rights Act 2003.[19] Regarding mental health law in particular, both the government[20] and the Law Society[21] acknowledged Ireland's non-compliance with the ECHR, and, in 2000, an Irish applicant argued in the European Court of Human Rights that the lack of an automatic, independent review of psychiatric detention breached ECHR rights (Chapter 2).[22] These developments contributed in large part to the emergence of the Mental Health Act 2001 and significant reform of Irish mental health services, with increased emphasis on rights.[23]

The EU's strong emphasis on human rights in *both* mental health law and policy merits particular attention, especially in light of the conclusion in Chapter 3 of this book that mental health legislation in England and Ireland provides robust protection for certain rights (e.g., right to liberty) but not others (e.g., economic and social rights). Does mental health *policy* have a particular role to play in protecting those rights which are not adequately protected through legislation?

A 'policy' is a principle or course of action proposed or adopted by a government, business, party or person.[24] *Mental health* policy is an especially broad term and may include matters relating to provision of mental health and social services, legal arrangements in relation to the mentally ill, and various

---

15 Universal Declaration of Human Rights, article 3.

16 ECHR, article 5.

17 Human Rights Act 1998, preamble.

18 Expert Committee, 1999; p. 120.

19 Bacik, 2001.

20 Department of Health, 1995; p. 13.

21 Law Reform Committee, 1999.

22 *Croke v Ireland* (2000) ECHR 680.

23 Mental Health Commission, *A Recovery Approach within the Irish Mental Health Services*, Dublin. Mental Health Commission, 2008

24 Pearsall & Trumble, 1996; p. 1120.

other activities aimed at promoting well-being, relieving suffering, controlling behaviour and responding to various kinds of distress, dysfunction and need.[25]

Mental health policy is, then, a complex concept, commonly involving multiple actors and layers of decision-making which can be difficult, if not impossible, to encapsulate fully.[26] In the midst of this complex matrix, however, it is readily apparent that mental health policy is inextricably linked with mental health legislation: like the EU, the WHO argues that mental health legislation is essential to reinforce and complement mental health policy, and provides an important legal framework for achieving policy goals.[27]

Legislation is especially important in the context of *mental* health owing to the long-standing existence of psychiatric institutions and specific legal arrangements between service-providers and service-users. This close relationship between law and policy can generate substantial tensions: as England's Mental Health Act 2007 evolved, for example, the Joint Parliamentary Scrutiny Committee on the English Mental Health Bill 2004 stated that the primary purpose of the legislation was to improve mental health services, while the government responded that its primary purpose was to bring people under compulsion.[28]

Consistent with these tight links between mental health policy and law, this book argues that, just as European-level factors (e.g., ECHR) have had a substantial influence on mental health *law* in England and Ireland (Chapters 2 and 3), so too are European-level actors (e.g., EU) starting to have similar influence on policy.[29] For the most part, this involvement in policy is strongly informed by human rights concerns: in 2011, for example, the EU reported on the 'EU Compass for Action of Mental Health and Well-Being',[30] an online resource aimed at influencing national mental health policy in directions outlined by the EU, with a strong emphasis on human rights in *both* law and policy.[31] Taken together, these various initiatives will hopefully increase consistency between law and policy, through a shared emphasis on human rights.

---

25 Rogers, A., Pilgrim, D., *Mental Health Policy in Britain (Second Edition)*, Basingstoke: Palgrave Macmillan, 2001; p. 226.

26 Lester, H., Glasby, J., *Mental Health Policy and Practice*, Basingstoke: Palgrave Macmillan, 2006; p. 18.

27 WHO, *Improving Health Systems and Services for Mental Health*, Geneva: WHO, 2009; p. 12.

28 Fennell, P., 'Mental health law: history, policy and regulation', in Gostin, L., McHale, J., Fennell, P., Mackay, R.D., and Bartlett, P. (eds), *Principles of Mental Health Law and Policy* (pp. 3–70), Oxford: Oxford University Press, 2010; p. 70.

29 Kelly, B.D., 'The emerging mental health strategy of the European Union', *Health Policy*, 2008, 85, 60–70.

30 http://ec.europa.eu/health/mental_health/eu_compass/index_en.htm (website verified, 30 May 2015).

31 EU, 2011; p. 18.

Increased EU involvement in mental health policy is consistent with the EU's broader engagement with general health policy at the national level, an increasing engagement which is mediated through both top-down and bottom-up approaches to shaping policy.[32] This has resulted in increased EU involvement in a broad range of health issues ranging from food safety[33] to bioethics,[34] and, increasingly, mental health law and policy.

Against this backdrop, it is possible that certain rights of the mentally ill which are poorly protected through mental health legislation (e.g., economic and social rights) might be more effectively addressed through mental health policy, which is also increasingly informed by human rights considerations, as emphasised by the EU and WHO. The position of voluntary patients, for example, is poorly addressed in current mental health legislation, which places strong emphasis on detained patients (Chapter 3). Perhaps a mental health policy that placed greater emphasis on the importance of effective mental health services for *all* patients would provide greater support for the economic and social rights and dignity of voluntary patients, who constitute the strong majority of those accessing mental health services.[35]

Protecting these economic and social rights of the mentally ill is an important task: there is strong evidence that people with mental illness in England, Ireland and elsewhere are at substantially increased risk of poverty, homelessness, unemployment, poor physical health and social exclusion, compared to those without mental illness.[36] This situation is attributable to both the historical exclusion of the mentally ill from full participation in society, and the fact that

---

32 Steffen, M., Lamping, W., Lehto, J., 'Introduction: the Europeanization of health policies', in Steffen, M. (ed.), *Health Governance in Europe* (pp. 1–17), London: Routledge, 2005; p. 6. See also: Hervey & McHale, 2004; McKee, M., MacLehose, L., Nolte, E., 'Health and enlargement', in McKee, M., MacLehose, L., and Nolte, E. (eds), *Health Policy and European Union Enlargement* (pp. 1–5), Berkshire, England: McGraw-Hill/Open University Press, 2004.

33 Clergeau, C., 'European food safety policies', in Steffen, M. (ed.), *Health Governance in Europe* (pp. 113–133), London: Routledge, 2005.

34 Lafond, F.D., 'Towards a European bioethics policy?', in Steffen, M. (ed.), *Health Governance in Europe* (pp. 152–173), London: Routledge, 2005.

35 Kelly et al., 2004; p. 67; McSherry, B., 'The right of access to mental health care: voluntary treatment and the role of law', in McSherry, B., and Weller, P. (eds), *Rethinking Rights-Based Mental Health Laws* (pp. 379–396), Oxford and Portland, Oregon: Hart Publishing, 2010.

36 Kelly, 2005; Scull, 2005; Kelly, B.D., 'Social justice, human rights and mental illness', *Irish Journal of Psychological Medicine*, 2007, 24, 3–4; p. 3. See also: Callard, F., Sartorius, N., Arboleda-Flórez, K., Bartlett, P., Helmchen, H., Stuart, H., Taborda, J., Thornicroft, G., *Mental Illness, Discrimination and the Law: Fighting for Social Justice*, Chichester: John Wiley and Sons, 2012.

people with mental illness occasionally lack capacity or opportunity adequately to assert their rights for themselves.[37]

These factors render it even more important that there are strong protections for all human rights, including economic and social rights, among the mentally ill. While both England and Ireland provide free legal representation to help protect the right to liberty for detained patients at appeals against detention, this representation is generally concerned only with the right to liberty (and, to a certain extent, treatment), and patients do not always benefit from legal representation or assertive advocacy in respect of other rights, such as economic and social rights.

As a result, while Chapter 3 demonstrated that mental health legislation provides protections for certain human rights (e.g., the right to liberty), and while other areas of law such as human rights law may provide protection for other rights (e.g., the right to life), there are still significant deficits in the protection of certain other rights among the mentally ill, such as economic and social rights, as envisioned by the WHO.[38]

This deficit might be remedied, at least in part, if the emphasis that the ECHR and EU place on human rights in law and policy was complemented by an emphasis on human dignity, a concept which is central to the CRPD but markedly absent from the processes leading to legislative reform in England and Ireland, and which receives scant attention in mental health legislation in both jurisdictions. As argued in Chapter 1, the enhancement of dignity is strongly linked with the opportunity to exercise human capabilities,[39] but the idea that mental health law might fundamentally aim to facilitate patients in exercising such capabilities does not feature significantly in either jurisdiction. While legislation in England and Ireland does provide free legal aid and advocacy services to certain patients (e.g., detained patients) in relation to specific matters (e.g., appealing detention orders), it does not provide robust support for exercise of capabilities more broadly (e.g., in relation to housing, employment, social participation, and various other issues of relevance to involuntary *and* voluntary patients).

Against the background of these deficits in mental health legislation, EU initiatives underpinning the importance of human rights in mental health *policy* are greatly to be welcomed. There is strong historical evidence to demonstrate the potential of policy and broad social change, rather than law, to effect transformational change in mental health services: in Ireland, for example, mental health legislation did not change significantly (in practice) between 1945 and 2006, and yet, between 1963 and 2003, the number of psychiatric inpatients

---

37 Sayce, 2000.

38 WHO, 2005.

39 Seedhouse and Gallagher, 2002; Nussbaum, 2011.

decreased by 81.5% (from 19,801 to 3,658).[40] This was a result of changes in policy and Irish society in general rather than law, and while it raises unresolved issues about access to treatment, it nonetheless demonstrates the power of mechanisms other than law to increase the liberty afforded to the mentally ill.[41]

That is not to suggest that legal protections of the right to liberty should be neglected, but rather that an exclusive focus on legal measures to protect the right to liberty alone fails to address or even acknowledge the broader range of social injustices and denials of rights commonly experienced by the mentally ill.[42] Other areas of public policy, such as social policy and equality policy,[43] may be well-suited to protecting some of these rights,[44] but mental health policy is now also recognised by the EU and WHO as a uniquely important vehicle for protecting and promoting rights among the mentally ill – and rightly so.

Findings from the analysis presented in this book, especially Chapter 3, confirm that economic and social rights, among others, are not adequately protected through mental health legislation alone. It is likely that mental health policy, informed by an awareness of human rights as outlined by the ECHR and EU, can help to remedy these deficits, and, most importantly, help promote the dignity and capabilities of involuntary *and* voluntary users of mental health services.

Key Values Underpinning Human Rights

Chapter 3 of this book presented a detailed consideration of mental health legislation in England and Ireland within a human rights-based framework, and the current chapter demonstrates the ongoing emphasis on human rights at the European level, in terms of both mental health law and policy. It is important

---

40   Kelly, B.D., 'Penrose's Law in Ireland: an ecological analysis of psychiatric inpatients and prisoners', *Irish Medical Journal*, 2007, 100, 373–374. 'Penrose's Law' suggests that as psychiatric inpatient populations decline, prison populations rise. In Ireland, the psychiatric inpatient population declined by 16,143 between 1963 and 2003, and the prison population rose by just 16.4% of this number (2,642); even if all of the increase in the prison population was attributable to discharged psychiatric patients, there was still a net 'liberation' of 13,501.

41   Department of Health, *The Psychiatric Services: Planning for the Future*, Dublin: Stationery Office, 1984. See also: Viney, M., 'Mental illness', *Irish Times*, 1968, 23–30 October.

42   Kelly, B.D., 'Social justice, human rights and mental illness', *Irish Journal of Psychological Medicine*, 2007, 24, 3–4; p. 3. See also: Callard et al., 2012; p. 185.

43   Sayce, 2000.

44   Alwan A., 'Foreword', in WHO, *Mental Health and Development* (p. vii), Geneva: WHO, 2010.

to emphasise, however, that rights-based approaches to any matter, including mental health-care, occur in specific social and political contexts, and these contexts may limit opportunity to articulate and observe such rights in practice. The legal observance of many civil rights, for example, requires relatively ready access to an independent court system.[45]

Mental health legislation may meet this requirement, at least in part, by ensuring access to mental health tribunals, free legal representation and advocacy,[46] but these measures presume the *existence* of an independent court system and *availability* of public resources to fund legal representation and advocacy for the underprivileged. On this basis, while human rights themselves may be 'universal',[47] the effectiveness of human rights-based approaches to specific issues, such as mental health care, relies on a set of assumptions which all societies may not meet; such as the existence of an independent court system, clear legislative provisions relating to mental illness, a certain standard of democratic governance and the (related) likelihood that human rights concerns will inform change.[48]

Many of these requirements reflect other human rights: the necessity for an independent court system, for example, is underlined in the ECHR, which states that 'in the determination of his civil rights and obligations or of any criminal charge against him, everyone is entitled to a fair and public hearing within a reasonable time by an independent and impartial tribunal established by law'.[49] In addition, 'everyone who is deprived of his liberty by arrest or detention' shall be entitled to 'take proceedings by which the lawfulness of his detention shall be decided speedily by a court'.[50] On this basis, the rights that mental health legislation may seek to protect (e.g., right to liberty) are inextricably linked with other rights (e.g., right to access a court system).

---

45 Osiatyński, 2009; p. 103.

46 In England and Ireland, detained individuals have free legal representation at mental health tribunals. In England, the Mental Health Act 2007 requires that the 'appropriate national authority shall make such arrangements as it considers reasonable to enable persons ('independent mental health advocates') to be available to help qualifying patients', although not all patients qualify (Mental Health Act 2007, section 30(2), amending Mental Health Act 1983, section 130A(1)).

47 Universal Declaration of Human Rights, preamble; Cassese, 1992.

48 Prins, H., 'Can the law serve as the solution to social ills?', *Medicine, Science and Law*, 1996, 36, 217–220; Richardson, G., 'Rights-based legalism: some thoughts from the research', in McSherry, B., and Weller, P. (eds), *Rethinking Rights-Based Mental Health Laws* (pp. 181–202), Oxford and Portland, Oregon: Hart Publishing, 2010; Rose, N., 'Unreasonable rights: mental illness and the limits of law', *Journal of Law and Society*, 1985, 12, 199–218.

49 ECHR, article 6(1).

50 ECHR, article 5(4).

The situation is rendered more complex in countries where a rights-based approach to mental health care may not rest easily with certain societal practices and cultural beliefs, especially countries with different cultural, professional and resource contexts than the socio-economically advantaged countries in which human rights discourse is most prevalent (e.g., UK, Ireland, US).[51] This emphasises the importance of human rights as *one element* within a broader approach to social justice, combined with political activity and social advocacy.[52]

As discussed in Chapter 1, the idea of dignity is central to the idea of rights,[53] and the idea of shared human capabilities is, in turn, central to the idea of dignity.[54] Dignity is, of course, important to *all* persons with mental disorder and not just the minority who are subjected to involuntary detention and treatment.[55] For the majority of patients, who engage *voluntarily* with mental health services, the key issue is *not* loss of dignity through violation of rights by mental health professionals or the state, but simple access to services.[56] An approach which recognises human dignity as a key value underpinning human rights permits a nuanced response to such a situation, aiming to achieve optimal observance of rights and, if not quite a *right* to medical care,[57] at least a reasonable expectation of a basic level of care consistent with human dignity.[58]

There may, however, be tensions between differing approaches to dignity in mental health settings, especially when the person in question lacks insight into his or her situation and temporarily lacks the capability to exercise his or her own rights or promote his or her own dignity.[59] For example, a person

---

51 Bartlett, P., 'Thinking about the rest of the world: mental health and rights outside the "first world"', in McSherry, B., and Weller, P. (eds), *Rethinking Rights-Based Mental Health Laws* (pp. 397–418), Oxford and Portland, Oregon: Hart Publishing, 2010; pp. 397–398; Fennell, P., 'Institutionalising the community: the codification of clinical authority and the limits of rights-based approaches', in McSherry, B., and Weller, P. (eds), *Rethinking Rights-Based Mental Health Laws* (pp. 13–50), Oxford and Portland, Oregon: Hart Publishing, 2010.

52 Bartlett, 2010; pp. 417–418.

53 Feldman, 2002; p. 130.

54 Feldman, 2002; p. 129.

55 Kelly et al., 2004; p. 67.

56 Petrila, J., 'Rights-based legalism and the limits of mental health law', in McSherry, B., and Weller, P. (eds), *Rethinking Rights-Based Mental Health Laws* (pp. 357–378), Oxford and Portland, Oregon: Hart Publishing, 2010; p. 377.

57 UDHR, article 25(1).

58 McSherry, B., 'The right of access to mental health care: voluntary treatment and the role of law', in McSherry, B., and Weller, P. (eds), *Rethinking Rights-Based Mental Health Laws* (pp. 379–396), Oxford and Portland, Oregon: Hart Publishing, 2010.

59 Insight is defined as the patient's degree of understanding and awareness that he or she is ill (Kaplan, H.I., Sadock, B.J., *Concise Textbook of Clinical Psychiatry*, Baltimore:

with schizophrenia who is untreated, homeless and shouting at passers-by on the street is, by most objective standards, in an undignified position, but the person may not perceive this indignity subjectively, owing to the effects of illness. A person *without* schizophrenia in a similar position is more likely to perceive his or her situation differently, experience subjective indignity, and take remedial action.

This situation highlights both conceptualisations of dignity outlined by Beyleveld and Brownsword; that is, 'dignity as empowerment' and 'dignity as constraint' (Chapter 1).[60] The idea of 'dignity as empowerment' focuses on advancing the person's autonomy, whereas 'dignity as constraint' reflects the idea that dignity can represent an objective value or good that reaches beyond the person and which, if violated, means that human dignity is compromised irrespective of whether the person agreed to perform the act in question.[61] If the person with mental disorder lacks insight into his or her situation, he or she may violate this shared, objective idea of dignity, possibly resulting in involuntary detention and treatment.

Feldman notes the importance of this objective aspect of dignity in people with incompletely formed or impaired mental capacity (e.g., young children, patients in vegetative states), especially in relation to the moral and, often, legal duty to have regard to their rights and interests when decisions are made regarding their welfare.[62] The objective conceptualisation of dignity may, however, be interpreted with excessive paternalism, and this, in turn, points to a broader problem with legislation-based solutions to problems experienced by persons with mental disorder who have reduced insight into their own mental state or behaviour: much of the law presumes that an autonomous and fully rational person is its subject, and this may not be the case for certain persons with mental disorder at certain times.[63]

Ireland has an especially strong tradition of this kind of 'paternalism' in mental health law, reflecting the emphasis that the Constitution of Ireland places on welfare-based concern for the vulnerable.[64] Consistent with this, the Irish Supreme Court makes it explicit that the Court should approach certain

---

Williams and Wilkins, 1996; p. 11).

60 Beyleveld & Brownsword, 2001; p. vii.

61 Beyleveld & Brownsword, 2001; p. 34.

62 Feldman, 2002; p. 127.

63 Weller, P., 'Lost in translation: human rights and mental health law', in McSherry, B., and Weller, P. (eds), *Rethinking Rights-Based Mental Health Laws* (pp. 51–72), Oxford and Portland, Oregon: Hart Publishing, 2010; pp. 71–72.

64 Constitution of Ireland, article 40(1) and (3). See also: Whelan, 2009; pp. 26–31.

medical matters 'from the standpoint of a prudent, good and loving parent'.[65] Against this background, some argue that Irish courts have interpreted the Mental Health Act 2001 with excessive paternalism, although this is by no means agreed (Chapter 2).

This explicit paternalism may, on the one hand, reflect the Irish state's constitutional obligation to protect the vulnerable,[66] but may also represent a disproportionately disempowering interpretation of the Constitution, at least in certain cases. In England, the tendency towards paternalism is less pronounced overall, and trends in this direction in England are generally attributable to public safety concerns rather than any perceived obligation to protect the vulnerable (Chapter 2). In both jurisdictions, however, there is clear difficulty achieving an optimal balance between measures fundamentally rooted in the advancement of patient autonomy and measures stemming from paternalistic or welfare-based concerns.

This difficulty may be addressed, at least in part, by mental capacity legislation which assumes a nuanced approach to mental capacity, facilitates careful evaluation of the person's capacity to make specific decisions, and offers supported decision-making procedures when they are needed.[67] Even in England, however, which has revised both its capacity and mental health legislation relatively recently, there is still evidence of significant paternalism in mental health law (Chapter 2), reflecting a real difficulty integrating the concepts of human rights, dignity, capabilities and welfare-based concerns in a balanced fashion that promotes both autonomy and dignity.

Any proposed solution to this dilemma that is based solely in mental health or capacity legislation will be subject to the intrinsic limitations of legal approaches to such problems; that is, requirements for an independent court system, financial resources to access courts, and certain standards of democratic governance. In addition, developing ever more detailed mental health or capacity legislation has the distinct demerit of expanding the remit and complexity of such legislatio,[68] and potentially reinforcing the discriminatory assumption that individuals with mental illness or impaired capacity are sufficiently dangerous as to require elaborate legislation in order to maintain public safety.[69]

---

65 *Re A Ward of Court (Withholding Medical Treatment) (No. 2)* [1996] 2 IR [1995] 2 ILRM 40; p. 99.

66 Kennedy, 2012.

67 In England: the Mental Capacity Act 2005. In Ireland: see Chapter 5.

68 Certain parts of the Mental Capacity Act 2005, as amended by the Mental Health Act 2007 (England), are undeniably long, complex and bureaucratic (Bowen, 2007; p. 150).

69 Campbell, T., Heginbotham, C., *Mental Illness: Prejudice, Discrimination and the Law*, Aldershot: Dartmouth Publishing Group, 1991; Campbell, T., 'Mental health law:

A further complexity associated with exclusively legal solutions to dilemmas relating to mental disorder or impaired capacity stems from the fact that not all human needs are best met through dedicated legal assurances of specific rights; many are much better met through alternative mechanisms of exchange or charity, and judicious political allocation of public resources.[70]

This situation is reflected, at least in part, in the rights-based analysis presented in this book: while revisions of mental health legislation in England and Ireland have resulted in stronger protections for the civil rights of the mentally ill, the greatest deficit is in the protection of social and economic rights *through mental health law* (Chapter 3). This supports the idea that mental health legislation may be best suited to the protection of 'negative rights' (e.g., prohibitions on torture and degrading treatment) rather than 'positive rights' (e.g., right to access health-care) for the mentally ill.[71]

In other words, while 'constitutional rights' may be suited to guaranteeing basic needs and protecting the vulnerable who are excluded from the political process,[72] other approaches, such as regulation and policy, are likely more suited to protecting other rights and addressing other needs.[73] This emphasis on human *needs* may be usefully complemented by an emphasis on human *nature*; that is, a combination of shared observations about the state of being human, including, for example, the existence of human needs *and* an individual sense of human dignity. This is consistent with the importance Nussbaum attaches to human capabilities,[74] which were discussed in Chapter 1 and are especially relevant in relation to dignity, but which were notably absent from the process of legislative reform in England and Ireland in recent years.

Broader recognition of these kinds of values (especially dignity and capabilities) would not only complement rights-based considerations of mental health care (such as that presented in this book) and help realise the 'general principles' of the CRPD,[75] but also acknowledge the intrinsically complex, multi-faceted nature of mental health care and decision-making.

---

institutionalised discrimination', *Australian and New Zealand Journal of Psychiatry*, 1994, 28, 554–559.

70 Osiatyński, 2009; p. 104.

71 Edmundson, 2004; Ishay, 2004; Hunt, 2007. ECHR principles have been evoked in relation to treatment, but while rulings indicate that treatment, when provided, must be based on medical necessity and in the patient's best interests (*R (PS) v Responsible Medical Officer* [2003] EWHC 2335 (Admin)), there is no automatic right to treatment (e.g., for an individual with untreatable personality disorder, detained on the basis of public protection) (*Hutchison Reid v UK* (2003) 37 EHRR 211).

72 Osiatyński, 2009; p. 142.

73 Osiatyński, 2009; p. 142.

74 Nussbaum, 1992; 2000; 2011.

75 UN, 2006, article 3; Kämpf, 2010; p. 150.

In the absence of this kind of broader recognition of the centrality of dignity and capabilities in protecting and promoting the rights of the mentally ill, at least some of the deficits in current legislation could still be addressed through relatively minor modifications of existing legal mechanisms. The examination of national mental health legislation in Chapter 3, for example, highlights deficits in 'oversight and review' procedures, related chiefly to the existing complaint mechanisms which lack the robustness recommended by the WHO (see Table 1, Appendix). Complaints mechanisms already exist in both English and Irish mental health services, but placing them on a stronger and more accountable footing would bring both jurisdictions into greater accordance with the WHO human rights standards.

Mental health tribunals represent another existing legal mechanism which might be modified to address some of these concerns and promote patient dignity and exercise of capabilities. The role of tribunals could, for example, be broadened to place greater emphasis on the involvement of carers, families and friends in treatment of mental illness and promotion of mental wellness.[76] As a result, reformed tribunals could offer enhanced opportunity to both protect basic rights and help shape treatment that is accessible, participative and sustainable.[77] This could be achieved through tribunals making non-binding treatment recommendations at the level of the individual and policy recommendations at the level of the institution, or providing opportunity for resolution of complaints, thus enhancing observance of other rights.[78]

This approach is consistent with the broader use of international human rights documents (such as the WHO checklist, explored in Chapter 3) to focus mental health laws more on positive rights of social participation,[79] with particular emphases on promoting dignity and autonomous exercise of capabilities by the mentally ill, not least through the provision of effective and acceptable treatments for mental disorder. The extent to which quite a wide

---

76 Carney, T., 'Involuntary mental health treatment laws: the "rights" and the wrongs of competing models?', in McSherry, B., and Weller, P. (eds), *Rethinking Rights-Based Mental Health Laws* (pp. 257–274), Oxford and Portland, Oregon: Hart Publishing, 2010; pp. 272–274.

77 Donnelly, M., 'Reviews of treatment decisions: legalism, process and the protection of rights', in McSherry, B., and Weller, P. (eds), *Rethinking Rights-Based Mental Health Laws* (pp. 275–298), Oxford and Portland, Oregon: Hart Publishing, 2010; p. 295.

78 Zuckerberg, J., 'Mental health law and its discontents: a reappraisal of the Canadian experience', in McSherry, B., and Weller, P. (eds), *Rethinking Rights-Based Mental Health Laws* (pp. 299–326), Oxford and Portland, Oregon: Hart Publishing, 2010; p. 326.

79 McSherry & Weller, 2010; p. 10.

array of state and non-state actors is relevant to this process is reflected further in the idea of a 'third wave' in human rights,[80] which is considered next.

Human Rights and Mental Disorder: The Third Wave

Klug describes the emergence of three 'waves' of rights over the past two centuries.[81] The first wave concerned concepts that emerged from the Enlightenment and focussed on civil and political rights. The second developed in response to the Second World War and focussed not just on protecting individuals from tyranny but also creating a sense of moral purpose for mankind and a fairer world for everyone, rooted in the concept of dignity. This was associated with increased emphasis on social and economic rights in the Universal Declaration of Human Rights[82] (the second generation of human rights) *and* an emergent emphasis on the achieving of equality between individuals, as opposed to simply equality before the law (a feature of the first wave).

Klug contends that there is now a third wave emerging, rooted in the concepts of mutuality or participation, with a broader range of actors increasingly seen as responsible for upholding rights (e.g., corporations, charities, private individuals) even if this is indirectly, through their governments.[83] This idea suggests that states are by no means the only or even the main potential abusers of power, and that rights may need to be upheld not only through law but also through persuasion, education, trade agreements and various other mechanisms.

In England, the Human Rights Act 1998 can, arguably, be construed as reflecting certain elements of this 'third wave'. For example, the Human Rights Act 1998 implicitly recognises the potential for bodies other than the state to infringe on human right, and makes it unlawful for public authorities in the UK to act in a way that is incompatible with the ECHR[84] (unless an act of Parliament dictates otherwise, in which case a 'declaration of incompatibility' can be made by a higher court).[85]

The extent of this provision is not entirely clear, however, owing to certain issues regarding the term 'public authority'. The term includes bodies such as courts, tribunals,[86] local authorities, NHS trusts and parole boards. Individuals,

---

80 Klug, 2000.

81 Klug, 2000; 2001.

82 UN, 1948.

83 Klug, 2001; p. 367.

84 Human Rights Act 1998, section 6(1).

85 Human Rights Act 1998, section 6(2).

86 Human Rights Act 1998, section 6(3)(a).

some of whose functions are of a public nature,[87] are 'public authorities' in respect of those activities only; doctors, for example, may be 'public authorities' in respect of public but not private patients.[88]

Difficulties with this distinction were highlighted in *R (Heather) v Leonard Cheshire Foundation*, in which a care home (in receipt of government funding and regulated by government) was deemed not to be a public authority for the purposes of the Human Rights Act 1998; the word 'public' being interpreted as meaning 'governmental'.[89] The law was amended in 2008 so that all private care homes are now covered by the Human Rights Act 1998.[90] This change is broadly consistent with Klug's suggestion that liability for protection of rights is broadening significantly.[91] It is notable that, in this instance, this is occurring through the will of parliament rather than the courts, arguably indicating significant governmental commitment to protecting human rights (at least at that time).

There is also evidence that this liability is substantial in magnitude, especially in the context of mental health care. As discussed in Chapter 2, the case of *Savage v South Essex Partnership NHS Foundation Trust*[92] involved the suicide of a detained patient who escaped from a mental health facility, and it was alleged that the NHS Trust had failed to protect the patient's ECHR right to life.[93] The House of Lords concluded that the NHS Trust indeed had a duty to reasonably protect psychiatric patients from taking their own lives.

In addition, it can be argued that the Human Rights Act 1998 exerts a 'horizontal effect' relevant to disputes between *private* parties, not by creating new rights in relation to private parties (direct horizontal effect) but requiring courts (which are public bodies) to act in accordance with the ECHR[94] (indirect horizontal effect).[95]

---

87 Human Rights Act 1998, section 6(3)(b).

88 Wadham et al., 2007; pp. 72–76.

89 *R (Heather) v Leonard Cheshire Foundation* [2002] EWCA Civ 366 [2002] 2 All ER 936. See also: *Aston Cantlow and Wilmcote with Billesley PCC Church Council v Wallbank* [2003] UKHL 37 [2004] 1 AC 546.

90 Health and Social Care Act 2008, section 145.

91 Klug, 2001; p. 367.

92 *Savage v South Essex Partnership NHS Foundation Trust* [2008] UKHL 74; *Savage v South Essex Partnership NHS Foundation Trust* [2010] EWHC 865 (QB). The UK Supreme Court later declared that this obligation can extend to voluntary patients, even when on home leave (*Rabone and Anor v Pennine Care NHS Trust* [2012] UKSC 2).

93 ECHR, article 2(1): 'Everyone's right to life shall be protected by law'.

94 Human Rights Act 1998, sections 6(1) and 8. In Ireland, by contrast, courts are not covered by the analogous provision of the European Convention on Human Rights Act 2003.

95 Morgan, J., 'Privacy in the House of Lords, Again', *Law Quarterly Review*, 2004, 120, 563–566. See: *Campbell v Mirror Group Newspapers Ltd.* [2004] UKHL 22,[2004] 2

Do these developments have particular relevance in the field of mental disorder and disability rights? In the first instance, O'Brien notes that the first UN convention of the twenty-first century, the CRPD, focused on the rights of disabled people and was consistent with the themes of social solidarity and interdependence in observance of rights, consistent with Klug's 'third wave'.[96]

People with mental disability and/or mental disorder are often engaged with a broad range of health and social care providers, including psychiatrists, nurses, social workers and various others, as well as, on occasion, mental health tribunals, lawyers and judges.[97] This diverse network of individuals and services has a substantive influence on the experiences of people with mental disorder and, in some cases, the extent to which they can enjoy both civil and political rights (e.g., right to liberty) as well as social and economic rights.

The majority of such actors are, however, agents of the state to greater or lesser degrees, and would be considered public bodies under the Human Rights Act 1998. Consistent with this, Carpenter argues that the 1998 Act still fundamentally belongs to the second wave of human rights; that is, it emphasises equality between individuals and strengthens anti-discrimination measure, but does not have *sufficient* regard for the diverse network of factors and actors which create the landscape in which rights are articulated, protected and/ or infringed.[98] Not least among these actors are people with mental disorder themselves, whose perspectives on their own rights provide an additional and vital dimension to the emergence of a meaningful third wave of human rights in this group, but whose voices are often ignored.[99]

In Ireland, these kinds of concerns about the rights of minority groups have tended to focus on a number of specific groupings, including the Irish 'travelling community',[100] migrants,[101] and people with mental disorder.[102] In 2004, Amnesty International drew particular attention to the position of people with mental disorder in Ireland, concluding that Ireland's mental health provisions and policy did not meet international best practice and human rights

---

AC 457 (HL).

96   O'Brien, N., 'Equality and human rights', *Political Quarterly*, 2008, 79, 27–35; pp. 31–32.

97   Gabbard, G.O., Kay, J., 'The fate of integrated treatment', *American Journal of Psychiatry*, 2001, 158, 1956–1963.

98   Carpenter, 2009; p. 223.

99   Lewis, 2009; Spander, H., Calton, T., 'Psychosis and human rights', *Social Policy and Society*, 2009, 8, 245–256.

100   Hughes et al., 2007.

101   Fanning, B., 'Racism, rules and rights', in Fanning, B. (ed.), *Immigration and Social Change in the Republic of Ireland* (pp. 6–26), Manchester and New York: Manchester University Press, 2007.

102   Kelly, 2001.

standards.[103] This book argues that the implementation of the Mental Health Act 2001 (between 2001 and 2006) has helped protect the rights of the mentally ill in Ireland to a significant extent, but that there are still areas of notable deficit (Chapters 2 and 3). A similar situation pertains in England, where the Mental Health Act 2007 has helped address some but not all human rights concerns.

The concept of a 'third wave' is of relevance here owing to its expansive recognition of the myriad actors involved in observing or violating rights. Persons with mental disorder, however, appear notably reliant on a broad range of *state* rather than *private* actors for the protection of rights, a situation they share with certain other groups whose rights are commonly the subject of concern, for example, children in care, migrants, prisoners.[104] Consistent with this, it is increasingly apparent that *all* actors engaged in 'functions of a public nature'[105] in England have quite substantial obligations to prevent violations of ECHR rights. Although welcome in terms of human rights protections, this situation is subject to the considerable caveat that judicial interpretations of the term 'functions of a public nature' in England are both complex and evolving.[106]

In Ireland, the analogous requirement that 'every organ of the State shall perform its functions in a manner compatible with the State's obligations under the Convention provisions'[107] is also limited by a relatively restrictive definition of 'organ of the State', which explicitly excludes courts.[108] Other aspects of this definition have not yet been comprehensively clarified in the Irish parliament or courts, so it remains unclear what, precisely, constitutes an 'organ of the State', although it is reasonable to assume that public health services, which provide the majority of mental health services in Ireland, constitute 'organs of the State'[109] and thus have a positive obligation to protect ECHR rights.

Overall, then, it is apparent that Klug's idea of a 'third wave' of human rights[110] has considerable significance in relation to the mentally ill, not least because individuals with mental disorder commonly experience discrimination and social exclusion at the hands of state *and* non-state actors alike,[111] and may

---

103   Amnesty International, *Amnesty International Report 2004*, London: Amnesty International Publications, 2004; p. 228.

104   Amnesty International, 2004.

105   Human Rights Act 1998, section 6(3)(b).

106   Wadham et al., 2007; pp. 72–76; R *(Heather) v Leonard Cheshire Foundation* [2002] EWCA Civ 366, [2002] 2 All ER 936; *Aston Cantlow and Wilmcote with Billesley PCC Church Council v Wallbank* [2003] UKHL 37 [2004] 1 AC 546.

107   European Convention on Human Rights Act 2003, section 3(1).

108   European Convention on Human Rights Act 2003, section 1(1).

109   Mullan, 2008.

110   Klug, 2000.

111   In relation to employment for example; 3% of people attending secondary mental health services in the UK are employed for 16 hours or more per week, compared

also lack the opportunity or support to challenge this discrimination in a robust or effective fashion.[112] Acknowledging the broad diversity of actors relevant to the violation or promotion of rights in this group is an important step forward in promoting dignity and the autonomous exercise of capabilities among the mentally ill.

Conclusions

This chapter examined three key themes which have informed the emerging emphasis on human rights in mental health law in England and Ireland over the past decade, have cropped up repeatedly throughout earlier chapters in this book, and are likely to continue to inform change in the future. These are: the European dimension to recent developments in human rights protections through mental health law and policy in England and Ireland (stemming especially from the ECHR and EU); key values underpinning human rights (especially dignity, human capabilities, and paternalistic or welfare-based concerns); and the potential relevance of a 'third wave' of human rights[113] in the context of mental disorder.

Regarding the European dimension of recent developments, the emphasis on human rights in the reform processes in both England and Ireland is consistent with the ECHR and the EU's emphasis on human rights in many areas of law and policy, including mental health. This reflects a broader convergence of national, European and global concern about the human rights of the mentally il, as reflected in the UN Principles for the Protection of Persons with Mental Illness and the Improvement of Mental Health Care[114] and WHO Resource Book on Mental Health, Human Rights and Legislation[115] (Chapter 3).

The EU places particular emphasis on the role of human rights in shaping mental health policy as well as law. This is consistent with the idea that mental health policy complements law in promoting the rights, dignity and capabilities of the mentally ill; mental health law already provides robust protections for certain rights (e.g., right to liberty) but not others (e.g., economic and social rights) (Chapter 3), and it is possible that mental health policy may be better

---

to 72.5% of the population as a whole (National Mental Health Development Unit, 2009). See also: Kelly, 2005; Kelly, B.D., 'The power gap: freedom, power and mental illness', *Social Science and Medicine*, 2006, 63, 2118–2128.

112 Kelly, B.D., 'The power gap: freedom, power and mental illness', *Social Science and Medicine*, 2006, 63, 2118–2128; Callard et al., 2012.

113 Klug, 2000; 2001.

114 UN, 1991.

115 WHO, 2005.

suited to the promotion of rights not adequately addressed through legislation, especially rights of particular concern to voluntary patients (e.g., access to treatment).

Given the EU's growing engagement with other areas of health policy and law, it is likely that the EU will increase its involvement in mental health policy in future years, further elaborating its emphasis on policy as a vehicle for advancing the rights of the mentally ill and, hopefully, promoting the dignity and autonomous exercise of capabilities in this group.

Regarding values underpinning human rights, it is readily apparent that protection of specific rights (e.g., right to liberty) is intrinsically linked with other rights (e.g., right to access a court system). The idea of dignity is central to all of these rights and critically important to voluntary and involuntary mental health patients alike. The fact that certain persons with mental disorder may have an impaired subjective sense of dignity has commonly contributed to paternalistic or welfare-based interpretations of mental health legislation; this trend is especially apparent in Ireland, where it also finds roots in the emphasis that Ireland's Constitution places on protecting the vulnerable.

As a result, both England and Ireland demonstrate real difficulty integrating the concepts of human rights, dignity, capabilities and welfare-based concerns in a balanced fashion that both ensures treatment and empowers patients. Law is not the only mechanism for addressing this dilemma, however, and solutions rooted in social or mental health policy, in addition to law, as recommended by the EU, are likely to help significantly. In addition, relatively minor adjustments to existing legal frameworks could also assist in further promoting rights and dignity. These adjustments could reasonably include strengthening complaints procedures in mental health services and altering the nature and purpose of mental health tribunals so as to promote broader participation, enhancement of dignity, and advancement of patients' exercise of their own capabilities.[116]

The idea of a 'third wave' of human rights[117] is also useful in this broader context, chiefly through its expansive recognition of the myriad actors involved in observing or violating the rights of the mentally ill. Persons with mental illness, however, similar to migrants, prisoners and certain other groups, are especially likely to be reliant on a broad range of *state* rather than private actors, including mental health and social services, tribunals and courts.

Most bodies engaged in such activities come under the remit of the Human Rights Act 1998 in England[118] and European Convention on Human Rights Act 2003 in Ireland, and have a resultant positive obligation to protect ECHR rights,

---

116 Zuckerberg, 2010.

117 Klug, 2000; 2001.

118 Subject to the caveat that judicial interpretations of the term 'functions of a public nature' in England are both complex and evolving.

with the notable exception of the courts in Ireland, which are not covered by this positive obligation.[119] Nonetheless, the recognition of a broad range of state and non-state actors as being relevant to human rights still makes the idea of the 'third wave' fundamentally important for the mentally ill, who commonly experience discrimination and social exclusion at the hands of state *and* non-state actors alike (see above), and may also lack the opportunity, resources or support to challenge this discrimination in a robust or effective fashion.[120]

Overall, the growing emphasis placed on the human rights of the mentally ill by national and trans-national bodies, the potential to modify mental health policy and existing legal mechanisms to enhance observance of dignity and rights, and the reliance of the mentally ill on myriad actors for the protection of rights, all converge on the importance of mental health law, human rights law *and* mental health policy in articulating and protecting the rights of the mentally il, as well as promoting their dignity and autonomous exercise of capabilities.

This situation, which is both complex and filled with possibility, is further explored in the final chapter of this book, which sets out overall conclusions and suggests useful directions for future work in this area.

---

119 European Convention on Human Rights Act 2003, sections 1(1) and 3(1).

120 Kelly, B.D., 'The power gap: freedom, power and mental illness', *Social Science and Medicine*, 2006, 63, 2118–2128; Callard et al., 2012.

Chapter 7
Conclusions:
Mental Disorder and Human Rights

Introduction

This book began by highlighting the plight of the mentally ill in early nineteenth-century Ireland, when a person with mental illness was likely to be consigned to 'a hole in the floor of the cabin, not high enough for the person to stand up in, with a crib over it to prevent his getting up. This hole is about five feet deep, and they give this wretched being his food there, and there he generally dies'.[1]

Two centuries later, in central London, a man with schizophrenia was found dead, with heart disease and hypothermia, in 'a dirty, damp and freezing flat, with mould growing on the floor and exposed electrical wires hanging off the walls. His boiler had broken, the bathroom ceiling had collapsed, and neighbours began to complain about the smell. His brother, Anthony Coombe, describing the scene as "squalor", said: "Even an animal couldn't have lived in that"'.[2]

This book focused on the two centuries between these two reports and examined two key questions. First, to what extent, if any, have human rights concerns influenced recent revisions of mental health legislation in England and Ireland? Second, to what extent, if any, have recent developments in mental health law in both jurisdictions assisted in protecting and promoting the human rights of the mentally ill?

Chapter 1 commenced by outlining the relationship between mental disorder and human rights and, from an historical perspective, argued that the history of the mentally ill is largely a history of social exclusion and denial of rights: while social and legal reforms relating to the mentally ill gathered pace throughout the nineteenth century, these often involved expansive institutional provision, associated with further denial of rights and erosion of dignity, rather than enhancing opportunity for autonomous exercise of capabilities. An approach to mental disorder informed explicitly by human rights only gathered strength

---

1 Committee of the House of Commons (of Great Britain, then including Ireland), quoted in Shorter, 1997; pp 1–2

2 Harding, 2010.

following the Universal Declaration of Human Rights[3] and ECHR,[4] and, in 1991, the UN's Principles for the Protection of Persons with Mental Illness and the Improvement of Mental Health Care.[5]

Three key concepts were explored in Chapter 1: human rights, human dignity and paternalism. Human rights are entitlements which one may legally or morally claim because one is a human being. Human dignity, which has both subjective and objective dimensions, results from the match between circumstances and capabilities: an individual experiences dignity if he or she is in circumstances which permit exercise of his or her capabilities.[6] This is consistent with Nussbaum's theory of human capabilities, which proposes that certain human capabilities are intrinsic to the definition of a 'human being'.[7] Paternalism is the claim by government or others to take responsibility for the welfare of a given individual. Ireland has a particularly strong history of paternalism in mental health law, stemming, at least in part, from the Irish Constitution's emphasis on the State's responsibility to protect its citizens and meet welfare obligations towards the vulnerable. The extent to which mental health law in England and Ireland is or is not disproportionately paternalistic recurs repeatedly through this book, and is linked with the ideas of both dignity and human rights.

Chapter 2 explored mental health legislation in England and Ireland and concluded that both England's Mental Health Act 2007 and Ireland's Mental Health Act 2001 introduced important reforms with clear potential to advance dignity and human rights, albeit with certain limitations and caveats. Chapter 3 examined the extent to which such legislation meets human rights standards as reflected in the *WHO Resource Book on Mental Health, Human Rights and Legislation.*[8] Areas of high compliance include definitions of mental disorder, involuntary treatment procedures, and offences and penalties. Areas of medium compliance relate to capacity and consent, oversight and review, and rules governing special treatments, seclusion and restraint. Areas of low compliance relate to promoting rights, voluntary treatment, vulnerable groups and emergency treatment. The greatest single deficit relates to economic and social rights which are not addressed substantively in the mental health laws of England or Ireland.

Overall, compliance with WHO standards is highest in areas of traditional concern in *asylum-based* mental health services (involuntary detention and

---

3 UN, 1948.
4 Council of Europe, 1950.
5 UN, 1991.
6 Seedhouse & Gallagher, 2002; p. 371.
7 Nussbaum, 1992; 2000; 2011.
8 WHO, 2005.

treatment) and lowest in areas of relevance to modern *community-based* mental health services (e.g., rights of voluntary patients, economic and social rights, rights to a minimum standard of care). Moreover, mental health legislation in both jurisdictions not only focuses on specific rights (e.g., right to liberty) to the virtual exclusion of certain others, but does so in a fashion commonly shaped by paternalism rather than autonomy. In England this situation stems primarily from the emphasis on public safety during the development of the Mental Health Act 2007, and in Ireland it stems from a long-standing welfare-based and paternalistic tradition in mental health law. If mental health legislation focussed more broadly on economic and social rights, as the WHO suggests, it might well remedy this situation by affording greater protection of dignity and promoting a broader array of rights and capabilities in areas other than strictly defined mental health care (i.e., in areas such as housing, employment and social participation, which are commonly problematic for the mentally ill).[9]

Chapter 4 examined the provisions of the CRPD[10], which is the most significant development in the field of mental disability, mental disorder and human rights in recent years. The CRPD is an important and empowering document for persons with disabilities, although it is not yet clear to what extent it applies to persons with mental disorder. It appears, nonetheless, to have significant implications for mental health legislation in England and Ireland in that it strongly discourages, if not precludes, *any* deprivation of liberty on the basis of disability. This is a dramatic change in the human rights landscape for people with mental disorder in England and Ireland and may have far-reaching effects for future revisions of mental health and capacity legislation in ratifying countries.

Chapter 5 went on to explore the revision of mental capacity legislation currently underway in Ireland, with specific focus on the Assisted Decision-Making (Capacity) Bill 2013, which proposes an entirely new legislative framework to govern decision-making by persons with impaired mental capacity. The 2013 Bill is clearly an important step forward in protecting and promoting the rights of individuals with disabilities. There are, however, several areas in need of clarification, stemming from both a series of specific issues in the Bill and the Bill's interaction with the Mental Health Act 2001 (which is also being revised).

From an international perspective, the 2013 Bill goes a considerable way towards meeting certain international human rights standards, of which the CRPD is the most notable. In particular, the Bill's shift in emphasis from a 'bests interests' approach to one based on 'will and preferences'[11] has been welcomed

---

9 Callard et al., 2012.

10 UN, 2006.

11 Assisted Decision-Making (Capacity) Bill 2013, section 8(7)(b).

in this regard[12] and interpreted as a significant move away from 'paternalism'.[13] This apparent shift contrasts strongly, however, with the emphasis on 'best interests' in the Mental Capacity Act 2005 in England and Wales,[14] and apparently paternalistic provisions of the Irish Constitution[15] which, arguably, serve as a means to ensure that the executive meets its welfare obligations towards citizens, including the mentally ill or incapacitated.[16] On this basis, the principle of 'best interests', if interpreted with care, is an important and empowering concept, especially for patients, families and carers who struggle daily with complex dilemmas.[17]

Chapter 6 drew together these and other key themes from the first five chapters of this book by focussing on three areas of relevance to recent and future developments in mental health law in England and Ireland. These are: the influence of European factors (e.g., ECHR, EU) on mental health legislation, case-law and policy; the interactions between the concepts of human rights, dignity, capabilities and paternalistic or welfare-based approaches to mental health law; and the relevance of a 'third wave' of human rights for the mentally ill.[18] This chapter concluded that the growing emphasis that both the ECHR and EU place on human rights in mental health law *and* policy could be usefully complemented by an emphasis on human dignity, a concept which is central to the CRPD but was markedly absent from the processes of legislative reform in England and Ireland, and receives scant attention in mental health legislation and policy in both jurisdictions.

This is regrettable: the enhancement of dignity is strongly linked with the opportunity to exercise human capabilities and autonomy, but the idea that mental health law might fundamentally aim to facilitate such autonomous exercise of capabilities does not feature sufficiently in mental health legislation in either jurisdiction. While legislation in England and Ireland does provide free legal aid and advocacy services to certain patients (e.g., detained patients) in relation to specific matters (e.g., appealing detention orders), it does not provide robust support for exercise of capabilities more broadly (e.g., in relation to housing, employment, social participation, or issues of particular relevance to voluntary patients).

Part of the solution may lie in further revisions to legislation and policy which emphasise not only rights at issue for detained patient, but also those

---

12 Shannon, 2013.
13 Costello, 2013.
14 Mental Capacity Act 2005, section 1(5); see also: Hughes, 2013.
15 Constitution of Ireland, article 40(3).
16 Kennedy, 2012.
17 Kelly, 2013.
18 Klug, 2000.

at issue for voluntary patients (e.g., rights to treatment, economic and social rights), which may be best addressed through policy (as recommended by the EU) rather than just through law.

Regarding the core values underpinning such reforms, it is readily apparent that both England and Ireland wrestle with the challenge of integrating the concepts of human rights, dignity, capabilities and welfare-based concern in an empowering, balanced fashion. Law is not the only mechanism for addressing this dilemma, however, and solutions rooted in social policy or mental health policy, in addition to law, are likely to help to a much greater extent in many important respects, in combination with relatively minor adjustments to existing legal frameworks (e.g., strengthening complaints procedures and altering the nature and purpose of mental health tribunals).

Such revisions of law or policy, especially looking at economic and social rights, could usefully take account of Klug's 'third wave' of human rights, owing the fact that certain persons with mental disorder have a relatively high level of reliance on a broad array of actors (chiefly but not exclusively state actors) for protection of rights and facilitating social participation.[19] Legislative requirements that public bodies act in accordance with ECHR rights go some distance towards ensuring that most actors affecting the lives of the mentally ill protect and promote their rights, but a greater overall emphasis on dignity and capabilities throughout law and policy would undoubtedly assist further, not least by simply acknowledging the broad array of state and non-state actors involved in promoting, protecting or violating the rights and dignity of the mentally ill.

What overall conclusions can be drawn from these arguments and discussions?

Key Conclusions

This book examined two key questions. First, to what extent, if any, have human rights concerns influenced recent revisions of mental health legislation in England and Ireland? Second, to what extent, if any, have recent developments in mental health law in both jurisdictions assisted in protecting and promoting the human rights of the mentally ill? The answers to these two questions are now considered, in turn.

---

19 Klug, 2000.

Human Rights Considerations Have Helped Shape Mental Health Legislation

The first key conclusion from this book is that human rights considerations have played significant and possibly even substantial roles in shaping recent revisions of mental health legislation in England and, especially, Ireland.

This is important: the history of society's treatment of the mentally ill demonstrates that the human rights of the mentally ill require special protection, not least because most jurisdictions have laws which permit involuntary detention and treatment of the mentally ill. This explains, at least in part, why mental health legislation provides relatively strong protection of the right to liberty in contrast to other rights: it is a legacy of the tradition of detention which dominates so much of the history of asylum-based psychiatry in England and Ireland.

The concepts of human rights and human rights law are critically important for addressing these matters,[20] and the analysis presented in Chapters 2 and 3 demonstrates that the evolution of mental health law in England and Ireland over the past six decades has been influenced strongly by human rights concerns mediated, in large part, through the ECHR and related case law. The WHO has also emphasised the importance of human rights in informing mental health legislation and policy.

In England, these rights-based considerations provided strong impetus for changes to mental health legislation. The Richardson Committee, advising on the new English legislation, was 'determined to include sufficient safeguards to ensure appropriate protection of the patient's individual dignity, autonomy and human rights'.[21] This concern with human rights was combined with concern about public safety, which also helped shape the Mental Health Act 2007, but, notwithstanding the strength of the public safety agenda, the influence of human rights concerns was still clearly apparent in the resultant legislation.

In Ireland, rights-based considerations dominated the reform debate single-handedly (Chapter 2) and remain the central driver of change today: when a review of the Mental Health Act 2001 was launched in 2011, the government emphasised the centrality of 'a human rights-based approach to mental health legislation'.[22] In 2012, the *Interim Report of the Steering Group on the Review of the*

---

20 Gable, L., Gostin, L., 'Human rights of persons with mental disabilities: The European Convention on Human Rights', in Gostin, L., McHale, J., Fennell, P., Mackay, R.D., and Bartlett, P. (eds), *Principles of Mental Health Law and Policy* (pp. 103–166), Oxford: Oxford University Press, 2010; p. 104.

21 Expert Committee, 1999; p. 44.

22 Culliton, G., 'Review of Act is to be built on "human rights"', *Irish Medical Times*, 2011, 27 May.

Mental Health Act 2001 confirmed that a 'rights-based approach to mental health law should be adopted'.[23] Overall, the growing emphasis on human rights in Ireland over the past twenty years has been central to the generally positive reform of mental health legislation introduced in the Mental Health Act 2001.

This is the first key conclusion from this book: human rights concerns clearly played a key role in recent revisions of mental health legislation in England and Ireland, and continue to do so. This is a welcome development, which plainly reflects growing recognition of the need to protect and promote the human rights of the mentally ill. There is, however, a need to examine not only how law is determined but also how law is implemented, because, as this book argues, there is strong evidence of possibly disproportionate paternalism and welfare-based approaches to the implementation and interpretation of mental health legislation in, for example, Ireland (Chapter 2). This topic, relating to the *outcome* of mental health law, is considered later in this chapter in the recommendations for future research.

In this context, the issue of paternalism in especially important because it reflects one of the key, recurring tensions in mental health law and services, which is evident repeatedly throughout this book: the need to renegotiate constantly the tensions between care and treatment on the one hand, and autonomy and liberty on the other.[24] This constant renegotiation involves not only mental health law, but also mental health policy, social policy and other areas of law (apart from dedicated mental health law). These matters are considered next, in relation to the second key conclusion of the present book.

Mental Health Legislation Protects Certain Human Rights

The second key conclusion of this book is that recent revisions of mental health legislation in England and Ireland protect some but not all of the human rights of the mentally ill. The strongest protections relate to the right to liberty: both jurisdictions are now highly compliant with WHO standards in relation to definitions of mental disorder and involuntary treatment, and moderately compliant in relation to systems for oversight and review, with the chief deficit in the latter area relating to deficient complaints procedures and *not* core processes for review of psychiatric detention per se (Chapter 3).

This high level of compliance is an especially recent development in Ireland: Ireland's Mental Health Act 2001, which introduced mental health tribunals for the first time, was only fully enacted in 2006. Prior to that, Ireland's Mental Treatment Act 1945 was in gross violation of international human rights standards, and was later declared unconstitutional. The situation in England

---

23 Steering Group on the Review of the Mental Health Act 2001, 2012; p. 11
24 Gostin et al., 2010; p. vi.

prior to its Mental Health Act 2007 was slightly better than in Ireland, but England's Mental Health Act 2007 still introduced several important advances in relation to protection of human rights, albeit with qualifications (Chapters 2 and 3).

The analysis presented in this book, however, demonstrates several areas of low compliance with WHO human rights standards, especially in relation to promoting rights, voluntary treatment and vulnerable groups. The greatest single deficit relates to economic and social rights which are not addressed substantively in the mental health laws of England or Ireland.

Interestingly, it is *not* the case that mental health legislation in England and Ireland tries and fails to protect rights in most of these areas. Rather, the legislation does not concern itself with these matters in the first instance, apart from some rather general statements of principle, especially in England.[25] For the most part, mental health legislation in both jurisdictions adequately protects rights *in areas addressed by the legislation*, which are generally the areas of traditional historical concern in asylum-based mental health services (i.e., involuntary detention and treatment).

Certain other areas which the WHO includes in its 'Checklist for Mental Health Legislation',[26] such as economic and social rights, are not addressed in any substantive fashion in mental health legislation in either England or Ireland. This prompts a question: *Should* such areas be addressed in mental health legislation at al, or are general legislative measures or policy initiatives sufficient to protect these rights amongst the mentally ill?

As discussed in Chapter 1, the historical experiences of the mentally ill, especially their increased rates of incarceration, indicate a need for dedicated, pro-active protection of human rights in this group. Efforts to meet this need have generally involved dedicated mental health legislation focussed on protecting the right to liberty, a right commonly and demonstrably at issue for certain persons with mental illness. This is consistent with an important role for mental health law in *protecting*, as opposed to just *not infringing*, certain rights, such as the right to liberty. In addition, of course, other areas of law, apart from dedicated mental health law, must also play a substantial role in protecting the rights of the mentally ill.

As discussed in Chapter 2, for example, the English Supreme Court, in 2012, found that an NHS Trust had breached its duty of care to a voluntary psychiatric inpatient who died by suicide while on leave home from a psychiatry unit in Stockport.[27] This case did not involve dedicated mental health legislation,

---

25 Mental Health Act 2007, section 8.

26 WHO, 2005.

27 *Rabone and Anor v Pennine Care NHS Trust* [2012] UKSC 2. See also: *Osman v UK* (2000) 29 EHRR 245; Bowcott, O., 'Hospital breached duty of care to psychiatric

but, rather, the ECHR and Human Rights Act 1998, demonstrating that rights protections for the mentally ill can be effective even if located in law other than dedicated mental health law. The *Rabone* case demonstrated this in relation to the right to life, but does it hold true for other rights? Do the protections of economic and social rights located in law other than dedicated mental health law (e.g., housing law) serve, in similar fashion, to protect the economic and social rights of the mentally ill?

Chapter 6 argued that, notwithstanding general legislation relating to equality, housing, and so forth, individuals with mental illness still experience difficulty availing of this legislation, resulting in increased rates of poverty, homelessness, unemployment, poor physical health and social exclusion. Chapter 6 went on to argue that mental health policy, especially if informed by human rights concerns (as recommended by the EU, among others), may assist with addressing deficits in relation to rights for the mentally ill. The experience of psychiatric de-institutionalisation in late twentieth-century Ireland, which found its roots in policy and broader social change rather than law, clearly demonstrates the potentially transformative effect of mechanisms other than law on patients' experiences of mental health services and enjoyment of liberty.

These arguments underline the second conclusion of this book: that the protection of human rights through dedicated mental health legislation alone is limited, and other mechanisms are highly relevant for human rights protections for the mentally ill. These mechanisms include areas of law other than mental health law (e.g., human rights law), mental health policy and social policy. Among these mechanisms, certain ones (e.g., human rights law) may be especially relevant to the protection of certain rights (e.g., right to life), while other mechanisms (e.g., mental health policy, social policy) may be more relevant to the protection of other rights (e.g., economic and social rights, and rights of particular relevance to voluntary patients).

In addition, a greater overall emphasis on dignity and capabilities throughout both law and policy would undoubtedly assist with the promotion of rights more broadly, not least by acknowledging the wide array of state and non-state stakeholders involved in protecting, promoting or violating the rights of the mentally ill, consistent with Klug's expansive vision of a 'third wave' in human rights [28] and the CRPD's emphasis on dignity. [29]

---

patient, supreme court rules', *Guardian*, 2012, 8 February; Madden, E., 'Important UK Supreme Court decision on human rights', *Irish Medical Times*, 2012, 18, 26. A similar positive obligation in relation to a *detained* patient who died by suicide was articulated by the House of Lords (*Savage v South Essex Partnership NHS Foundation Trust* [2008] UKHL 74); *Savage v South Essex Partnership NHS Foundation Trust* [2010] EWHC 865 (QB)).

28   Klug, 2000.
29   CRPD, article 1.

Useful Directions for Future Research

Future research about human rights protection for the mentally ill through mental health law in England and Ireland could usefully focus on the *outcomes* of mental health legislation in both jurisdictions; the relevance of concepts such as Klug's 'third wave' of human rights;[30] and the growing trans-national influences on national mental health law. To conclude, each of these areas is examined in turn.

The Outcome of Mental Health Legislation

The examination of human rights protection for the mentally ill through mental health law in England and Ireland presented in this book focused not only on the content of legislation but also, to a significant extent, on its outcome in case law, in order to demonstrate how the legislation works in practice. This element of the book is extremely important: regardless of the theoretical provisions of mental health law or policy, it is the lived experience of mental disorder that matters most to the mentally ill; that is, real-life service provision, social exclusion or denial of rights.[31] In other words, it is the *realisation* of human rights protections and experience of day-to-day justice that matter most to people with mental disorder and their families.[32]

For people with mental disorder, issues such as involuntary detention and levels of service provision have exceptionally profound effects on the kind of lives they can actually lead. With this in mind, it is imperative that the outcomes of revisions of mental health legislation are observed with greater care: the Mental Health Act 2007 (England) and Mental Health Act 2001 (Ireland) may have been strongly influenced by the ECHR and related case-law (as demonstrated in earlier chapters), but what are the real-life outcomes of these influences and reforms? Have they actually resulted in greater protection of human rights for the mentally ill on a day-to-day basis?

The analyses presented in Chapters 2 and 3 demonstrate that revisions of legislation in both jurisdictions occurred, at least in part, in response to human rights concerns and ECHR case-law, and that both jurisdictions are now generally compliant with WHO standards in key areas of traditional concern in asylum-based mental health services (i.e., involuntary admission and treatment). The most notable deficits relate to economic and social rights, which are not dealt with in any detail in the mental health laws of either jurisdiction and are

---

30 Klug, 2001.
31 Kelly, 2005.
32 Sen, 2009; p. 10.

of increasing relevance to the majority of mental health service-users (i.e., voluntary patients) in modern, community-based mental health services.

Again, however, *both* law and policy matter in relation to outcomes. As discussed in Chapter 6, for example, mental health legislation did not change significantly (in practice) in Ireland between 1945 and 2006 and yet, between 1963 and 2003, the number of psychiatric inpatients decreased by 81.5%, chiefly as a result of policy rather than legislative change, allied with broader changes across Irish society.[33] At individual level, the role of mental health legislation in relation to liberty is more readily apparent: in the first eleven months following full implementation of the Mental Health Act 2001, approximately 12% of detention orders examined by tribunals were revoked.[34]

These developments raise important research questions, many of which remain unanswered today. Does this apparently increased observance of the right to liberty impact negatively on access to treatment? Does it impact on public safety? Do those who are no longer inpatients access effective outpatient treatment and social services? Does their mental health deteriorate or improve? More research is needed on these kinds of outcomes following legislative change, in Ireland and elsewhere.

The 'Third Wave' of Human Rights in Mental Health

Future research could also usefully focus on the relevance of Klug's 'third wave' of human rights in the context of the mentally ill (Chapter 6).[35] People with mental disorder commonly find their lives shaped by not only mental health services and law, but also general health services, social services and societal attitudes. There is strong evidence that people with enduring mental disorder face challenges in all of these areas, which, along with the enduring stigma of mental illness, constitute a form of 'structural violence' which limits their participation in civil and social life, and constrains many to live lives shaped by discrimination, exclusion and denial of rights, by state and non-state actors alike.[36]

---

33 Kelly, B.D., 'Penrose's Law in Ireland: an ecological analysis of psychiatric inpatients and prisoners', *Irish Medical Journal*, 2007, 100, 373–374. See also: Viney, 1968; Department of Health, 1984.

34 McGuinness, I., 'Tribunals revoke 12 per cent of detentions', *Irish Medical Times*, 2007, 43, 3.

35 Klug, 2000; 2001.

36 Kelly, 2005; Kelly, B.D., 'The power gap: freedom, power and mental illness', *Social Science and Medicine*, 2006, 63, 2118–2128; Callard et al., 2012.

The broader network of responsibility for the protection of the rights of the mentally ill, articulated by Klug,[37] merits closer study, especially in relation to the positive obligation of public authorities to take reasonable measures to prevent violations of ECHR rights.[38] Is this positive obligation being met by all of the diverse authorities and agencies involved in shaping the lives of the mentally ill? How enforceable is this positive obligation, in real terms? Does the deficit in the protection of economic and social rights, identified in this book (Chapter 3), indicate that this positive obligation is not being met?

Trans-national Influences on National Mental Health Law

Future research could also usefully focus on the increased role of international bodies such as the EU and WHO in shaping mental health law and policy. Arguments and analyses presented in this book have demonstrated the role of the ECHR in shaping recent revisions of mental health law in England and Ireland (Chapters 2), the effect of WHO guidelines in shaping regulatory practice (Chapter 3), and the increasing role of the EU in mental health policy (Chapter 6). Greater research is needed, however, in order to elucidate more clearly the mental health policy-making processes within the EU and WHO, and their likely effects on national law and policy in member states.[39]

There is a particular need to identify the policy processes and values which underpin these developments, with particular reference to values such as human dignity[40] and capabilities[41] in the protection of the rights of the mentally ill. The rights-based analysis presented throughout this book demonstrates that mental health legislation in England and Ireland is now generally compliant with WHO standards in key areas of traditional concern (e.g., involuntary admission and treatment) but notable deficits remain in certain other areas, such as economic and social rights (Chapter 3).

Might approaches to both law and policy which are more clearly rooted in the concepts of dignity and capabilities help remedy these deficits (Chapter 6)? Do developments at the level of the EU, Council of Europe, WHO and UN support these values? Might approaches rooted in *both* mental health law and

---

37 Klug, 2001; p. 367.

38 Wadham et al., 2007.

39 Kelly, B.D., 'The emerging mental health strategy of the European Union', *Health Policy*, 2008, 85, 60–70; Callard, F., Rose, D., 'The mental health strategy for Europe: why service user leadership in research is indispensable', *Journal of Mental Health*, 2012, 21, 219–226.

40 Carozza, 2008; Klug, 2000; pp. 100–101; Osiatyński, 2009; p. 189.

41 Nussbaum, 1992; 2000; 2011.

policy reach the domains of human experience which mental health legislation alone fails adequately to address in both jurisdictions?

Finally, future research could also usefully examine legal and other mechanisms which have evolved in diverse societies to deal with the challenges presented to societies by individuals with severe mental disorder. More specifically, there is a need to examine comparatively the ways in which other jurisdictions, apart from England and Ireland, attempt to balance the need for treatment with the right to liberty, and the public's expectation of safety with the complex therapeutic decision-making required in individual cases of mental disorder.

Appendix
World Health Organization's 'Checklist on Mental Health Legislation': Ireland and England

Table 1   World Health Organization's 'Checklist on Mental Health Legislation': Ireland and England (World Health Organization, *WHO Resource Book on Mental Health, Human Rights and Legislation*, Geneva: World Health Organization, 2005).

Legislative issue			Ireland	England
A	Preamble and objectives	1a	Does the legislation have a preamble which emphasizes the human rights of people with mental disorders?	✗	✗
		1b	Does the legislation have a preamble which emphasizes the importance of accessible mental health services for all?	✗	✗
		2a	Does the legislation specify that the purpose and objectives to be achieved include non-discrimination against people with mental disorders?	✗	✓
		2b	Does the legislation specify that the purpose and objectives to be achieved include promotion and protection of the rights of people with mental disorders?	✗	✗
		2c	Does the legislation specify that the purpose and objectives to be achieved include improved access to mental health services?	✗	✗
		2d	Does the legislation specify that the purpose and objectives to be achieved include a community-based approach?	✓	✓
B	Definitions	1	Is there a clear definition of mental disorder/mental illness/mental disability/mental incapacity?	✓	✓
		2	Is it evident from the legislation why the particular term (above) has been chosen?	✗	✗
		3	Is the legislation clear on whether or not mental retardation/intellectual disability, personality disorders and substance abuse are being covered in the legislation?	✓	✓
		4	Are all key terms in the legislation clearly defined?	✓	✓
		5	Are all the key terms used consistently throughout the legislation (i.e., not interchanged with other terms with similar meanings)?	✓	✓
		6	Are all 'interpretable' terms (i.e., terms that may have several possible interpretations or meanings or may be ambiguous in terms of their meaning) in the legislation defined?	✓	✓
C	Access to mental health care	1	Does the legislation make provision for the financing of mental health services?	✗	✗
		2	Does the legislation state that mental health services should be provided on an equal basis with physical health care?	✗	✗

Legislative issue		(Table 1, continued)	Ireland	England
	3	Does the legislation ensure allocation of resources to underserved populations and specify that these services should be culturally appropriate?	✗	✓
	4	Does the legislation promote mental health within primary health care?	✗	✗
	5	Does the legislation promote access to psychotropic drugs?	✗	✗
	6	Does the legislation promote a psychosocial, rehabilitative approach?	✗	✗
	7	Does the legislation promote access to health insurance in the private and public health sector for people with mental disorders?	✗	✗
	8	Does the legislation promote community care and deinstitutionalization?	✓	✓
D	Rights of users of mental health services			
	1	Does the legislation include the rights to respect, dignity and to be treated in a humane way?	✓	✓
	2	Is the right to patients' confidentiality regarding information about themselves, their illness and treatment included?	✓	✗
	2a	Are there sanctions and penalties for people who contravene patients' confidentiality?	✗	✗
	2b	Does the legislation lay down exceptional circumstances when confidentiality may be legally breached?	✗	✓
	2c	Does the legislation allow patients and their personal representatives the right to ask for judicial review of, or appeal against, decisions to release information?	✗	✗
	3	Does the legislation provide patients free and full access to information about themselves (including access to their clinical records)?	✗	✗
	3a	Are circumstances in which such access can be denied outlined?	✗	✗
	3b	Does the legislation allow patients and their personal representatives the right to ask for judicial review of, or appeal against, decisions to withhold information?	✗	✗
	4	Does the law specify the right to be protected from cruel, inhuman and degrading treatment?	✓	✓
	5	Does the legislation set out the minimal conditions to be maintained in mental health facilities for a safe, therapeutic and hygienic environment?	✗	✗
	6	Does the law insist on the privacy of people with mental disorders?	✓	✗

Legislative issue *(Table 1, continued)*		Ireland	England
	6a	Is the law clear on minimal levels of privacy to be respected?	✗	✗
	7	Does the legislation outlaw forced or inadequately remunerated labour within mental health institutions?	✗	✗
	8	Does the law make provision for educational activities; vocational training; leisure and recreational activities; and religious or cultural needs of people with mental disorders?	✗	✗
	9	Are the health authorities compelled by the law to inform patients of their rights?	✓	✓
	10	Does legislation ensure that users of mental health services are involved in mental health policy, legislation development and service planning?	✗	✓
E Rights of families or other carers	1	Does law entitle families or other primary carers to information about the person with mental disorder (unless patient refuses the divulging of such information)?	✗	✓
	2	Are family members or other primary carers encouraged to become involved in the formulation and implementation of patient's individualized treatment plan?	✗	✗
	3	Do families or other primary carers have the right to appeal involuntary admission and treatment decisions?	✗	✓
	5	Does legislation ensure that family members or other carers are involved in the development of mental health policy, legislation and service planning?	✗	✓
F Competence, capacity and guardianship	1	Does legislation make provision for the management of the affairs of people with mental disorders if they are unable to do so?	✓	✓
	2	Does the law define 'competence' and 'capacity'?	✗	✓
	3	Does the law lay down a procedure and criteria for determining a person's incapacity/incompetence with respect to issues such as treatment decisions, selection of a substitute decision-maker, making financial decisions?	✓	✓
	4	Are procedures laid down for appeals against decisions of incapacity/incompetence, and for periodic reviews of decisions?	✗	✗
	5	Does the law lay down procedures for the appointment, duration, duties and responsibilities of a guardian to act on behalf of a patient?	✓	✓
	6	Does the law determine a process for establishing in which areas a guardian may take decisions on behalf of a patient?	✓	✓
	7	Does the law make provision for a systematic review of the need for a guardian?	✗	✗

Legislative issue	(Table 1, continued)		Ireland	England
G	Voluntary admission and treatment	8	Does law make provision for patient to appeal against appointment of guardian?	✓	✓
		1	Does the law promote voluntary admission and treatment as a preferred alternative to involuntary admission and treatment?	✓	✓
		2	Does the law state that all voluntary patients can only be treated after obtaining informed consent?	✗	✗
		3	Does law state that people admitted as voluntary mental health users should be cared for in a way that is equitable with patients with physical health problems?	✗	✗
		4	Does the law state that voluntary admission and treatment also implies the right to voluntary discharge/refusal of treatment?	✗	✗
		5	Does the law state that voluntary patients should be informed at the time of admission that they may only be denied the right to leave if they meet the conditions for involuntary care?	✗	✗
H	Non-protesting patients	1	Does law make provision for patients who are incapable of making informed decisions about admission or treatment, but do not refuse admission or treatment?	✗	✓
		2	Are the conditions under which a non-protesting patient may be admitted and treated specified?	✗	✓
		3	Does the law state that if users admitted or treated under this provision object to their admission or treatment they must be discharged or treatment stopped unless the criteria for involuntary admission are met?	✓	✗
I	Involuntary admission (when separate from treatment) and involuntary treatment (where admission and treatment are combined)	1a	Does the law state that involuntary admission may only be allowed if there is evidence of mental disorder of specified severity?	✓	✓
		1b	Does the law state that involuntary admission may only be allowed if there is serious likelihood of harm to self or others and/or substantial likelihood of serious deterioration in the patient's condition if treatment is not given?	✓	✓
		1c	Does the law state that involuntary admission may only be allowed if admission is for a therapeutic purpose?	✓	✓
		2	Does the law state that two accredited mental health care practitioners must certify that the criteria for involuntary admission have been met?	✓	✓
		3	Does the law insist on accreditation of a facility before it can admit involuntary patients?	✓	✓

Legislative issue *(Table 1, continued)*			Ireland	England
	4	Is the principle of the least restrictive environment applied to involuntary admissions?	✓	✓
	5	Does the law make provision for an independent authority (e.g., review body or tribunal) to authorize all involuntary admissions?	✓	✓
	6	Are speedy time frames laid down within which the independent authority must make a decision?	✓	✓
	7	Does the law insist that patients, families and legal representatives be informed of the reasons for admission and of their rights of appeal?	✗	✗
	8	Does the law provide for a right to appeal an involuntary admission?	✓	✓
	9	Does the law include a provision for time-bound periodic reviews of involuntary (and long-term 'voluntary') admission by an independent authority?	✗	✗
	10	Does the law specify that patients must be discharged from involuntary admission as soon as they no longer fulfil the criteria for involuntary admission?	✓	✓
J Involuntary treatment (when separate from involuntary admission)	1a	Does the law set out the criteria that must be met for involuntary treatment, including: Patient suffers from a mental disorder?	✓	✓
	1b	Does the law set out the criteria that must be met for involuntary treatment, including: Patient lacks the capacity to make informed treatment decisions?	✓	✓
	1c	Does the law set out the criteria that must be met for involuntary treatment, including: Treatment is necessary to bring about an improvement in the patient's condition, and/or restore the capacity to make treatment decisions, and/or prevent serious deterioration, and/or prevent injury or harm to self or others?	✓	✓
	2	Does the law ensure that a treatment plan is proposed by an accredited practitioner with expertise and knowledge to provide the treatment?	✓	✓
	3	Does the law make provision for a second practitioner to agree on the treatment plan?	✗	✗
	4	Has an independent body been set up to authorize involuntary treatment?	✓	✓
	5	Does the law ensure that treatment is for a limited time period only?	✓	✓
	6	Does the law provide for a right to appeal involuntary treatment?	✓	✓

Legislative issue	(Table 1, continued)		Ireland	England
		7	Are there speedy, time-bound, periodic reviews of involuntary treatment in the legislation?	✓	✓
K	Proxy consent for treatment	1	Does the law provide for a person to consent to treatment on a patient's behalf if that patient has been found incapable of consenting?	✓	✓
		2	Is the patient given the right to appeal a treatment decision to which a proxy consent has been given?	✓	✓
		3	Does law provide for use of 'advance directives'; if so, is term clearly defined?	✓	✓
L	Involuntary treatment in community settings	1	Does the law provide for involuntary treatment in the community as a 'less restrictive' alternative to an inpatient mental health facility?	✓	✓
		2	Are all the criteria and safeguards required for involuntary inpatient treatment also included for involuntary community-based treatment?	✓	✓
M	Emergency situations	1	Are criteria for emergency admission/treatment limited to situations where there is high probability of immediate and imminent danger/harm to self and/or others?	✗	✓
		2	Is there a clear procedure in law for admission/treatment in emergency situations?	✓	✓
		3	Does the law allow any qualified and accredited medical or mental health practitioner to admit and treat emergency cases?	✓	✓
		4	Does the law specify a time limit for emergency admission (usually no longer than 72 hours)?	✗	✗
		5	Does the law specify the need to initiate procedures for involuntary admission and treatment, if needed, as soon as possible after the emergency situation has ended?	✓	✓
		6	Are treatments such as ECT, psychosurgery and sterilization, as well as participation in clinical or experimental trials outlawed for people held as emergency cases?	✗	✗
		7	Do patients, family members and personal representatives have the right to appeal against emergency admission/treatment?	✗	✗
N	Determinations of mental disorder	1a	Does the legislation define level of skills required to determine mental disorder?	✓	✓
		1b	Does the legislation specify the categories of professionals who may assess a person to determine the existence of a mental disorder?	✓	✓
		2	Is the accreditation of practitioners codified in law, and does this ensure that accreditation is operated by an independent body?	✓	✓

Legislative issue	*(Table 1, continued)*		Ireland	England
O	Special treatments	1	Does the law prohibit sterilization as a treatment for mental disorder?	✗	✗
		1a	Does the law specify that the mere fact of having a mental disorder should not be a reason for sterilization or abortion without informed consent?	✗	✗
		2	Does the law require informed consent for major medical and surgical procedures on persons with a mental disorder?	✓	✓
		2a	Does the law allow medical and surgical procedures without informed consent, if waiting for informed consent would put the patient's life at risk?	✓	✓
		2b	In cases where inability to consent is likely to be long term, does the law allow authorization for medical and surgical procedures from an independent review body or by proxy consent of a guardian?	✓	✓
		3	Are psychosurgery and other irreversible treatments outlawed on involuntary patients?	✗	✗
		3a	Is there an independent body that makes sure there is indeed informed consent for psychosurgery or other irreversible treatments on involuntary patients?	✗	✓
		4	Does the law specify the need for informed consent when using ECT?	✓	✓
		5	Does the law prohibit the use of unmodified ECT?	✗	✗
		6	Does the law prohibit the use of ECT in minors?	✗	✗
P	Seclusion and restraint	1	Does the law state that seclusion and restraint should only be utilized in exceptional cases to prevent immediate or imminent harm to self or others?	✓	✗
		2	Does the law state that seclusion and restraint should never be used as a means of punishment or for the convenience of staff?	✓	✗
		3	Does the law specify a restricted maximum time period for which seclusion and restraints can be used?	✓	✗
		4	Does the law ensure that one period of seclusion and restraint is not followed immediately by another?	✗	✗
		5	Does the law encourage the development of appropriate structural and human resource requirements that minimize the need to use seclusion and restraints in mental health facilities?	✓	✗

Legislative issue	(Table 1, continued)		Ireland	England
	6	Does law lay down adequate procedures for use of seclusion and restraints including: who should authorize it; facility should be accredited; that the reasons and duration of each incident be recorded in a database and made available to a review board; and that family members/carers and personal representatives be immediately informed when the patient is subject to seclusion and/or restraint?	✓	✗
Q Clinical and experimental research	1	Does the law state that informed consent must be obtained for participation in clinical or experimental research from both voluntary and involuntary patients who have the ability to consent?	✗	✗
	2a	Where a person is unable to give informed consent (and where a decision has been made that research can be conducted): Does the law ensure that proxy consent is obtained from either the legally appointed guardian or family member, or from an independent authority constituted for this purpose?	✗	✓
	2b	Where a person is unable to give informed consent (and where a decision has been made that research can be conducted): Does the law state that the research cannot be conducted if the same research could be conducted on people capable of consenting, and that the research is necessary to promote the health of the individual and that of the population represented?	✗	✓
R Oversight and review mechanisms	1	Does the law set up a judicial or quasi-judicial body to review processes related to involuntary admission or treatment and other restrictions of rights?	✓	✓
	1a(i)	Does the above body assess each involuntary admission/treatment?	✓	✓
	1a(ii)	Does the above body entertain appeals against involuntary admission and/or involuntary treatment?	✓	✓
	1a(iii)	Does the above body review the cases of patients admitted on an involuntary basis (and long-term voluntary patients)?	✗	✗
	1a(iv)	Regularly monitor patients receiving treatment against their will?	✓	✓
	1a(v)	Authorize or prohibit intrusive and irreversible treatments (such as psychosurgery and ECT)?	✓	✓
	1b	Does the composition of this body include an experienced legal practitioner and an experienced health care practitioner, and a 'wise person' reflecting the 'community' perspective?	✓	✓

Legislative issue	(Table 1, continued)	Ireland	England
1c	Does the law allow for appeal of this body's decisions to a higher court?	✓	✓
2	Does the law set up a regulatory and oversight body to protect the rights of people with mental disorders within and outside mental health facilities?	✓	✓
2a(i)	Does the above body conduct regular inspections of mental health facilities?	✓	✓
2a(ii)	Provide guidance on minimizing intrusive treatments?	✓	✗
2a(iii)	Maintain statistics; on, for example, the use of intrusive and irreversible treatments, seclusion and restraints?	✓	✓
2a(iv)	Maintain registers of accredited facilities and professionals?	✗	✗
2a(v)	Report and make recommendations directly to the appropriate government minister?	✓	✓
2a(vi)	Publish findings on a regular basis?	✓	✓
2b	Does the composition of the body include professionals (in mental health, legal, social work), representatives of users of mental health facilities, members representing families of people with mental disorders, advocates and lay persons?	✗	✓
2c	Is this body's authority clearly stated in the legislation?	✓	✓
3a	Does the legislation outline procedures for submissions, investigations and resolutions of complaints?	✗	✗
3b(i)	Does the law stipulate the time period from the occurrence of the incident within which the complaint should be made?	✗	✗
3b(ii)	Does the law stipulate a maximum time period within which the complaint should be responded to, by whom and how?	✗	✗
3b(iii)	Does the law stipulate the right of patients to choose and appoint a personal representative and/or legal counsel to represent them in any appeals or complaints procedures?	✗	✗
3b(iv)	Does the law stipulate the right of patients to an interpreter during the proceedings, if necessary?	✗	✗

Legislative issue		(Table 1, continued)	Ireland	England
	3b(v)	Does the law stipulate the right of patients and their counsel to access copies of their medical records and any other relevant reports and documents during the complaints or appeals procedures?	✗	✗
	3b(vi)	Does the law stipulate the right of patients and their counsel to attend and participate in complaints and appeals procedures?	✗	✗
S Police responsibilities	1	Does the law place restrictions on the activities of the police to ensure that persons with mental disorders are protected against unlawful arrest and detention and are directed towards the appropriate health care services?	✓	✓
	2	Does the legislation allow family members, carers or health professionals to obtain police assistance in situations where a patient is highly aggressive or is showing out-of-control behaviour?	✓	✓
	3	Does the law allow for persons arrested for criminal acts, and in police custody, to be promptly assessed for mental disorder if there is suspicion of mental disorder?	✓	✓
	4	Does the law make provision for the police to assist in taking a person to a mental health facility who has been involuntarily admitted to the facility?	✓	✓
	5	Does legislation make provision for the police to find an involuntarily committed person who has absconded and return him/her to the mental health facility?	✓	✓
U Discrimination	1	Does the law include provisions aimed at stopping discrimination against people with mental disorders?	✗	✓
V Housing	1	Does the law ensure non-discrimination of people with mental disorders in the allocation of housing?	✗	✓
	2	Does the law make provision for housing of people with mental disorders in state housing schemes or through subsidized housing?	✗	✗
	3	Does the legislation make provision for housing in halfway homes and long-stay, supported homes for people with mental disorders?	✗	✗
W Employment	1	Does the law make provision for the protection of persons with mental disorders from discrimination and exploitation in the work place?	✗	✓
	2	Does the law provide for 'reasonable accommodation' for employees with mental disorders, for example, by providing for a degree of flexibility in working hours to enable those employees to seek mental health treatment?	✗	✗

Legislative issue	*(Table 1, continued)*		Ireland	England
	3	Does the law provide for equal employment opportunities for people with mental disorders?	✗	✗
	4	Does the law make provision for the establishment of vocational rehabilitation programmes and other programmes that provide jobs and employment in the community for people with mental disorders?	✗	✗
X Social security	1	Does legislation provide for disability grants and pensions for people with mental disabilities?	✗	✗
	2	Does the law provide for disability grants and pensions for people with mental disorders at similar rates as those for people with physical disabilities?	✗	✗
Y Civil issues	1	Does the law uphold the rights of people with mental disorders to the full range of civil, political, economic, social and cultural rights to which all people are entitled?	✗	✗
Z Protection of vulnerable groups (minors)	1	Does the law limit the involuntary placement of minors in mental health facilities to instances where all feasible community alternatives have been tried?	✓	✓
	2a	If minors are placed in mental health facilities, does the legislation stipulate that they should have a separate living area from adults?	✗	✗
	2b	If minors are placed in mental health facilities, does the legislation stipulate that the environment is age-appropriate and takes into consideration the developmental needs of minors?	✗	✓
	3	Does the law ensure that all minors have an adult to represent them in all matters affecting them, including consenting to treatment?	✗	✗
	4	Does the law stipulate the need to take the opinions of minors into consideration on all issues affecting them (including consent to treatment), depending on their age and maturity?	✗	✓
	5	Does legislation ban all irreversible treatments for children?	✗	✗
Protection of vulnerable groups (women)	1	Does legislation allow women with mental disorders equal rights with men in all matters relating to civil, political, economic, social and cultural rights?	✓	✓
	2a	Does the law ensure women in mental health facilities have adequate privacy?	✓	✗
	2b	Does the law ensure that women in mental health facilities are provided with separate sleeping facilities from men?	✗	✗

Legislative issue	*(Table 1, continued)*		Ireland	England
	3	Does legislation state that women with mental disorders should receive equal mental health treatment and care as men, including access to mental health services and care in the community, and in relation to voluntary and involuntary admission and treatment?	✗	✗
Protection of vulnerable groups (minorities)	1	Does legislation specifically state that persons with mental disorders should not be discriminated against on the grounds of race, colour, language, religion, political or other opinions, national, ethnic or social origin, legal or social status?	✗	✓
	2	Does the legislation provide for a review body to monitor involuntary admission and treatment of minorities and ensure non-discrimination on all matters?	✗	✗
	3	Does the law stipulate that refugees and asylum seekers are entitled to the same mental health treatment as other citizens of the host country?	✗	✗
AZ Offences and penalties	1	Does the law have a section dealing with offences and appropriate penalties?	✓	✓
	2	Does the law provide appropriate sanctions against individuals who violate any of the rights of patients as established in the law?	✓	✓

Notes:

- This table comprises the World Health Organization's 'Checklist on Mental Health Legislation' (World Health Organization, *WHO Resource Book on Mental Health, Human Rights and Legislation*, Geneva: World Health Organization, 2005).
- The table indicates whether legislation in Ireland and England meets (✓) or does not meet (✗) specific standards.
- See text for details and references in relation to individual standards (Chapter 3).
- This book focuses on civil detention, so standards which relate solely to mentally ill offenders (E4; T1-6) are omitted.

Bibliography

Adams, G.B., *The Origin of the English Constitution*, New Haven: Yale University Press, 1912.

Alwan, A., 'Foreword', in World Health Organization, *Mental Health and Development* (p. vii), Geneva: World Health Organization, 2010.

Amnesty International, *Amnesty International Report 2004*, London: Amnesty International Publications, 2004.

Ashcroft, R.E., 'Making sense of dignity', *Journal of Medical Ethics*, 2005, 31, 679–682.

Bacik, I., 'A human rights culture for Ireland?', in Bacik, I., and Livingstone, S. (eds), *Towards a Culture of Human Rights in Ireland* (pp. 1–45), Cork: Cork University Press in association with the Centre for Cross Border Studies (Armagh), 2001.

Bainbridge, E., Byrne, F., Hallahan, B., McDonald, C., 'Clinical stability in the community associated with long-term approved leave under the Mental Health Act 2001', *Irish Journal of Psychological Medicine*, 2014, 31, 143–148.

Baker, N., 'Psychiatrists seek to readmit patients released by tribunals', *Irish Examiner*, 2009, 7 April.

Bamrah, J.S., Datta, S., Rahim, A., Harris, M., McKenzie, K., 'UK's Mental Health Bill', *Lancet*, 2007, 370, 1029.

Barber, L., 'Spread of freedom leaves human rights court fighting fires', *Financial Times*, 2008, 19/20 April.

Barnes, J.-A., 'Mental health chief confident HSE will meet legal obligations', *Irish Medical News*, 2006, 40, 24.

Barnes, J.-A., 'Mental health tribunals cost €2.56m', *Irish Medical News*, 2007, 22, 12.

Barnes, J.-A., 'Red-letter day for mental health?', *Irish Medical News*, 2006, 41, 4.

Barrington, R., *Health, Medicine and Politics in Ireland 1900–1970*, Dublin: Institute of Public Administration, 1987.

Bartlett, P., *Blackstone's Guide to the Mental Capacity Act 2005*, Oxford: Oxford University Press, 2005.

Bartlett, P., 'Thinking about the rest of the world: mental health and rights outside the "first world"', in McSherry, B., and Weller, P. (eds), *Rethinking Rights-Based Mental Health Laws* (pp. 397–418), Oxford and Portland, OR: Hart Publishing, 2010.

Bartlett, P., 'Informal admissions and deprivation of liberty under the Mental Capacity Act 2005', in Gostin, L., McHale, J., Fennell, P., Mackay, R.D., and Bartlett, P. (eds), *Principles of Mental Health Law and Policy* (pp. 385–412), Oxford: Oxford University Press, 2010.

Bartlett, P., 'The United Nations Convention on the Rights of Persons with Disabilities and mental health law', *Modern Law Review*, 2012, 75, 752–778.

Bartlett, P., Lewis, O., Thorold, O., Mental Disability and the European Convention on Human Rights (International Studies in Human Rights, Volume 90), Leiden/Boston: Martinus Nijhofs, 2007.

Bartlett, P., McHale, J., 'Mental incapacity and mental health: the development of legal reform and the need for joined-up thinking', *Journal of Social Welfare and Family Law*, 2003, 25, 313–324.

Bartlett, P., Sandland, R., *Mental Health Law: Policy and Practice (Third Edition)*, Oxford: Oxford University Press, 2007.

Batty, D., 'Law "reinforced mental health stereotypes"' *Guardian*, 2008, 18 February.

Bernstein, R.A., Manchester, R.A., Weaver, L.A., 'The effect of visiting on psychiatric patients in a general hospital', *Community Mental Health Journal*, 1980, 16, 235–240.

Beyleveld, D., Brownsword, R., 'Human dignity, human rights, and human genetics', *Modern Law Review*, 1998, 61, 661–680.

Beyleveld, D., Brownsword, R., 'My body, my body parts, my property?', *Health Care Analysis*, 2000, 8, 87–99.

Beyleveld, D., Brownsword, R., *Human Dignity in Bioethics and Biolaw*, Oxford: Oxford University Press, 2001.

Beyleveld, D., Brownsword, R., Wallace, S., 'Clinical ethics committees: clinician support or crisis management?', *HEC Forum*, 2002, 14, 13–25.

Bhugra, D., Appleby, L., 'Mental illness, the law and rudeness', *Guardian*, 2008, 3 November.

Bindman, J., Maingay, S., Szmukler, G., 'The Human Rights Act and mental health legislation', *British Journal of Psychiatry*, 2003, 182, 91–94.

Bloch, S., Reddaway, P., *Soviet Psychiatric Abuse*, Boulder, CO: Westview Press, 1985.

Bluglass, R., 'The origins of The Mental Health Act 1983', *Bulletin of the Royal College of Psychiatrists*, 1984, 8, 127–134.

Blumenthal, S., Wessely, S., 'The cost of Mental Health Review Tribunals', *Psychiatric Bulletin*, 1994, 18, 274–276.

Bowcott, O., 'Hospital breached duty of care to psychiatric patient, supreme court rules', *Guardian*, 2012, 8 February.

Bowen, P., *Blackstone's Guide to the Mental Health Act 2007*, Oxford: Oxford University Press, 2007.

Brindle, D., 'A new act, but mental health battles remain', *Guardian*, 2007, 11 July.

Buchanan, A., Grounds, A., 'Forensic psychiatry and public protection', *British Journal of Psychiatry*, 2011, 198, 420–423.

Butcher, J., 'Controversial Mental Health Bill reaches the finishing line', *Lancet*, 2007, 370, 117–118.

Callard, F., Rose, D., 'The mental health strategy for Europe: Why service user leadership in research is indispensable', *Journal of Mental Health*, 2012, 21, 219–226.

Callard, F., Sartorius, N., Arboleda-Flórez, K., Bartlett, P., Helmchen, H., Stuart, H., Taborda, J., Thornicroft, G., *Mental Illness, Discrimination and the Law: Fighting for Social Justice*, Chichester: John Wiley and Son., 2012.

Campbell, T., 'Mental health law: institutionalised discrimination', *Australian and New Zealand Journal of Psychiatry*, 1994, 28, 554–559.

Campbell, T., Heginbotham, C., *Mental Illness: Prejudice, Discrimination and the Law*, Aldershot: Dartmouth Publishing Group, 1991.

Care Quality Commission, *How to Complain About a Health Care or Social Care Service*, Newcastle upon Tyne: Care Quality Commission, 2009.

Carey, P., *Data Protection (Third Edition)*, Oxford: Oxford University Press, 2009.

Carney, T., 'Involuntary mental health treatment laws: the "rights" and the wrongs of competing models?', in McSherry, B., and Weller, P. (eds), *Rethinking Rights-Based Mental Health Laws* (pp. 257–274), Oxford and Portland, OR.

Carolan, M., 'Psychiatric patient takes case against involuntary detention in hospital', *Irish Times*, 2008, 16 October.

Carolan, M., 'Woman's hospital detention ruled unlawful by court', *Irish Times*, 2008, 1 November.

Carozza, P., 'Human dignity and judicial interpretation of human rights: a reply', *European Journal of International Law*, 2008, 19, 931–944.

Carpenter, M., 'A third wave, not a third way?', *Social Policy and Society*, 2009, 8, 215–230.

Cass, E., Robbins, D., Richardson, A., *Dignity in Care*, London: Social Care Institute for Excellence, 2006.

Cassese, A., 'The General Assembly', in Alston, P. (ed.), *The United Nations and Human Rights: A Critical Appraisal* (pp. 25–54), Oxford: Clarendon Press, 1992.

Clergeau, C., 'European food safety policies', in Steffen, M. (ed.), *Health Governance in Europe* (pp. 113–133), London: Routledge, 2005.

Coid, J.W., 'The Christopher Clunis enquiry', *Psychiatric Bulletin*, 1994, 18, 449–452.

Collins, S., 'Emergency mental health law rushed through Dáil', *Irish Times*, 2008, 31 October.

Committee on the Rights of Persons with Disabilities, *Concluding Observations of the Committee on the Rights of Persons with Disabilities: Spain*, Geneva: United Nations, 2011.

Conrady, J., Roeder, T., 'The legal point of view', in Kallert, T.W., and Torres-González, F. (eds), *Legislation on Coercive Mental Health Care in Europe* (pp. 349–374), Frankfurt: Peter Lang, 2006.

Cooney, T., O'Neill, O., *Kritik 1: Psychiatric Detention: Civil Commitment in Ireland*, Delgany, Wicklow: Baikonur, 1996.

Costello, J., 'Bill on assisted decision-making will support the vulnerable', *Irish Times*, 2013, 29 July.

Coulter, C., 'Government and judge combine to clear up loophole', *Irish Times*, 2008, 1 November.

Coulter, C., 'Legal rights of mental health sufferers ignored', *Irish Times*, 2005, 1 November.

Council of Europe, *European Convention on Human Rights (Convention for the Protection of Human Rights and Fundamental Freedoms)*, Strasbourg: Council of Europe, 1950.

Council of Europe, *Recommendation (818) on the Situation of the Mentally Ill*, Strasbourg: Council of Europe, 1977.

Council of Europe, *Recommendation 1235 on Psychiatry and Human Rights*, Strasbourg: Council of Europe, 1994.

Council of Europe, *Recommendation R(83)2 of the Committee of Ministers to Member States Concerning the Legal Protection of Persons Suffering from Mental Disorder Placed as Involuntary Patients*, Strasbourg: Council of Europe, 1983.

Council of Europe, *White Paper on the Protection of the Human Rights and Dignity of People Suffering from Mental Disorder*, Strasbourg: Council of Europe, 2000.

Council of Europe, *White Paper Regarding a Draft Recommendation on Legal Protection of Persons Suffering from Mental Disorder*, Strasbourg: Council of Europe, 2000.

Council of Europe. *ETS 164 Convention on Human Rights and Biomedicine 4, IV*. Strasbourg: Council of Europe, 1997.

Court Service, *Office of Wards of Court*, Dublin: Courts Information Service, 2003.

Court, C., 'Clunis inquiry cites "catalogue of failure"', *British Medical Journal*, 1994, 308, 613.

Craven, C., 'Signs of paternalist approach to the mentally ill persist', *Irish Times*, 2009, 27 July.

Culliton, G., 'Review of Act is to be built on "human rights"', *Irish Medical Times*, 2011, 27 May.

Cummings, E., O'Conor, O., 'The SM judgment and the Mental Health Act 2008', *Irish Medical Journal*, 2009, 7, 234.

Curtice, M.J.R., 'Medical treatment under Part IV of the Mental Health Act 1983 and the Human Rights Act 1998', *Psychiatric Bulletin*, 2009, 33, 111–115.

Daly, A., Walsh, D., *HRB Statistics Series 15: Activities of Irish Psychiatric Units and Hospitals 2010*, Dublin: Health Research Board, 2011.

Daly, A., Walsh D., *HRB Statistics Series 25: Activities of Irish Psychiatric Units and Hospitals 2013*. Dublin: Health Research Board, 2014.

De Búrca, G., 'The drafting of the European Union Charter of Fundamental Rights', *European Law Review*, 2001, 26, 126–138.

Department for Constitutional Affairs, *The Mental Capacity Act Code of Practice*, London: The Stationery Office, 2007.

Department of Health, *The Psychiatric Services: Planning for the Future*, Dublin: Stationery Office, 1984.

Department of Health, *White Paper: A New Mental Health Act*, Dublin: The Stationery Office, 1995.

Department of Health, *Post-Legislative Assessment of the Mental Health Act 2007 (Cm 8408)*. London: The Stationery Office, 2012.

Department of Health and Children, *Review of the Operation of the Mental Health Act 2001*, Dublin: Department of Health and Children, 2007.

Department of Health and Social Security, *Better Services for the Mentally Ill. Cmnd 6233*, London: Her Majesty's Stationery Office, 1975.

Department of Health and Social Security, *Care in the Community. A Consultative Document on Moving Resources for Care in England*, London: Her Majesty's Stationery Office, 1981.

Department of Health and Social Security, *Mental Health (Hospital, Guardianship and Consent to Treatment) Regulations*, London: Her Majesty's Stationery Office, 1983.

Department of Health and Social Security, *Mental Health Act 2007 Explanatory Notes*, London: Her Majesty's Stationery Office, 2007.

Department of Health and Social Security, *Reform of Mental Health Legislation*, London: Her Majesty's Stationery Office, 1981.

Department of Health and Social Security, *Review of the Mental Health Act 1959*, London: Her Majesty's Stationery Office, 1975.

Department of Health and Social Security, *Royal Commission on the Law Relating to Mental Illness and Mental Deficiency. Cmnd 169*. London: Her Majesty's Stationery Office, 1957.

Dhanda, A., 'Legal capacity in the disability rights convention: stranglehold of the past or lodestar for the future?', *Syracuse Journal of International Law and Commerce*, 2007, 34, 429–461.

Division of Mental Health and Prevention of Substance Abuse (World Health Organization), *Guidelines for the Promotion of Human Rights of Persons with Mental Disorders*, Geneva: World Health Organization, 1996.

Division of Mental Health and Prevention of Substance Abuse (World Health Organization), *Mental Health Care Law: Ten Basic Principles*, Geneva: World Health Organization, 1996.

Donnelly, M., 'Reviews of treatment decisions: legalism, process and the protection of rights', in McSherry, B., and Weller, P. (eds), *Rethinking Rights-Based Mental Health Laws* (pp. 275–298), Oxford and Portland, OR: Hart Publishing, 2010.

Duggan, C., 'Dangerous and severe personality disorder', *British Journal of Psychiatry*, 2011, 198, 431–433.

Dworkin, R., *Life's Dominion*, London: Harper Collins, 1995.

Dyer, C., 'Ruling could free dozens of mentally ill offenders', *Guardian*, 2001, 29 March.

Dyer, J.A.T., 'Rehabilitation and community care,' i, Kendell, R.E., and Zealley, A.K. (eds) *Companion to Psychiatric Studies (Fifth Edition)* (pp. 927–941), Edinburgh: Churchill Livingstone, 1996.

Eastman, E., Peay, J., 'Bournewood: an indefensible gap in mental health law', *British Medical Journal*, 1998, 317, 94–95.

Edmundson, W., *An Introduction to Rights*, Cambridge: Cambridge University Press, 2004.

Eldergill, A., 'The best is the enemy of the good', *Journal of Mental Health Law*, 2008, May, 21–37.

El-Hai, J., *The Lobotomist*, Hoboken, NJ: Wiley and Sons, 2005.

Elliott, L., 'Mental health issues "cost UK £70bn a year", claims thinktank', *Guardian*, 2011, 11 February.

European Union, *European Pact for Mental Health and Well-Being*, Brussels: European Union, 2008.

European Union, *Mental Well-Being: For a Smart, Inclusive and Sustainable Europe*, Brussels: European Union, 2011.

Expert Committee, *Review of the Mental Health Act 1983*, London: Department of Health, 1999.

Expert Group on Mental Health Policy, *A Vision for Change*, Dublin: The Stationery Office, 2006.

Fadden, G., Bebbington, P., Kuipers, L., 'The burden of care', *British Journal of Psychiatry*, 1987, 150, 285–292.

Fanning, B., 'Racism, rules and rights', in Fanning, B. (ed.), *Immigration and Social Change in the Republic of Ireland* (pp. 6–26), Manchester and New York: Manchester University Press, 2007.

Fazel, S., Seewald, K., 'Severe mental illness in 33,588 prisoners worldwide: systematic review and meta-regression analysis', *British Journal of Psychiatry*, 2012, 200: 364–373.

Feldman, D., *Civil Liberties and Human Rights in England and Wales (Second Edition)*, Oxford: Oxford University Press, 2002.

Fennell, P., 'Institutionalising the community: the codification of clinical authority and the limits of rights-based approaches', in McSherry, B., and Weller, P. (eds), *Rethinking Rights-Based Mental Health Laws* (pp. 13–50), Oxford and Portland, OR: Hart Publishing, 2010.

Fennell, P., 'Mental health law: history, policy and regulation', in Gostin, L., McHale, J., Fennell, P., Mackay, R.D., and Bartlett, P. (eds), *Principles of Mental Health Law and Policy* (pp. 3–70), Oxford: Oxford University Press, 2010.

Fennell, P., *Mental Health: The New Law*, Bristol: Jordan Publishing, 2007.

Fenwick, H., *Civil Liberties and Human Rights (Fourth Edition)*, Oxon and New York: Routledge-Cavendish, 2007.

Ferriter, D., *The Transformation of Ireland 1900–2000*, London: Profile Books, 2004.

Finnane, P., *Insanity and the Insane in Post-Famine Ireland*, London: Croon Helm, 1981.

Fistein, E.C., Holland, A.J., Clare, I.C.H., Gunn, M.J., 'A comparison of Mental health legislation from diverse Commonwealth jurisdictions', *International Journal of Law and Psychiatry*, 2009, 32, 147–155.

Fitzsimons, K., 'Right to treatment should not be forgotten in psychiatry', *Irish Medical News*, 2007, 45, 4.

Foley, S., Kelly, B.D., Clarke, M., McTigue, O., Gervin, M., Kamali, M., Larkin, C., O'Callaghan, E., Browne, S., 'Incidence and clinical correlates of aggression and violence in patients with first episode psychosis', *Schizophrenia Research*, 2005, 72, 161–168.

Freeman, M., *Human Rights*, Cambridge: Polity Press, 2002.

Gabbard, G.O., Kay, J., 'The fate of integrated treatment,' *American Journal of Psychiatry*, 2001, 158, 1956–1963.

Gable, L., Gostin, L., 'Human rights of persons with mental disabilities: The European Convention on Human Rights', in Gostin, L., McHale, J., Fennell,

P., Mackay, R.D., and Bartlett, P. (eds), *Principles of Mental Health Law and Policy* (pp. 103–166), Oxford: Oxford University Press, 2010.

Gallagher, A., 'Dignity and respect for dignity – two key health professional values: implications for nursing practice', *Nursing Ethics*, 2004, 11, 587–599.

Gallagher, A., Seedhouse, D., 'Dignity in care: the views of patients and relatives', *Nursing Times*, 2002, 98, 38–40.

Ganter, K., 'Funding for Mental Health Act is a human rights issue', *Medicine Weekly*, 2005, 13, 26.

Ganter, K., Daly, I., Owens, J., 'Implementing the Mental Health Act 2001', *Irish Journal of Psychological Medicine*, 2005, 22, 79–82.

Gillon, R., *Philosophical Medical Ethics*, London: Wiley, 1997.

Goldman, H.H., 'Implementing the lessons of mental health service demonstrations: human rights issues', *Acta Psychiatrica Scandinavica*, 2000, 399 (suppl.), 51–54.

Gostin, L., Gable, L., 'The human rights of persons with mental disabilities', *Maryland Law Review*, 2004, 63, 20–121.

Gostin, L., McHale, J., Fennell, P., Mackay, R.D., Bartlett, P., 'Preface', in Gostin, L., McHale, J., Fennell, P., Mackay, R.D., and Bartlett, P. (eds), *Principles of Mental Health Law and Policy* (pp. v-viii), Oxford: Oxford University Press, 2010.

Gostin, L.O., *A Human Condition: The Law Relating to Mentally Abnormal Offenders. Observations, Analysis and Proposals for Reform. Volume 2*, Leeds: National Association for Mental Health (MIND), 1975.

Gostin, L.O., *A Human Condition: The Mental Health Act from 1959 to 1975, Volume 1*, Leeds: National Association for Mental Health (MIND), 1975.

Gray, J., *Liberalism*, Milton Keynes: Open University Press, 1986.

Gunn, J., 'Reform of mental health legislation', *British Medical Journal*, 1981, 283, 1487–1488.

Guruswamy, S., Kelly, B.D., 'A change of vision? Mental health policy', *Irish Medical Journal*, 2006, 99, 164–166.

Hall, I., Ali, A., 'Changes to the Mental Health and Mental Capacity Acts', *Psychiatric Bulletin*, 2009, 33, 226–230.

Hallaran, W.S., *An Enquiry into the Causes producing the Extraordinary Addition to the Number of Insane*, Cork: Edwards and Savage, 1810.

Harding, E., 'Acts of contradiction', *Guardian (Society)*, 2010, 31 March.

Häyry, M., 'Another look at dignity', *Cambridge Quarterly of Healthcare Ethics*, 2004, 13, 7–14.

Health and Consumer Protectorate Director-General, *Improving the Mental Health of the Population: Towards a Strategy on Mental Health for the European Union*, Brussels: European Commission, 2005.

Health and Social Care Information Centre. *In-patients Formally Detained in Hospitals under the Mental Health Act 1983 and Patients Subject to Supervised Community Treatment*. London: Health and Social Care Information Centre, 2013.

Helfer, L.R., 'Redesigning the European Court of Human Rights', *European Journal of International Law*, 2008, 19, 125–59.

Hervey, T.K., 'We don't see a connection: the "right to health" in the EU Charter and European Social Charter', in de Búrca, G., and de Witte, B. (eds), *Social Rights in Europe* (pp. 305–338), Oxford: Oxford University Press, 2005.

Hervey, T.K., Kenner, J. (eds), *Economic and Social Rights under the EU Charter of Fundamental Rights: A Legal Perspective*, Oxford: Hart Publishing, 2003.

Hervey, T.K., McHale, J.V., *Health Law and the European Union*, Cambridge: Cambridge University Press, 2004.

Hill, S., Pang, T., 'Leading by example', *Lancet*, 2007, 369, 1842–1844.

Hogan, G., Whyte, G., *J.M. Kelly: The Irish Constitution (Fourth Revised Edition)*, Dublin: Tottel Publishing, 2003.

Horowitz, A.V., *Creating Mental Illness*, Chicago: University of Chicago Press, 2002.

Hotopf, M., 'The assessment of mental capacity', in Jacob, R., Gunn, N., and Holland, A. (eds), *Mental Capacity Legislation: Principles and Practice* (pp. 15–32), London: RCPsych Publications, 2013.

Hughes, I., Clancy, P., Harris, C., Beetham, D., *Power to the People*, Dublin: TASC, 2007.

Hughes, J.C., 'Best interests', in Jacob, R., Gunn, N., and Holland, A. (eds), *Mental Capacity Legislation: Principles and Practice* (pp. 33–53), London: RCPsych Publications, 2013.

Hunt, L., *Inventing Human Rights*, New York and London: W.W. Norton and Company, 2007.

Information Centre, *In-patients Formally Detained in Hospitals Under the Mental Health Act 1983 and Other Legislation*, London: Information Centre/Government Statistical Service, 2007.

Inspectors of Lunatics, *The Forty-Second Report (With Appendices) of the Inspector of Lunatics (Ireland)*, Dublin: Thom & Co. for Her Majesty's Stationery Office, 1893.

Irish Human Rights Commission, *Annual Report 2006*, Dublin: Irish Human Rights Commission, 2007.

Ishay, M.R., *The History of Human Rights*, Berkeley and Los Angeles: University of California Press, 2004.

Jabbar, F., Kelly, B.D., Casey, P., 'National survey of psychiatrists' responses to implementation of the Mental Health Act 2001 in Ireland', *Irish Journal of Medical Science*, 2010, 179, 291–294.

Jacob, R., Fistein. E. 'Clinical ambiguities in the assessment of capacity', in Jacob, R., Gunn, N., and Holland, A. (eds), *Mental Capacity Legislation: Principles and Practice* (pp. 96–108), London: RCPsych Publications, 2013.

Jacob, R., Holland, A., 'Introduction', in Jacob, R., Gunn, N., and Holland, A. (eds), *Mental Capacity Legislation: Principles and Practice* (pp. 1–14), London: RCPsych Publications, 2013.

Jans, J.H., De Lange, R., Prechal, S., Widdershoven, R., *Europeanisation of Public Law*, Groningen: Europa Law Publishing, 2006.

Joint Committee on Justice, Defence and Equality, *Report on Hearings in relation to the Scheme of the Mental Capacity Bill*, Dublin: Houses of the Oireachtas, 2012.

Kämpf, A., 'Involuntary treatment decisions: using negotiated silence to facilitate change?', in McSherry, B., and Weller, P. (eds), *Rethinking Rights-Based Mental Health Laws* (pp. 129–150), Oxford and Portland, OR: Hart Publishing, 2010.

Kanter, A.S., 'The promise and challenge of the United Nations Convention on the Rights of Persons with Disabilities', *Syracuse Journal of International Law and Commerce*, 2007, 34, 287–321.

Kaplan, H.I., Sadock, B.J., *Concise Textbook of Clinical Psychiatry*, Baltimore: Williams and Wilkins, 1996.

Kelleher, D., *Privacy and Data Protection Law in Ireland*, Dublin: Tottel Publishing, 2006.

Kelly, B.D., 'Viewpoint: The Mental Health Act 2001', *Irish Medical Journal*, 2002, 95, 151–152.

Kelly, B.D., 'Mental health policy in Ireland, 1984–2004', *Irish Journal of Psychological Medicine*, 2004, 21, 61–68.

Kelly, B.D., 'Mental illness in nineteenth-century Ireland: a qualitative study of workhouse records', *Irish Journal of Medical Science*, 2004, 173, 53–55.

Kelly, B.D., 'Structural violence and schizophrenia', *Social Science and Medicine*, 2005, 61, 721–730.

Kelly, B.D., 'Irish mental health law', *Irish Psychiatrist*, 2006, 7, 29–30.

Kelly, B.D., 'The power gap: freedom, power and mental illness', *Social Science and Medicine*, 2006, 63, 2118–2128.

Kelly, B.D., 'Penrose's Law in Ireland: an ecological analysis of psychiatric inpatients and prisoners', *Irish Medical Journal*, 2007, 100, 373–374.

Kelly, B.D., 'Social justice, human rights and mental illness', *Irish Journal of Psychological Medicine*, 2007, 24, 3–4.

Kelly, B.D., 'The Irish Mental Health Act 2001', *Psychiatric Bulletin*, 2007, 31, 21–24.

Kelly, B.D., 'The emerging mental health strategy of the European Union', *Health Policy*, 2008, 85, 60–70.

Kelly, B.D., 'Mental health law in Ireland, 1945 to 2001: Reformation and renewal?' *Medico-Legal Journal*, 2008; 76, 65–72.

Kelly, B.D., 'Mental health law in Ireland, 1821–1902: building the asylums', *Medico-Legal Journal*, 2008, 76, 19–25.

Kelly, B.D., 'The Mental Treatment Act 1945 in Ireland: An historical enquiry', *History of Psychiatry*, 2008, 19, 47–67.

Kelly, B.D., 'The Mental Health Act 2001', *Irish Medical News*, 2009, 20, 29.

Kelly, B.D., 'Community treatment orders under the Mental Health Act 2007 in England and Wales: what are the lessons for Irish mental health legislation?', *Medico-Legal Journal of Ireland*, 2009, 15, 43–48.

Kelly, B.D., 'Mental health legislation and human rights in England, Wales and the Republic of Ireland', *International Journal of Law and Psychiatry*, 2011, 34, 439–454.

Kelly, B.D., 'Human rights and the obligation to prevent suicide', *Irish Times*, 2012, 23 July.

Kelly, B.D., 'Progressive Bill on assisted decision-making offers real hope for families and carers', *Irish Times*, 2013, 28 October.

Kelly, B.D., 'An end to psychiatric detention? Implications of the United Nations Convention on the Rights of Persons with Disabilities', *British Journal of Psychiatry*, 2014, 204, 174–175.

Kelly, B.D., 'Dignity, human rights and the limits of mental health legislation', *Irish Journal of Psychological Medicine*, 2014, 31, 75–81.

Kelly, B.D., 'The Assisted Decision-Making (Capacity) Bill 2013: content, commentary, controversy', *Irish Journal of Medical Science*, 2015, 184, 31–46.

Kelly, B.D., 'Mental capacity and participation in research', *Irish Medical Times*, 2014, 18, 20.

Kelly, B.D., Clarke, M., Browne, S., Gervin, M., Kinsella, A., Lane, A., Larkin, C., O'Callaghan, E., 'Clinical predictors of admission status in first episode schizophrenia', *European Psychiatry*, 2004, 19, 67–71.

Kelly, B.D., Lenihan, F., 'Attitudes towards the implementation of the Mental Health Act 2001', *Irish Journal of Psychological Medicine*, 2006, 23, 82–84.

Kennedy, H., '"Libertarian" groupthink not helping mentally ill', *Irish Times*, 2012, 12 September.

Kennedy, H., *The Annotated Mental Health Acts*, Dublin: Blackhall Publishing, 2007.

Kennedy, L., Ell, P.S., Crawford, E.M., Clarkson, L.A., *Mapping the Great Irish Famine*, Dublin: Four Courts Press, 1999.

Kessler, R.C., Üstün, T.B., *WHO World Mental Health Surveys*, Cambridge: Cambridge University Press, 2008.

Kettle, M., 'Britain must beware the dystopic drift towards a US-style judiciary', *Guardian*, 2012, 28 March.

Keys, M., *Annotated Legislation: Mental Health Act 2001*, Dublin: Round Hall, Sweet and Maxwell, 2002.

King's Fund, *Briefing: Mental Health Act 2007*, London: The King's Fund, 2008.

Kingdon, D., Jones, R., Lönnqvist, J., 'Protecting the human rights of people with mental disorder', *British Journal of Psychiatry*, 2004, 185, 277–279.

Kisely, S., Campbell, L.A., Preston, N., 'Compulsory community and involuntary outpatient treatment for people with severe mental disorders', *Cochrane Database of Systematic Reviews*, 2005, 3, CD004408.

Klug, F., 'The Human Rights Act – a "third way" or "third wave" Bill of Rights', *European Human Rights Law Review*, 2001, 4, 361–372.

Klug, F., *Values for a Godless Age: The History of the Human Rights Act and Its Political and Legal Consequences*, London: Penguin, 2000.

Knapp, M., 'Mental ill-health: cost implications', in Cooper, C.L., Field, J., Goswami, U., Jenkins, R., and Sahakian, B.J. (eds), *Mental Capital and Wellbeing* (pp. 515–527), Chichester, West Sussex: Wiley-Blackwell, 2010.

Lafond, F.D., 'Towards a European bioethics policy?', in Steffen, M. (ed.), *Health Governance in Europe* (pp. 152–173), London: Routledge, 2005.

Laing, J.M., 'Reforming mental health law and the ECHR', *Journal of Social Welfare and Family Law*, 2003, 25, 325–340.

Laing, J.M., *Care or Custody? Mentally Disordered Offenders in the Criminal Justice System*, Oxford: Oxford University Press, 1999.

Law Reform Commission, *Vulnerable Adults and the Law (LRC 83–2006)*, Dublin: Law Reform Commission, 2006.

Law Reform Committee, *Mental Health: The Case for Reform*, Dublin: The Law Society, 1999.

Lawson, A., 'The United Nations Convention on the Rights of Persons with Disabilities: new era or false dawn?', *Syracuse Journal of International Law and Commerce*, 2007, 34, 563–619.

Lawton-Smith, S., Dawson, J., Burns, T., 'Community treatment orders are not a good thing', *British Journal of Psychiatry*, 2008, 193, 96–100.

Leahy, T., 'Challenges with new mental health law', *Forum*, 2007, 24, 14–15.

Lee, G., 'Far from the madding crowd', *Law Society Gazette*, 2008, 6, 40–43.

Leonard, P., McLaughlin, M., 'Capacity legislation for Ireland: filling the legislative gaps', *Irish Journal of Psychological Medicine*, 2009, 26, 165–168.

Lester, H., Glasby, J., *Mental Health Policy and Practice*, Basingstoke: Palgrave MacMillan, 2006.

Letsas, G., *A Theory of Interpretation of the European Convention on Human Rights*, Oxford: Oxford University Press, 2007.

Lewis, L., 'Politics of recognition,' *Social Policy and Society*, 2009, 8, 257–274.

Lewis, O., 'The expressive, educational and proactive roles of human rights', in McSherry, B., and Weller, P. (eds), *Rethinking Rights-Based Mental Health Laws* (pp. 97–128), Oxford and Portland, OR: Hart Publishing, 2010.

Lord Goldsmith, Q.C., 'A charter of rights, freedoms and principles', *Common Market Law Review*, 2001, 38, 1201–1216.

Lynch, K., 'Balancing the scales of justice', *Irish Examiner*, 2013, 24 September.

Lynch, P., 'GPs in revolt over psychiatric admissions', *Irish Medical News*, 2007, 39, 1.

Lyons, F.S.L., *Ireland Since the Famine*, London: Fontana, 1985.

MacBride, S., 'The imperatives of survival,' in Abrams, I., and Frängsmyr, T. (eds), *Nobel Lectures: Peace, 1971–1980* (pp. 86–101), Singapore: World Scientific Publishing, 1997.

Madden, E., 'Important UK Supreme Court decision on human rights', *Irish Medical Times*, 2012, 18, 26.

Madden, E., 'Involuntary detention found admissible in the High Court', *Irish Medical Times*, 2007, 28, 20.

Madden, E., 'Judge commends action of hospital staff in detention', *Irish Medical Times*, 2008, 37, 28.

Madden, E., 'Section of Mental Health Act was unconstitutional', *Irish Medical Times*, 2009, 30, 15.

Madden, E., 'Supreme Court critical of case taken against St Vincent's Hospital', *Irish Medical Times*, 2009, 28, 18.

Madden, E., 'Supreme Court rules on Mental Health Act', *Irish Medical Times*, 2008, 22, 26.

Madden, E., 'Important UK Supreme Court decision on human rights', *Irish Medical Times*, 2012, 18, 26.

Mandelstam, M., *Community Care Practice and the Law (Third Edition)*, London: Jessica Kingsley Publishers, 2005.

Maritain, J., *The Rights of Man and Natural Law*, New York: Charles Scribner's Sons, 1951.

McGuinness, I., 'Consultants not to apply for mental health tribunal positions', *Irish Medical Times*, 2005, 10, 1.

McGuinness, I., 'Litany of failures', *Irish Medical News*, 2007, 6, 1.

McGuinness, I., 'More court appeals', *Irish Medical Times*, 2007, 24, 3.

McGuinness, I., 'Penny-pinching delays', *Irish Medical Times*, 2007, 25, 1.

McGuinness, I., 'Tribunals revoke 12 per cent of detentions', *Irish Medical Times*, 2007, 43, 3.

McGuinness, I., 'Tribunals to decide on legal representation', *Irish Medical Times*, 2006, 45, 1.

McHale, J., 'Fundamental rights and health care', in Mossialos, E., Permanand, G., Baeten, R., and Hervey, T. (eds), *Health Systems Governance in Europe: The Role of EU Law and Policy* (pp. 282–314), Cambridge: Cambridge University Press, 2009.

McHale, J., Fox, M., Gunn, M., Wilkinson, S., *Health Care Law: Text and Materials (Second Edition)*, London: Sweet and Maxwell, 2006.

McKee, M., MacLehose, L., Nolte, E., 'Health and enlargement', in McKee, M., MacLehose, L., and Nolte, E. (eds), *Health Policy and European Union Enlargement* (pp. 1–5), Berkshire, England: McGraw-Hill/Open University Press, 2004.

McSherry, B., 'The right of access to mental health care: voluntary treatment and the role of law', in McSherry, B., and Weller, P. (eds), *Rethinking Rights-Based Mental Health Laws* (pp. 379–396), Oxford and Portland, OR: Hart Publishing, 2010.

McSherry, B., Weller, P., 'Rethinking rights-based mental health laws', in McSherry, B., and Weller, P. (eds), *Rethinking Rights-Based Mental Health Laws* (pp. 3–10), Oxford and Portland, OR: Hart Publishing, 2010.

Medical Council, *Guide to Professional Conduct and Ethics for Registered Practitioners (Seventh Edition)*, Dublin: Medical Council, 2009.

Menéndez, A.J., 'Chartering Europe: legal status and policy implications of the Charter of Fundamental Rights of the European Union', *Journal of Common Market Studies*, 2002, 40, 471–490.

Mental Health Act Commission, *Placed Amongst Strangers*, London: The Stationery Office, 2003.

Mental Health Alliance, *Mental Health Act 2007: Report Stage Briefing, House of Commons*, London: Mental Health Alliance, 2006.

Mental Health Commission, *A Recovery Approach Within the Irish Mental Health Services*, Dublin: Mental Health Commission, 2008.

Mental Health Commission, *Code of Practice on the Use of Physical Restraint in Approved Centres*, Dublin: Mental Health Commission, 2009.

Mental Health Commission, *Code of Practice Relating to Admission of Children under the Mental Health Act 2001*, Dublin: Mental Health Commission, 2006.

Mental Health Commission, *Report on the Operation of Part 2 of the Mental Health Act 2001*, Dublin: Mental Health Commission, 2008.

Mental Health Commission, *Report on the Use of Electroconvulsive Therapy in Approved Centres in 2008*, Dublin: Mental Health Commission, 2009.

Mental Health Commission, *Report on the Use of Seclusion, Mechanical Means of Bodily Restraint and Physical Restraint in Approved Centres in 2008*, Dublin: Mental Health Commission, 2009.

Mental Health Commission, *Rules Governing the Use of Electro-Convulsive Therapy*, Dublin: Mental Health Commission, 2009.

Mental Health Commission, *Rules Governing the Use of Seclusion and Mechanical Means of Bodily Restraint*, Dublin: Mental Health Commission, 2009.

Mental Health Subcommittee, 'Advising a mentally disordered client', *Law Society Gazette*, 2009, 103, 44–45.

Millon, T., *Masters of the Mind*, Hoboken, New Jersey: John Wiley & Son, 2004.

Mills, S., 'The Mental Health Act 2001', *Irish Psychiatrist*, 2004, 5, 49–55.

Minkowitz, T., 'The United Nations Convention on the Rights of Persons with Disabilities and the right to be free from non-consensual psychiatric interventions', *Syracuse Journal of International Law and Commerce*, 2007, 34, 405–428.

Minkowitz, T., 'Abolishing mental health laws to comply with the Convention on the Rights of Persons with Disabilities', in McSherry, B., and Weller, P. (eds), *Rethinking Rights-Based Mental Health Laws* (pp. 151–177), Oxford and Portland, OR: Hart Publishing, 2010.

Mollica, R.F., 'From asylum to community', *New England Journal of Medicine*, 1983, 308, 367–373.

Moncrieff, J., 'The politics of a new Mental Health Act', *British Journal of Psychiatry*, 2003, 183, 8–9.

Morgan, J., 'Privacy in the House of Lords, Again', *Law Quarterly Review*, 2004, 120, 563–566.

Morris, F., 'Mental health law after *Bournewood*', *Journal of Mental Health Law*, 1999, February, 41–47.

Morsink, J., *The Universal Declaration of Human Rights*, Philadelphia: University of Pennsylvania Press, 1999.

Mudiwa, L., 'Ireland signs WHO declaration on mental health', *Medicine Weekly*, 2005, 3, 18.

Mulholland, C., *A Socialist History of the NHS*, Saarbrücken: VDM Verlag, 2009.

Mulholland, P., 'ECT amendment proposal sent to the government', *Irish Medical News*, 2010, 35, 3.

Mullan, G., 'Incorporation of the ECHR into Irish law', in Moriarity, B., and Massa, E. (eds), *Human Rights Law (Second Edition)* (pp. 69–81), Oxford: Oxford University Press/Law Society of Ireland, 2008.

Munro, R., *Dangerous Minds*, New York: Human Rights Watch and Geneva Initiative on Psychiatry, 2002.

National Institute for Clinical Excellence, *Guidance on the Use of Electroconvulsive Therapy (Update: May 2010).* London: National Institute for Clinical Excellence, 2010.

National Mental Health Development Unit, *Work, Recovery and Inclusion*, London: National Mental Health Development Unit, 2009.

Neier, A., 'Social and economic rights', *Human Rights Brief*, 2006, 13, 1–3.

NHS Information Centre for Health and Social Care, *In-patients Formally Detained in Hospitals under the Mental Health Act 1983*, London: NHS/National Statistics, 2011.

Ní Mhaoláin, Á., Kelly, B.D., 'Ireland's Mental Health Act 2001', *Psychiatric Bulletin*, 2009, 33, 161–164.

Nilforooshan, R., Amin, R., Warner, J., 'Ethnicity and outcome of appeal after detention under the Mental Health Act 1983', *Psychiatric Bulletin*, 2009, 33, 288–290.

Nimmagadda, S., Jones, C.N., 'Consultant psychiatrists' knowledge of their role as representatives of the responsible authority at mental health review tribunals', *Psychiatric Bulletin*, 2008, 32, 366–369.

Nolan, N., 'Case law on the Mental Health Act 2001: part 1', *Irish Psychiatrist*, 2008, 3, 176–182.

Nussbaum, M.C., 'Human functioning and social justice: In defence of Aristotelian essentialism', *Political Theory*, 1992, 20, 202–246.

Nussbaum, M.C., *Creating Capabilities: The Human Development Approach*, Cambridge, MA: Harvard University Press, 2011.

Nussbaum, M.C., *Women and Human Development: The Capabilities Approach*, Cambridge: Cambridge University Press, 2000.

Ó Cionnaith, F, 'Consultants not responsible for harm under Act', *Medicine Weekly*, 2006, 43, 1.

O'Brien, C., 'Reviews for mental patients in detention', *Irish Times*, 2006, 1 November.

O'Brien, N., 'Equality and human rights', *The Political Quarterly*, 2008, 79, 27–35.

O'Donoghue, B., Moran, P., 'Consultant psychiatrists' experiences and attitudes following the introduction of the Mental Health Act 2001', *Irish Journal of Psychological Medicine*, 2009, 26, 23–26.

O'Donovan, D., *The Atlas of Health*, London: Earthscan, 2008.

O'Malley, T. (Minister of State at the Department of Health and Children), 'Mental Health Services', *Dáil Éireann Debate*, 2005 (10 February), 597, 4.

O'Neill, A.-M., *Irish Mental Health Law*, Dublin: First Law Ltd, 2005.

O'Reilly, B., 'Congratulations to IMT for raising the issues of mental health tribunals', *Irish Medical Times*, 2007, 14, 19.

O'Shea, E., Kennelly, B., *The Economics of Mental Health Care in Ireland*, Dublin: Mental Health Commission/Irish Centre for Social Gerontology/ Department of Economics, NUI Galway, 2008.

Office for Disability Issues, *UK Initial Report on the UN Convention on the Rights of Persons with Disabilities*, London: HM Government, 2009.

Organisation for Economic Cooperation and Development, 'Making mental health count', *Focus on Health*, 2014, July.

Organisation of the Islamic Conference, *Cairo Declaration on Human Rights in Islam*, Cairo: Organisation of the Islamic Conference, 1990.

Osiatyński, W., *Human Rights and Their Limits*, Cambridge: Cambridge University Press, 2009.

Owens, J., 'Mental health services crying out for reform', *Irish Times*, 2005, 21 November.

Oxman, A.D., 'Use of evidence in WHO recommendations', *Lancet*, 2007, 369, 1883–1889.

Pearsall, J., Trumble, B. (eds), *The Oxford Reference English Dictionary (Second Edition)*, Oxford: Oxford University Press, 1996.

Peay, J., 'Civil admission following a finding of unfitness to plead', in McSherry, B., and Weller, P. (eds), *Rethinking Rights-Based Mental Health Laws* (pp. 231–254), Oxford and Portland, OR: Hart Publishing, 2010.

Peers, S., Ward, A. (eds), *The EU Charter of Fundamental Rights*, Oxford and Portland, OR: Hart Publishing, 2004.

Perlin, M.L., 'International human rights law and comparative mental disability law: the universal factors', *Syracuse Journal of International Law and Commerce*, 2007, 34, 333–357.

Perlin, M.L., Kanter, A.S., Treuthart, M.P., Szeli, E., Gledhill, K., *International Human Rights and Comparative Mental Disability Law*, Durham, NC: Carolina Academic Press, 2006.

Perlin, M.L., Kanter, A.S., Treuthart, M.P., Szeli, E., Gledhill, K., *International Human Rights and Comparative Mental Disability Law: Documents Supplement*, Durham, NC: Carolina Academic Press, 2006.

Petrila, J., 'Rights-based legalism and the limits of mental health law', in McSherry, B., and Weller, P. (eds), *Rethinking Rights-Based Mental Health Laws* (pp. 357–378), Oxford and Portland, OR: Hart Publishing, 2010.

Phillips, P., Nasr, S.J., 'Seclusion and restraint and prediction of violence', *American Journal of Psychiatry*, 1983, 140, 229–232.

Picton, T., 'Learning disabilities and the new Mental Health Act', *Psychiatric Bulletin*, 2008, 32, 316.

Pidd, H., 'Grim tip of a forced marriage iceberg', *Guardian*, 2013, 10 August.

Pilgrim, D., 'New "mental health" legislation for England and Wales', *Journal of Social Policy*, 2007, 36, 79–95.

Pinto-Duschinsky, M., 'The hijacking of the human rights debate', *Standpoint*, 2012, 42, 34–37.

Porter, R. *Madmen: A Social History of Madhouses, Mad-Doctors and Lunatics*, Gloucestershire, UK: Tempus, 2004.

Porter, R., *Madness*, Oxford: Oxford University Press, 2002.

Powell, G., Caan, W., Crowe, M., 'What events precede violent incidents in psychiatric hospitals?', *British Journal of Psychiatry*, 1994, 165, 107–112.

Prins, H., 'Can the law serve as the solution to social ills?', *Medicine, Science and Law*, 1996, 36, 217 220.

Prior, P.M., 'Dangerous lunacy: The misuse of mental health law in nineteenth-century Ireland', *Journal of Forensic Psychiatry and Psychology*, 2003, 14, 525–541.

Prior, P.M., 'Mentally disordered offenders and the European Court of Human Rights', *International Journal of Law and Psychiatry*, 2007, 30, 546–557.

Psychiatrist, 'Insanity in Ireland', *The Bell*, 1944, 7, 303–310.

Puta-Chekwe, C., Flood, N., 'From division to integration', in Merali, I., and Oosterveld, V. (eds), *Giving Meaning to Economic Social and Cultural Rights* (pp. 39–51), Philadelphia: University of Pennsylvania Press, 2001.

Rahman, M.S., Wolferstan, N., 'A human right to be detained? Mental healthcare after "Savage" and "Rabone"', *The Psychiatrist*, 2013, 37, 294–296.

Rapaport, J., Manthorpe, J., 'Family matters: Developments concerning the role of the nearest relative and social worker under mental health law in England and Wales', *British Journal of Social Work*, 2008, 38, 1115–1131.

Rausing, S., 'Yes to reforming the European court of human rights. No to overriding it', *Guardian*, 2011, 7 December.

Reynolds, J., *Grangegorman*, Dublin: Institute of Public Administration, 1992.

Richards, F., Dale, J., 'The Mental Health Act 1983 and incapacity', *Psychiatric Bulletin*, 2009, 33, 176–178.

Richardson, G., 'Rights-based legalism: some thoughts from the research', in McSherry, B., and Weller, P. (eds), *Rethinking Rights-Based Mental Health Laws* (pp. 181–202), Oxford and Portland, OR: Hart Publishing, 2010.

Richardson, G., 'The European convention and mental health law in England and Wales', *International Journal of Law and Psychiatry*, 2005, 28, 127–139.

Ritchie, J.H., Dick, D., Lingham, R., *The Report of the Inquiry into the Care and Treatment of Christopher Clunis*, London: Her Majesty's Stationery Office, 1994.

Robins, J., *Fools and Mad*, Dublin: Institute of Public Administration, 1986.

Robinson, R., Scott-Moncrieff, L., 'Making sense of Bournewood', *Journal of Mental Health Law*, 2005, May, 17–25.

Rogers, A., Pilgrim, D., *Mental Health Policy in Britain (Second Edition)*, Basingstoke: Palgrave Macmillan, 2001.

Rose, N., 'Unreasonable rights: mental illness and the limits of law', *Journal of Law and Society*, 1985, 12, 199–218.

Rosen, A., Rosen, T., McGorry, P., 'The human rights of people with severe and persistent mental illness', in Dudley, M., Silove, D., and Gale, F. (eds), *Mental Health and Human Rights* (pp. 297–320), Oxford: Oxford University Press, 2012.

Rosen, M., *Dignity: Its History and Meaning*, Cambridge, MA: Harvard University Press, 2012.

Royal Commission, *Report of the Royal Commission on Lunacy and Mental Disorders (Cmd. 2700)*, London: Stationery Office, 1926.

Rutherdale, A., 'Detention in mental hospital after 6 month period without new order invalid', *Irish Times*, 1994, 26 September.

Ryan, D., *The Mental Health Acts 2001–2009*, Dublin: Blackhall Publishing, 2010.

Sainsbury Centre for Mental Health, *Mental Health at Work*, London: Sainsbury Centre for Mental Health, 2007.

Samsi, K., Manthorpe, J., Nagendran, T., Heath, H., 'Challenges and expectations of the Mental Capacity Act 2005: an interview-based study of community-based specialist nurses working in dementia care', *Journal of Clinical Nursing*, 2012, 21, 1697–1705.

Sarkar, S.P., Adshead, G., 'Black robes and white coats', *British Journal of Psychiatry*, 2005, 186, 96–98.

Sayce, L., *From Psychiatric Patient to Citizen*, Basingstoke: Palgrave Macmillan, 2000.

Scull, A., *The Most Solitary of Afflictions*, New Haven: Yale University Press, 2005.

Seedhouse, D., Gallagher, A., 'Clinical ethics: undignifying institutions', *Journal of Medical Ethics*, 2002, 28, 368–372. 368.

Sen, A., *The Idea of Justice*, London: Allen Lane, 2009.

Shannon, J, 'Getting one's Act together', *Medicine Weekly*, 2006, 43, 20.

Shannon, J, 'Mental Health Act is in breach of human rights', *Medicine Weekly*, 2006, 45, 1.

Shannon, J., 'New capacity Bill has gaps in human rights protection', *Irish Medical News*, 2013, 34, 4.

Shorter, E., *A History of Psychiatry*, New York: John Wiley and Sons, 1997.

Singh, D.K., Moncrieff, J., 'Trends in mental health review tribunal and hospital managers' hearings in north-east London 1997–2007', *Psychiatric Bulletin*, 2009, 33, 15–17.

Singh, S.P., Greenwood, N., White, S., Churchill, R., 'Ethnicity and the Mental Health Act 1983', *British Journal of Psychiatry*, 2007, 191, 99–105.

Smith, R.K.M., *Textbook on International Human Rights (Third Edition)*, Oxford: Oxford University Press, 2007.

Spander, H., Calton, T., 'Psychosis and human rights', *Social Policy and Society*, 2009, 8, 245–256.

Spellman, J., 'Section 260 of the Mental Treatment Act, 1945 Reviewed', *Medico-Legal Journal of Ireland*, 1998, 4, 20–24.

Steadman, H.J., Mulvey, E.P., Monahan, J., Clark Robbins, P., Applebaum, P.S., Grisso, T., Roth, L.H., Silver, E., 'Violence by people discharged from acute psychiatric inpatient facilities and by others in the same neighbourhoods', *Archives of General Psychiatry*, 1998, 55, 393–401.

Steering Group on the Review of the Mental Health Act 2001. *Interim Report of the Steering Group on the Review of the Mental Health Act 2001*. Dublin: Department of Health, 2012.

Steffen, M., Lamping,W., Lehto, J., 'Introduction: the Europeanization of health policies', in Steffen, M. (ed.), *Health Governance in Europe* (pp. 1–17), London: Routledge, 2005.

Stone, M.H. *Healing the Mind*, London: Pimlico, 1998.

Szmukler, G., 'Homicide enquiries', *Psychiatric Bulletin*, 2000, 24, 6–10.

Szmukler, G., Richardson, G., Owen, G., '"Rabone" and four unresolved problems in mental health law', *Psychiatric Bulletin*, 2013, 37, 297–301.

Szmukler, G., Daw, R., Callard, F., 'Mental health law and the UN Convention on the rights of persons with disabilities', *International Journal of Law and Psychiatry*, 2014, 37, 245–252.

Tacket, A., *Health Equity, Social Justice and Human Rights*, London and New York, Routledge, 2012.

Tomuschat, C., *Human Rights (Second Edition)*, Oxford: Oxford University Press, 2008.

Torrey, E.F., Miller, J., *The Invisible Plague*, New Jersey: Rutgers University Press, 2001.

Torrey, E.F., *Surviving Schizophrenia (Fourth Edition)*, New York: Quill/ HarperCollins, 2001.

Travis, A., Wintour, P., 'Deadlock likely on commission pondering a British bill of rights', *Guardian*, 2011, 18 March.

United Nations, *Universal Declaration of Human Rights*, Geneva: United Nations, 1948.

United Nations, *Principles for the Protection of Persons with Mental Illness and the Improvement of Mental Health Care*, New York: United Nations, Secretariat Centre For Human Rights, 1991.

United Nations, *Convention on the Rights of Persons with Disabilities*, Geneva: United Nations, 2006.

United Nations High Commissioner for Human Rights, *Annual Report of the United Nations High Commissioner for Human Rights and Reports of the Office of the High Commissioner and the Secretary General: Thematic Study by the Office of the United Nations High Commissioner for Human Rights on Enhancing Awareness and Understanding of the Convention on the Rights of Persons with Disabilities*, Geneva: United Nations, 2009.

Unsworth, C., *The Politics of Mental Health Legislation*, Oxford: Clarendon Press, 1987.

US Bureau of the Census, *Historical Statistics of the United States, Colonial Times to 1970, Bicentennial Edition, Part .*, Washington, DC: GPO, 1975.

Viney, M., 'Mental illness', *Irish Times*, 1968, 23–30 October.

Vize, E., 'Pay threat to psychiatrists over mental health tribunals', *Medicine Weekly*, 2005, 41, 1.

Wadham, J., Mountfield, H., Edmundson, A., Gallagher, C., *Blackstone's Guide to The Human Rights Act 1998 (Fourth Edition)*, Oxford: Oxford University Press, 2007.

Wadham, J., Ruebain, D., Robinson, A., Uppal, S., *Blackstone's Guide to the Equality Act 2010*, Oxford: Oxford University Press, 2010.

Walsh, D., Daly, A., *Mental Illness in Ireland 1750–2002*, Dublin: Health Research Board, 2004.

Walsh, E., Buchannan, A., Fahy, T., 'Violence and schizophrenia', *British Journal of Psychiatry*, 2001, 180, 490–495.

Watters, E., *Crazy Like Us*, New York: Free Press, 2010.

Weller, P., 'Lost in translation: human rights and mental health law', in McSherry, B., and Weller, P. (eds), *Rethinking Rights-Based Mental Health Laws* (pp. 51–72), Oxford and Portland, OR: Hart Publishing, 2010.

Welsh, S.F., 'Provisions of the Mental Capacity Act 2005', in Jacob, R., Gunn, N., and Holland, A. (eds), *Mental Capacity Legislation: Principles and Practice* (pp. 54–77), London: RCPsych Publications, 2013.

Welsh, S.F., Keeling, A., 'The deprivation of liberty safeguards', in Jacob, R., Gunn, N., and Holland, A. (eds), *Mental Capacity Legislation: Principles and Practice* (pp. 78–95), London: RCPsych Publications, 2013.

Whelan, D., 'Legacy of unresolved legal issues on mental health', *Irish Times*, 2008, 4 November.

Whelan, D., 'Mental health tribunals', *Medico-Legal Journal of Ireland*, 2004, 10, 84–89.

Whelan, D., *Mental Health: Law and Practice*, Dublin: Round Hall, 2009.

Whitley, R., Henwood, B.F., 'Life, liberty, and the pursuit of happiness: reframing inequities experienced by people with severe mental illness', *Psychiatric Rehabilitation Journal*, 2014, 37, 68–70.

Wicks, E., *Human Rights and Healthcare*, Oxford and Portland, OR: Hart Publishing, 2007.

World Health Organization, *International Classification of Mental and Behavioural Disorders*, Geneva: World Health Organization, 1992.

World Health Organization, *Guidelines for the Promotion of Human Rights of Persons with Mental Disorders*, Geneva: World Health Organization, 1996.

World Health Organization, *ICD-10 Guide for Mental Retardation*, Geneva: World Health Organization, 1996.

World Health Organization, *Mental Health Law: Ten Basic Principles*, Geneva: World Health Organization, 1996.

World Health Organization, *Mental Health: New Understanding, New Hope*, Geneva: World Health Organization, 2001.

World Health Organization, *WHO Resource Book on Mental Health, Human Rights and Legislation*, Geneva: World Health Organization, 2005.

World Health Organization, *Improving Health Systems and Services for Mental Health*, Geneva: World Health Organization, 2009.

World Health Organization Ministerial Conference on Mental Health, *Mental Health Action Declaration for Europe: Facing the Challenges, Building Solutions*, Helsinki: World Health Organization, 2005.

World Health Organization Ministerial Conference on Mental Health, *Mental Health Declaration for Europe: Facing the Challenges, Building Solutions*, Helsinki: World Health Organization, 2005.

Wrigley, M., 'A state of unpreparedness', *Irish Medical Times*, 2006, 40, 1I.

Zuckerberg, J., 'Mental health law and its discontents: a reappraisal of the Canadian experience', in McSherry, B., and Weller, P. (eds), *Rethinking Rights-Based Mental Health Laws* (pp. 299–326), Oxford and Portland, OR: Hart Publishing, 2010.

Index